FRAGMENTS OF OLD COMEDY

II

LCL 514

FRAGMENTS OF OLD COMEDY

VOLUME II

DIOPEITHES TO PHERECRATES

EDITED AND TRANSLATED BY

IAN C. STOREY

HARVARD UNIVERSITY PRESS

CAMBRIDGE, MASSACHUSETTS

LONDON, ENGLAND

2011

Library of Congress Control Number 2010937704
CIP data available from the Library of Congress

ISBN 978-0-674-99663-2

CONTENTS

Abbreviations   vii

THE POETS OF OLD COMEDY

DIOPEITHES   2

ECPHANTIDES   4

EPILYCUS   14

EUETES   18

EUNICUS   20

EUPHRONIUS   24

EUPOLIS   26

EUXENIDES   268

HEGEMON   270

HERMIPPUS   276

ION OF CHIOS   316

LEUCON   320

LYCIS   328

LYSIPPUS   330

CONTENTS

MAGNES	338
METAGENES	354
MYLLUS	368
MYRTILUS	372
NICOCHARES	378
NICOPHON	396
PHERECRATES	410

ABBREVIATIONS

A&R	*Atene e Roma*
Aevum (Ant.)	*Aevum Antiquum*
AFLB	*Annali della Facoltà di Lettere e Filosofia di Bari*
AHB	*Ancient History Bulletin*
AION (fil.)	*Annali dell'Istituto Universitario Orientale di Napoli. Sezione filologico-letteraria.*
AJPh	*American Journal of Philology*
Bakola	E. Bakola, *Cratinus and the Art of Comedy* (Oxford 2010)
BICS	*Bulletin of the Institute of Classical Studies*
C&M	*Classica et Mediaevalia*
Campbell *GL*	D. A. Campbell (ed.), *Greek Lyric*, 5 vols. (1982–1993)
Capps	E. Capps, "Epigraphical Problems in the History of Comedy," *CPh* 28 (1907) 179–99
CGA	A. López Eire (ed.), *Sociedad, Política y Literatura: Comedia griega antigua* (Salamanca 1997)
CGFP	C. Austin (ed.), *Comicorum Graecorum Fragmenta in Papyris Reperta* (Berlin/New York 1973)

ABBREVIATIONS

Companion	G. W. Dobrov (ed.), *Brill's Companion to the Study of Greek Comedy* (Leiden 2010)
CPh	*Classical Philology*
CQ	*Classical Quarterly*
CW	*Classical World*
Demianczuk	J. Demianczuk (ed.), *Supplementum Comicum* (Krakow 1912)
Dobrov (*BA*)	G. Dobrov (ed.), *Beyond Aristophanes* (Atlanta 1993)
Dobrov (*City*)	G. Dobrov, *The City as Comedy* (Chapel Hill, NC 1995)
Edmonds	J. M. Edmonds (ed./tr.), *The Fragments of Attic Comedy*, vol. I (Leiden 1957)
Euripides VII	C. Collard and M. Cropp, *Euripides Fragments:* Aegeus–Meleager (Cambridge, MA 2008)
Euripides VIII	C. Collard and M. Cropp, *Euripides Fragments:* Oedipus–Chrysippus, *other fragments* (Cambridge, MA 2008)
G&R	*Greece and Rome*
Geissler	P. Geissler, *Chronologie der altattischen Komödie*, 2nd ed. (Dublin/Zurich 1969)
GRBS	*Greek, Roman and Byzantine Studies*
GrGr	*Grammatici Graeci*, ed. G. Uhlig and others, 4 vols., in 6 (Leipzig 1867–1910)
ICS	*Illinois Classical Studies*
IG	*Inscriptiones Graecae*
JHS	*Journal of Hellenic Studies*
Kaibel	Extracts from Kaibel's unpublished writings on Old Comedy appear *ad loc.* in *PCG*

ABBREVIATIONS

Kassel-Austin [K.-A.]	= *PCG*
Kock	T. Kock (ed.), *Comicorum Atticorum Fragmenta*, vol. I (Lepizig 1880)
Koster	W. J. W. Koster (ed.), *Scholia in Aristophanem, Pars I: fasc. IA. Prolegomena de Comoedia* (Groningen 1975)
ΚΩΜΩΙΔΟ-ΤΡΑΓΩΙΔΙΑ	E. Medda, M. S. Mirto, and M. P. Pattoni (eds.), ΚΩΜΩΙΔΟΤΡΑΓΩΙΔΙΑ *Intersezioni del tragico e del comico nel teatro del V secolo a.C.* (Pisa 2006)
LCM	*Liverpool Classical Monthly*
MCr	*Museum Criticum*
Meineke	A. Meineke (ed.), *Fragmenta Comicorum Graecorum.* (Berlin 1839–1857)
MH	*Museum Helveticum*
Norwood	G. Norwood, *Greek Comedy* (London 1931)
Olson	S. D. Olson, *Broken Laughter* (Oxford 2007)
PAA	J. Traill (ed.), *Persons of Ancient Athens*, 20 vols. (Toronto 1994–)
PCG	R. Kassel and C. Austin (eds.), *Poetae Comici Graeci* (Berlin 1983–)
PCPhS	*Proceedings of the Cambridge Philological Society*
Pellegrino (*Utopie*)	M. Pellegrino, *Utopie e immagini gastronomiche nei frammenti dell' archaia* (Bologna 2000)
PMG	D. L. Page (ed.), *Poetae Melici Graeci* (Oxford 1962)
P. Oxy.	Oxyrhynchus Papyrus

PSI	*Pubblicazioni della Società italiana per la ricerca dei papyri greci e latini in Egitto*
QUCC	*Quaderni Urbinati di Cultura Classica*
Revermann	M. Revermann, *Comic Business* (Oxford 2006)
RFIC	*Rivista di Filologia e di Istruzione Classica*
Rivals	D. Harvey and J. Wilkins (eds.), *The Rivals of Aristophanes* (London 2000)
Rothwell	K. S. Rothwell, *Nature, Culture and the Origins of Old Comedy* (Cambridge 2007)
RPh	*Révue de Philologie*
SemRom	*Seminaria Romana*
SIFC	*Studi Italiani di Filologia Classica*
SPhV	*Studia Philologica Valentina*
Storey	I. C. Storey, *Eupolis: Poet of Old Comedy* (Oxford 2003)
TCP	A. H. Sommerstein, S. Halliwell, J. Henderson, and B. Zimmermann (eds.), *Tragedy, Comedy and the Polis* (Bari 1993)
Tessere	A. M. Belardinelli et al. (eds.). *Tessere. Frammenti della commedia greca: studi e commenti* (Bari 1998)
Thompson (*Birds*)	D.W, Thompson, *A Glossary of Greek Birds* (London 1936)
Thompson (*Fishes*)	D. W. Thompson, *A Glossary of Greek Fishes* (London 1947)

TrGF	B. Snell (corrected edition by R. Kannicht), *Tragicorum Graecorum Fragmenta*, vol. I (Göttingen 1986)
Tsantsanoglou	K. Tsantsanoglou, *New Fragments of Greek Literature in the Lexicon of Photius* (Athens 1984)
ZPE	*Zeitschrift für Papyrologie und Epigraphik*

FRAGMENTS OF OLD COMEDY

II

[ΔΙΟΠ]ΕΙΘΗΣ

Testimonium

i *IG* ii² 2325.51

Διοπ]είθης II

[DIOP]EITHES

The list of victors at the Dionysia attributes two victories to a poet whose name ends in –eithes. He comes after Cratinus (debut 454) and before Crates and Callias, poets of the 440s. We are thus looking for a poet who won for the first time in the late 450s. Space on the inscription will allow for four or five characters before –eithes. The name is most commonly completed as Diopeithes, but other possibilities exist: an Axiopeithes, known to belong to a prominent family in the mid-fifth century (PAA 139645), and (more interestingly) Philopeithes (PAA 941940), who married the sister of Aeschylus and was the father of the tragic poet Philocles.

Testimonium

i [on the list of victors at the Dionysia]

Diop]eithes 2

ΕΚΦΑΝΤΙΔΗΣ

A minor comic poet of the early period, his name appears
on the list of victors at the Dionysia (T 1) after that of
Euphronius (victory known for 458) and before that of
Cratinus. His carer began, therefore, in the mid-450s. F 5
refers to one Androcles, a kōmōidoumenos of the 420s, and
if the allusion is correctly attributed, shows that he must
still have been active in the mid- to late 430s. As with many
of these early or lesser poets, only one or two plays were ac-
tually known and quoted from. In Ecphantides' case it was
his Satyrs. The recorded total of four victories, set against
only two known titles, confirms that he was more active
(and more successful) than the meagre remains suggest.

There appears to be an intertextual conversation going
on between Cratinus and Ecphantides. Cratinus quotes
the other poet by name (F 361.1 = T 7a) and at F 502

Testimonia

i *IG* ii² 2325.49

Ἐκφαν]τίδης ΙΙΙΙ

4

ECPHANTIDES

creates the comic compound Choerilecphantides, Choeri-
lus being the early tragic poet (TrGF I nr. 2, 66–67). We
may compare his linking of Euripides (tragedian) with
Aristophanes (comic poet) at F 342 in a similar compound,
euripidaristophanizein. *The scholiast to* Wasps *151 (T 5)*
implies that Cratinus had called Ecphantides "Smoky," the
metaphor being that of wine going stale. The point is pre-
sumably the same as that at Knights *507–40, successful*
poets of earlier days, now past their prime.

A vase of the late sixth century by Euphronius depicts
a scene at a symposium with a singer named Ecphanti-
des. Vermeule (Antike Kunst *8 [1965] 34–39) points out*
that fifty years later we find comic poets named Euphro-
nius and Ecphantides—grandsons of the vase painter and
singer?

Testimonia

i [list of victors at the Dionysia, from the late 450s]

   Ecphan]tides 4

ii *IG* ii² 3091.1–2

Ε.[. . . . . χορηγῶν ἐνίκα] κωμῳδοῖς·
Ἐχφαντίδης ἐδίδασκε * Πείρας.

iii Aristotle *Politics* 1341a30

καὶ μετὰ τὰ Μηδικὰ φρονηματισθέντες ἐκ τῶν ἔργων,
πάσης ἥπτοντο μαθήσεως, οὐδὲν διακρίνοντες ἀλλ'
ἐπιζητοῦντες. διὸ καὶ τὴν αὐλητικὴν ἤγαγον πρὸς τὰς
μαθήσεις. καὶ γὰρ ἐν Λακεδαίμονί τις χορηγὸς αὐτὸς
ηὔλησε τῷ χορῷ, καὶ περὶ Ἀθήνας οὕτως ἐπεχωρίασεν
ὥστε σχεδὸν οἱ πολλοὶ τῶν ἐλευθέρων μετεῖχον αὐτῆς·
δῆλον δὲ ἐκ τοῦ πίνακος ὃν ἀνέθηκε Θράσιππος Ἐκ-
φαντίδῃ χορηγήσας.

iv Anonymous *On Aristotle's* Nicomachean Ethics 4.6

Ἐκφαντίδης παλαιότατος ποιητὴς τῶν ἀρχαίων.

v Σ *Wasps* 151b

τὸν ὑπεκλυόμενον οἶνόν φασί τινες καπνίαν λέγε-
σθαι· ἐν δὲ τοῖς περὶ Κρατίνου διώρισται, ὅτι τὸν
ἀπόθετον ἢ καὶ παλαιόν. διὸ καὶ Ἐκφαντίδην Κα-
πνίαν καλοῦσιν.

ECPHANTIDES

ii [an inscription from Aexone listing victorious *chorēgoi* and poets]

E[. . . won as *chorēgus*] in comedy/Ecphantides produced his *Experiments*.

iii After the Persian Wars they [the Greeks], inspired by their achievements, devoted themselves to all sorts of learning, making no distinction but just pursuing research. And so they included *aulos* playing as a subject of learning. For at Sparta a certain *chorēgus* played the *aulos* himself for his chorus, and in Athens it became so popular that most freeborn citizens would know how to play it. This is clear from the tablet which Thrasippus put up when he served as a *chorēgus* for Ecphantides.

iv Ecphantides, a very early poet of Old Comedy.

v But some call wine that is starting to go off "smoky," but in the ‹notes› about Cratinus it is defined as "discarded" or "too old." That is why they call Ecphantides "Smoky."

vi

(a) Hesychius κ 716

Καπνίας· Ἐκφαντίδης ὁ τῆς κωμῳδίας ποιητὴς Καπνίας ἐπεκαλεῖτο διὰ τὸ μηδὲν λαμπρὸν γράφειν.

(b) Hesychius ε 1439

Ἐκφαντίδῃ γὰρ τῷ κωμικῷ Χοιρίλος θεράπων ἦν, ὃς συνεποιεῖτο κωμῳδίας.

vii

(a) Cratinus F 361.1

"εὔιε κισσοχαῖτ' ἄναξ χαῖρ'," ἔφασκ' Ἐκφαντίδης.

(b) Cratinus F 502

Χοιριλεκφαντίδης

Fragments

ΠΕΙΡΑΙ

8

vi

(a) Ecphantides, the comic poet, was nicknamed "Smoky" because he did not write anything brilliant.

(b) Ecphantides the comic poet had a servant called Choerilus, who helped him write his comedies.[1]

1 Compare the story of Euripides and Cephisophon at *Life of Euripides* 2, 6 and Aristophanes *Frogs* 944 + Σ and F 596.

vii

(a) "Hail, Lord Bacchus, with ivy in your hair," to quote Ecphantides [F 4].

(b) Chorilecphantides.

Fragments

EXPERIMENTS

We know about this comedy only from the records at Aexone (T 2). It is not readily apparent what this title means or what sort of form the chorus might have taken.

ΣΑΤΥΡΟΙ

1 Athenaeus 96bc

πόδας ἐπεὶ δέοι πριάμενον καταφαγεῖν ἐφθοὺς ὑός.

ΑΔΗΛΩΝ ΔΡΑΜΑΤΩΝ

3 Anonymous *On Aristotle's* Nichomachean Ethics 4.6

Μεγαρικῆς κωμῳδίας † ᾆσμα δίειμαι †
αἰσχυνόμενος τὸ δρᾶμα Μεγαρικὸν ποιεῖν.

4 Hephaestion *Handbook* 15.21 [= Cratinus F 361.1]

εὔιε κισσοχαῖτ᾽ ἄναξ, χαῖρε.

SATYRS

At least five comedies of the late fifth century were either named "Satyrs" (others by Callias, Cratinus, Phrynichus) or had a chorus of satyrs (Dionysalexander). This seems to have been the only comedy of Ecphantides which was cited or about which anything was known. If F 5, which mentions Androcles, comes from Satyrs, *then we may date this play in the 430s, when Callias (*Satyrs*) and Cratinus (Dionysalexander) were putting on their plays with satyrs in the chorus. Was Ecphantides' comedy another reaction perhaps to the satyrs missing from Euripides'* Alcestis *in 438?*

1 Whenever he had to buy and eat boiled pigs' feet.

Brief fragment: (F 2) "having shut out."

UNASSIGNED FRAGMENTS

3 A song of Megarian comedy I refuse to sing, being ashamed to write drama from Megara.[1]

1 While the text is uncertain, the sense is clear. See the summary by F. Conti Bizzarro, *MCr* 29 (1994) 155–56, who sees l. 2 as part of the commentary, not the text.

4 Hail, Lord [Bacchus], with ivy in your hair.

5 Aristophanes Σ *Wasps* 1187a

Ἀνδροκλέα δὲ Κρατῖνος Σεριφίοις φησὶ δοῦλον καὶ πτωχόν, ἐν δὲ Ὥραις ἡταιρηκότα, ‹εἰ› ἄρα τὸν αὐτόν· Τηλεκλείδης δὲ ἐν Ἡσιόδοις καὶ Ἐκφαντίδης βαλλαντιοτόμον.

6 Pollux 2.127

κακηγορίστατος

5 Cratinus in *Men of Seriphos* [F 223] calls Androcles a slave and a beggar, in *Seasons* [F 281] a sexual pervert, ‹if he means› the same person. Teleclides in *Hesiods* [F 16] and Ecphantides ‹call him› a cutpurse.

6 Very abusive.

ΕΠΙΛΥΚΟΣ

Testimonium

i *Suda* ε 2450

Ἐπίλυκος, κωμικὸς ποιητής. τῶν δραμάτων αὐτοῦ ἐστι Κοραλίσκος, ὡς Ἀθήναιος.

Fragments

ΚΩΡΑΛΙΣΚΟΣ

EPILYCUS

Crates is said (Suda κ 2339) to have had a brother Epilycus, an epic poet. Was he in fact (or also) a poet of Old Comedy? The perfumed ointments of F 1 are mentioned several times in the fragments of Old Comedy, but not exclusively so (see Athenaeus 690–91). But the other comic allusions to the Spartan kopis *(F 4) cited by Athenaeus (138e, 140a) are all from poets of Old Comedy (Cratinus F 175, Eupolis F 147, Philyllius F 15).*

Testimonium

i Epilycus: comic poet, whose plays include *Young'un*, according to Athenaeus [citing F 1, 2, 4, 5].

Fragments

YOUNG'UN

Photius (p. 198.15) records that kōraliskos *is a Cretan term for* meirakion *(youth). The speaker of F 4 is a Dorian Greek, perhaps a Cretan, but more likely in view of the* kopis *(a Spartan festival) to have been a Spartan. Compare the Doricisms in Eupolis'* Helots *(F 147, 149).*

1 Photius (z) p. 119 (Tsantsanoglou); Athenaeus 691c

μύρον δὲ βάκκαρίς τε καὶ ψάγδας ὁμοῦ.

2 Athenaeus 650e

μῆλα καὶ ῥόας λέγεις.

3 Photius (b, z) α 1308

                         πλοῖόν τε λαβὼν κατ᾽ ἐμαυτὸν
κἀμφίβληστρον τήν τε τρίαιναν.

4 Athenaeus 140a

ποττὰν κοπίδ᾽, οἰῶ, σῶμαι·
ἐν Ἀμύκλαισιν παρ᾽ Ἀπέλλω
βάρακες πολλοὶ κἄρτοι
καὶ δωμός τοι μάλα ἁδύς.

ΑΔΗΛΩΝ ΔΡΑΜΑΤΩΝ

7 Athenaeus 28d

Χῖος καὶ Θάσιος ἠθημένος

1 For perfume, asarabacca and sagda as well.

2 You [sing.] are talking about apples and pomegranates.[1]

> [1] At *Wasps* 1268 "apples and pomegranates" are a very simple meal.

3 And taking a boat by myself and a net and the trident.

4 I am off to the *kopis,* I reckon. At Amyclae, in Apollo's temple, there are many barley cakes and loaves of bread, and a very tasty broth.

Brief fragments: (F 5) "cicada," (F 6) "bailer."

UNASSIGNED FRAGMENTS

7 Chian and strained Thasian ⟨wine⟩.

Brief fragments: (F 8) "bone collector," (F 9) "morsel."

ΕΥΕΤΗΣ

The Suda (*T 1*) records three shadowy poets active at Athens at the same time as Epicharmus, whom he dates to "six years before the Persian Wars," that is in the mid-480s. As the list of tragic victors at the Dionysia (IG *ii²* 2325a.2) presented a ..]etes (TrGF 6) as a contemporary of Aeschy-

Testimonium

i *Suda* ε 2766

Ἐπίχαρμος . . . ἦν δὲ πρὸ τῶν Περσικῶν ἔτη ἔξ, διδάσκων ἐν Συρακούσαις· ἐν δὲ Ἀθήναις Εὐέτης καὶ Εὐξενίδης καὶ Μύλλος ἐπεδείκνυντο.

Fragment

ΕΠΙΚΛΗΡΟΣ

1 Photius (z) δ 144

ἀπελθεῖν με δεῖται.

EUETES

lus, it seemed possible that the Suda had misidentified an early tragic poet as a writer of comedy. But the fragment of Photius (citing F 1) gives not only a name but also a play title (Heiress), which sounds far more comic than tragic. With Tsantsanoglou I suspect that this may be a hitherto unknown poet of Middle or New Comedy.

Testimonium

i Epicharmus . . . he was active six years before the Persian Wars [486/5] producing plays in Syracuse. At Athens Euetes and Euxenides and Myllus were putting on plays.

Fragment

HEIRESS

A common title among the poets of Middle and New Comedy. An epikleros was a woman who had inherited money and property from her father, and as such could be the focus for all sorts of comedies of love and intrigue.

1 I must go away.

ΕΥΝΙΚΟΣ

Testimonium

i *Suda* αι 222

Αἴνικος, Ἀθηναῖος, κωμικός. ἔστι δὲ τῆς ἀρχαίας κωμῳδίας. δράματα αὐτοῦ Ἄντεια.

ΑΝΤΕΙΑ

EUNICUS

The Suda *(T 1) gives the name of a poet of Old Comedy as "Ainikos" and his one title as* Anteia. *As Athenaeus and Pollux assign an* Anteia *to a Eunicus (Eunikos), Meineke "corrected" the text of the* Suda *accordingly. At Aristotle* Eudemian Ethics *1238a32–39 a statement about lovers and loved ones (F 2) is attributed to someone whose name has been restored by Jackson as "Ainikos." Are all these references to one man, and is his name Eunikos or Ainikos? As the* hetaera *Anteia, who gave her name to the comedy, was active in the early fourth century, if Eunicus "belongs to the Old Comedy" (T 1), then he was active in the very last years of the genre.*

Testimonium

i Eunicus [MSS "Ainicus"]: of Athens, comic poet. He belongs to the Old Comedy. His plays include *Anteia*.

ANTEIA

At 567c and 586e Athenaeus lists comedies named after hetaerae, *including* Anteia *by "Eunicus or Philyllius."* Anteia *(PAA 131297) was a celebrated hetaera of the early fourth century, mentioned as a friend of Lais at Anaxandrides F 9 and the subject of a comedy by Antiphanes.*

21

THE POETS OF OLD COMEDY

Fragment

1 Pollux 10.100

λαβοῦσα τῶν ὤτων φίλησον τὴν χύτραν.

ΠΟΛΕΙΣ

ΑΔΗΛΩΝ ΔΡΑΜΑΤΩΝ

2 Aristotle *Eudemian Ethics* 1238b32

ἐρώμενος τοιαῦτ᾽ ἄν, οὐκ ἐρῶν λέγοι[1]

[1] Reading Jackson's εἴρηκεν Αἴνικος for the received text εὑρηκέναι νεῖκος in Aristotle.

EUNICUS

Fragment

1 Take hold of the ears and give a pot-kiss [or "take hold of the 'ears' and kiss the pot"].[1]

    [1] Pollux uses this passage to identify χύτρα as a sort of kiss that one gives children by seizing their ears, but it may just mean "take the pot by the ears and kiss it."

CITIES

Athenaeus mentions this comedy four times, each time with the author's identity in question. Four times Philyllius is named as a possible author, Aristophanes twice (86e, 140a), "whoever wrote the play" twice (92e, 381a), and Eunicus once (86e). As both Pollux and Hesychius confidently assert the authorship of Philyllius, that ascription should be accepted.

UNASSIGNED FRAGMENT

2 A loved one would say that, but not a lover.

ΕΥΦΡΟΝΙΟΣ

Testimonia

i *IG* ii² 2318.46–48

κωμῳδῶν
Εὐρυκλείδης ἐχορήγει
Εὐφρόνιος ἐδίδασκε

ii *IG* ii² 2325.48

Εὐφρόν]ιος I

EUPHRONIUS

This shadowy figure won a victory at the Dionysia of 458 (T 1). If his name is to be restored on the list of victors at the Dionysia before those of Ecphantides and Cratinus (first victory in 454), this was his only success. Vermeule (Antike Kunst 5 [1964] 34–39) calls attention to a late sixth century vase by Euphronius on which a singer, labelled "Ecphantides," performs at a symposium and wonders if the comic poets of the 450s, Euphronius and Ecphantides, could be the grandsons of vase painter and singer.

Testimonia

i [the results of the dramatic contests for the Dionysia of 458]

Of comic poets/Euryclides acted as *chorēgus*/Euphronius put on the play.

ii [from the list of victors at the Dionysia]

Euphron]ius 1

ΕΥΠΟΛΙΣ

Along with Cratinus and Aristophanes, Eupolis was one of
the canonical Three of Old Comedy (see T 16–20). T 2 sug-
gests that he began his career in 429. He was thus one of the
"next generation" of comic poets who would dominate the
420s and 410s and create the political and topical sort
of comedy that we now regard as typical of the genre. T 1
records his death "in a shipwreck in the Hellespont," the
context being that of military service. Since no play or ref-
erence in his surviving works demands a date of 410 or
later, it is commonly assumed that he died in the sea battle
of Cynossema, fought in the later part of 411 (Thucydides
8.104–6). In a career, then, of eighteen or nineteen years,
he performed fourteen (T 2) or seventeen (T 1) times and
won seven victories (T 1). The plays whose authenticity is
in no doubt add up to fourteen, fifteen if we include the per-
formance of the second Autolycus. Seven victories, three at
the Lenaea (T 11) and thus four at the Dionysia (T 10), in
fourteen starts is an enviable record. Eupolis seems to have
been especially productive in the 420s, when at least eight
of his comedies were produced. If the Suda (T 1) is correct
that he began to produce at age seventeen, then we have life
dates of 445–411.

As far as we can gather, his comedy resembled that of
his rival Aristophanes, but with one or two significant ex-
ceptions. His comedy was based on a great and fantastic

26

EUPOLIS

idea, often with a principal character engaged putting that idea into practice. In Demes *the idea was to bring back four leaders from the dead and thus improve things at Athens.* In Officers *it was "Dionysus joins the navy."* In Dyers *a new deity arrives at Athens, to be greeted by the appropriate chorus, cross-dressing dancing effeminates.* Also like Aristophanes and Cratinus, he wrote political comedy, especially in Demes *(where four political leaders are brought back from the dead),* Cities *(with a chorus of cities from the* archē*),* probably Golden Race *(where Athens of the 420s is anything but golden),* and certainly Maricas, *a demagogue comedy about Hyperbolus.*

Eupolis *was especially fond of bringing real people on stage as characters in his dramas and making the comedy turn on the comic possibilities they presented. In addition to the four leaders in* Demes, *only one of whom (Pericles) would have been known personally to the spectators, we may cite Callias and Protagoras in* Spongers, *Autolycus the boy victor and very possibly Callias again in* Autolycus, *Hyperbolus "disguised" as Maricas in that comedy, Phormion in* Officers, *and most notorious of all, Alcibiades in* Dyers. *It is very likely also that Socrates appeared as a character in Eupolis, but we cannot pin down a play for certain.*

But he does not seem to have followed Aristophanes

with the latter's obsession for parody, especially of Euripides. There are brief allusions to and parodies of epic and poetry and drama, but nothing on a large scale, nothing along the lines of Aristophanes' attempt to define his comic art in terms of tragedy. Like Aristophanes, Eupolis appears to have avoided the mythological burlesque that was so popular with Cratinus and Hermippus in the 430s. When he brings Dionysus on stage in Officers, *it is to a contemporary setting with an Athenian general in command. Unless* Golden Race *is an instance of the comic theme of the ideal existence, Eupolis also did not write comedies of utopia, again a very popular theme in the late fifth century.*

Testimonia

i *Suda* ε 3657

Εὔπολις, Σωσιπόλιδος, Ἀθηναῖος, κωμικός. ὃς ἑπτακαίδεκα ἔτη γεγονὼς ἤρξατο ἐπιδείκνυσθαι· καὶ ἐδίδαξε μὲν δράματα ιζʹ, ἐνίκησε δὲ ζʹ. καὶ ἀπέθανε ναυαγήσας κατὰ τὸν Ἑλλήσποντον ἐν τῷ πρὸς Λακεδαιμονίους πολέμῳ· καὶ ἐκ τούτου ἐκωλύθη στρατεύεσθαι ποιητήν. τὰ δὲ δράματα αὐτοῦ Αἶγες, Ἀστράτευτος ἢ Ἀνδρόγυνοι, καὶ ἄλλα.

ii Anonymous *On Comedy* (Koster III.9–13, 33–35)

τούτων δέ εἰσιν ἀξιολογώτατοι Ἐπίχαρμος, Μάγνης, Κρατῖνος, Κράτης, Φερεκράτης, Φρύνιχος, Εὔπολις, Ἀριστοφάνης.

His plays seem to be firmly rooted in Athens and its issues and denizens of the day.

Recent bibliography: E. M. Bowie, JHS *108 (1988) 183–85; L. P. E. Parker,* PCPhS *34 (1988) 115–22;* JHS *111 (1991) 203–8; M. Heath,* G&R *37 (1990) 143–58; I. C. Storey,* Phoenix *44 (1990) 1–30, in* TCP *373–96;* AHB *8 (1994) 107–20;* Eupolis. Poet of Old Comedy *(2003);* Lustrum *48 (2006) 73–108, 231–32; S. Dworacki,* Eupolis: i fragmenty jego komedii *(1991); K. Sidwell,* GRBS *34 (1993) 365–89; C&M *45 (1994) 71–115; H.-G. Nesselrath, in* Rivals *233–46; G. Kavvadias, in* Rivals *159–61;* Storey & Allan *204–6; N. Kyriakidi,* Aristophanes und Eupolis *(2007).*

Testimonia

i Eupolis: son of Sosipolis, of Athens, comic poet. He began to put on plays at the age of seventeen. He produced seventeen plays and won seven victories. He died in a shipwreck in the Hellespont during the Peloponnesian War. As a result poets were forbidden to serve in the military. His plays are *Nanny-Goats*, *Draft-Dodgers* or *Men-Women*, etc.

ii The most noteworthy poets [of Old Comedy] are Epicharmus, Magnes, Cratinus, Crates, Pherecrates, Phrynichus, Eupolis, and Aristophanes.

Εὔπολις Ἀθηναῖος. ἐδίδαξεν ἐπὶ ἄρχοντος Ἀπολλοδώ
ρου, ἐφ᾽ οὗ καὶ Φρύνιχος, γεγονὼς δυνατὸς τῇ λέξει
καὶ ζηλῶν Κρατῖνον· πολὺ γοῦν λοίδορον καὶ σκαιὸν
ἐπιφαίνει. γέγραπται δὲ αὐτῷ δράματα ιδ΄.

σκαιὸν codd., αἰσχρὸν Geel.

iii Canon of Comic Poets

κωμῳδοποιοὶ ἀρχαίας ζ΄· Ἐπίχαρμος, Κρατῖνος, Εὔ
πολις, Ἀριστοφάνης, Φερεκράτης, Κράτης, Πλάτων.

iv Pausanias 2.7.3

μετὰ δὲ τὸ μνῆμα τοῦ Λύκου διαβεβηκόσιν ἤδη τὸν
Ἀσωπόν, ἔστιν ἐν δεξιᾷ τὸ Ὀλύμπιον, ὀλίγον δὲ
ἔμπροσθεν ἐν ἀριστερᾷ τῆς ὁδοῦ τάφος Εὐπόλιδι
Ἀθηναίῳ ποιήσαντι κωμῳδίαν.

v

(a) Eusebius (Jerome)

Eupolis et Aristophanes scriptores comoediarum agnoscuntur.

(b) Eusebius (Armenian)

Eupolis und Aristophanes waren als Liederdichter gekannt.

Eupolis: of Athens. He produced in the archonship of
Apollodorus [430/29], the same year as Phrynichus, a pow-
erful poet in his language and an emulator of Cratinus. He
displays much that is abusive and clumsy ["repulsive"?].
Fourteen plays are written by him.

iii There are seven poets of Old Comedy: Epicharmus,
Cratinus, Eupolis, Aristophanes, Pherecrates, Crates,
Platon.

iv [in Sicyon] After the memorial to Lycus, once you have
crossed the Asopus on your right is the Olympium, and a
little farther on the left side of the road is the tomb of
Eupolis, the Athenian comic poet.

v

(a) [428/7] Eupolis and Aristophanes, the writers of com-
edy, are becoming known.

(b) [427/6] Eupolis and Aristophanes were becoming
known as poets.

vi Cyril of Alexandria *Against Julian* 1.13

ὀγδοηκοστῇ ὀγδόῃ Ὀλυμπιάδι τὸν κωμῳδὸν Ἀριστο-
φάνην, Εὔπολίν τε καὶ Πλάτωνα γενέσθαι φασίν.

vii Syncellus p. 309.15 Mosshammer

Εὔπολις καὶ Ἀριστοφάνης κωμικοὶ Σοφοκλῆς τε ὁ
τραγῳδοποιὸς ἐγνωρίζετο.

viii *Chronica Minora* I 266.4 Fr.

filosofi autem cognoscebantur temporibus Artaxerxis
Sofoclus . . . Euripidus cantoconpositor . . . Socratus Athi-
neus et Periclus et Eupolus et Aristofanus architector.

ix *Suda* π 1708

Πλάτων, Ἀθηναῖος, κωμικός, γεγονὼς τοῖς χρόνοις
κατὰ Ἀριστοφάνην καὶ Φρύνιχον, Εὔπολιν, Φερεκρά-
την.

x *IG* ii² 2325.59

Εὔ[πολις

xi *IG* ii² 2325.126

Εὔ]πολις IIII

vi In the 88th Olympiad [428/7–425/4] they say that Aristophanes the comic poet was active, also Eupolis and Platon.

vii [428/7–425/4] The comic poets, Eupolis and Aristophanes, and Sophocles the tragedian were becoming known.

viii In the time of Artaxerxes [464–423] the philosophers were becoming known, Sophocles . . . Euripides the writer of songs . . . Socrates of Athens and Pericles and Eupolis and Aristophanes the dramatist.

ix Platon: of Athens, comic poet, who lived at the same time as Aristophanes and Phrynichus, Eupolis, Pherecrates.

x [list of victors at the Dionysia, in the 420s]
     Eu[polis

xi [list of victors at the Lenaea, in the 420s]
     Eu]polis 4

xii Aelian *On the Nature of Animals* 10.41

Εὐπόλιδι τῷ τῆς κωμῳδίας ποιητῇ δίδωσι δῶρον Αὐ-
γέας ὁ Ἐλευσίνιος σκύλακα ἰδεῖν ὡραῖον, Μολοττὸν
τὸ γένος, καὶ καλεῖ τοῦτον ὁ Εὔπολις ὁμωνύμως τῷ
δωρησαμένῳ αὐτόν. κολακευθεὶς οὖν ταῖς τροφαῖς,
καὶ ἐκ τῆς συνηθείας ὑπαχθεὶς τῆς μακροτέρας, ἐφίλει
τὸν δεσπότην ὁ Αὐγέας ὁ κύων. καί ποτε ὁμόδουλος
αὐτῷ νεανίας, ὄνομα Ἐφιάλτης, ὑφαιρεῖται δράματά
τινα τοῦ Εὐπόλιδος, ἃ οὐκ ἔλαθε κλέπτων, ἀλλὰ εἶδεν
αὐτὸν ὁ κύων, καὶ ἐμπεσὼν ἀφειδέστατα δάκνων ἀπ-
έκτεινεν. χρόνῳ δὲ ὕστερον ἐν Αἰγίνῃ τὸν βίον ὁ
Εὔπολις κατέστρεψε, καὶ ἐτάφη ἐνταῦθα· ὁ δὲ κύων
ὠρυόμενός τε καὶ θρηνῶν τὸν τῶν κυνῶν θρῆνον, εἶτα
μέντοι λύπῃ καὶ λιμῷ ἑαυτὸν ἐκτήξας ἀπέθανεν ἐπὶ τῷ
τροφεῖ καὶ δεσπότῃ, μισήσας τὸν βίον ὁ κύων. καὶ ὅ
γε τόπος καλεῖται μνήμῃ τοῦ τότε πάθους Κυνὸς
Θρῆνος.

xiii

(a) Hypothesis I *Acharnians*

ἐδιδάχθη ἐπὶ Εὐθύνου ἄρχοντος ἐν Ληναίοις διὰ Καλ-
λιστράτου· καὶ πρῶτος ἦν· δεύτερος Κρατῖνος Χειμα-
ζομένοις. οὐ σῴζονται. τρίτος Εὔπολις Νουμηνίαις.

34

xii Augeas of Eleusis once gave a gift to Eupolis, the comic poet, a handsome Molossian puppy dog, and Eupolis called it "Augeas" after the man who had given it to him. Spoilt in its upbringing and becoming used to Eupolis over a long period of time, Augeas the dog came to love its master very much. On one occasion, a fellow slave named Ephialtes was stealing some of Eupolis' plays, but the thief did not get away with it, for the dog saw him, attacked and bit him without mercy, finally killing him. Later on Eupolis passed away in Aegina and was buried there. The dog howled and wailed the lament that dogs utter, then finally tired with life, starved itself through grief and hunger, expiring on the tomb of its lord and master. And the place is in fact called "Dog's Lament," in memory of its suffering.

xiii

(a) It [*Acharnians*] was produced in the archonship of Euthynus [426/5] at the Lenaea through Callistratus. It finished first. Cratinus ⟨was⟩ second with *Tempest-Tossed*—it is not extant. Eupolis ⟨was⟩ third with *New Moons*.

(b) Hypothesis II *Knights*

ἐδιδάχθη τὸ δρᾶμα ἐπὶ Στρατοκλέους ἄρχοντος δημο-
σίᾳ εἰς Λήναια δι' αὐτοῦ <τοῦ> Ἀριστοφάνους. πρῶ-
τος ἦν· ἐνίκα δεύτερος Κρατῖνος Σατύροις· τρίτος
Ἀριστομένης Ὑλοφόροις.

(c) Hypothesis III *Peace*

ἐνίκησε δὲ τῷ δράματι ὁ ποιητὴς ἐπὶ ἄρχοντος Ἀλ-
καίου ἐν ἄστει. πρῶτος Εὔπολις Κόλαξι, δεύτερος
Ἀριστοφάνης Εἰρήνῃ, τρίτος Λεύκων Φράτορσιν.

xiv *Suda* δ 756

διασκευαζόμενα. Εὔπολις, Ἀθηναῖος, κωμικός, ἔγραψε
τόσα καὶ ἄλλα διασκευαζόμενος.

xv Horace *Satires* 2.3.11–12

quorsum pertinuit stipare Platona Menandro?
Eupolin, Archilochum, comites educere tantos?

xvi Horace *Satires* 1.4.1–5

Eupolis atque Cratinus Aristophanesque poetae
atque alii, quorum comoedia prisca virorum est,
siquis erat dignus describi, quod malus ac fur,
quod moechus foret aut sicarius aut alioqui
famosus, multa cum libertate notabant.

(b) The play [*Knights*] was produced in the archonship of Stratocles at the Lenaia through Aristophanes in his own name. It was first. Kratinos won the second prize with *Satyrs*, Aristomenes the third with *Wood-Bearers*.

(c) The poet won a prize with his play at the City Dionysia in the archonship of Alcaeus [422/1]. Eupolis came first with *Spongers*, Aristophanes second with *Peace*, and Leukon third with *Phratry-Members*.

xiv "Revising": Eupolis, of Athens, the comic poet, wrote a number of comedies, revising some.

xv What was the purpose of packing Platon along with Menander, of bringing along such companions as Eupolis or Archilochus?

xvi Eupolis, Cratinus, and Aristophanes and indeed any of the other poets of Old Comedy, would single out with great freedom anyone who was worthy of being pointed out, for being a wicked man or a thief, an adulterer or a cutthroat or notorious for any other reason.

xvii Persius 1.122–24

        audaci quicumque adflate Cratino
iratum Eupolidem praegrandi cum sene palles,
aspice et haec, si forte aliquid decoctius audis.

xviii Velleius Paterculus 1.16.3

una priscam illam et ueterem sub Cratino Aristophaneque
et Eupolide comoediam.

xix Quintilian 10.1.65–66

antiqua comoedia cum sinceram illam sermonis Attici gra-
tiam prope sola retinet, tum facundissimae libertatis, et si
est ⟨in⟩ insectandis uitiis praecipua, plurimum tamen
uirium etiam in ceteris partibus habet. nam et grandis et
elegans et uenusta . . . plures eius auctores, Aristophanes
tamen et Eupolis Cratinusque praecipui.

xx [Dionysius of Halicarnassus] *Art of Rhetoric* 8.11

ἡ δέ γε κωμῳδία ὅτι πολιτεύεται ἐν τοῖς δράμασι καὶ
φιλοσοφεῖ, ἡ τῶν περὶ τὸν Κρατῖνον καὶ Ἀριστο-
φάνην καὶ Εὔπολιν, τί δεῖ καὶ λέγειν;

xxi Plutarch *Table-Talk* 7.8.3

οὕτω δεήσει γραμματικὸν ἑκάστῳ τὸ καθ' ἕκαστον
ἐξηγεῖσθαι, τίς ὁ Λαισποδίας παρ' Εὐπόλιδι καὶ ὁ

xvii You who get off on bold Cratinus, who are impressed by Eupolis as well as the grand old man [Aristophanes], turn your attention also to this, if you would hear something more distilled.

xviii One ‹generation has featured› that early Old Comedy under Cratinus, Aristophanes, and Eupolis.

xix Old Comedy is perhaps alone in preserving not only that pure grace of Attic language but also a very potent freedom, and if it is especially good in chasing down vice, it does have a very great deal of power, however, in other areas. For it is grand and elegant and charming . . . there are many authors but especially Aristophanes, Eupolis, and Cratinus.

xx It is hardly necessary to state that comedy in the time of Cratinus and Aristophanes and Eupolis engaged with politics and philosophy.

xxi We would need a learned scholar beside each guest to explain every reference, e.g., who Laespodias was in

THE POETS OF OLD COMEDY

Κινησίας παρὰ Πλάτωνι καὶ ὁ Λάμπων παρὰ Κρα-
τίνῳ, καὶ τῶν κωμῳδουμένων ἕκαστος, ὥστε γραμ-
ματοδιδασκαλεῖον ἡμῖν γενέσθαι τὸ συμπόσιον ἢ
κωφὰ καὶ ἄσημα τὰ σκώμματα διαφέρεσθαι.

xxii Lucian *To the Uneducated Man* 27

τὰ τοσαῦτα βιβλία ἔχων τί μάλιστα ἀναγιγνώσκεις
αὐτῶν; τὰ Πλάτωνος; τὰ Ἀντισθένους; τὰ Ἀρχιλόχου;
τὰ Ἱππώνακτος; ἢ τούτων μὲν ὑπερφρονεῖς, ῥήτορες
δὲ μάλιστά σοι διὰ χειρός· εἰπέ μοι, καὶ Αἰσχίνου τὸν
κατὰ Τιμάρχου λόγον ἀναγιγνώσκεις; ἢ ἐκεῖνά γε
πάντα οἶσθα καὶ γιγνώσκεις αὐτῶν ἕκαστον, τὸν δὲ
Ἀριστοφάνην καὶ τὸν Εὔπολιν ὑποδέδυκας;

xxiii Lucian *Twice Accused* 33

τὸ μὲν τραγικὸν ἐκεῖνο καὶ σωφρονικὸν προσωπεῖον
ἀφεῖλέ μου, κωμικὸν δὲ καὶ σατυρικὸν ἄλλο ἐπέθηκέ
μοι καὶ μικροῦ δεῖν γελοῖον. εἶτά μοι εἰς τὸ αὐτὸ
φέρων συγκαθεῖρξεν τὸ σκῶμμα καὶ τὸν ἴαμβον καὶ
κυνισμὸν καὶ τὸν Εὔπολιν καὶ τὸν Ἀριστοφάνην, δει-
νοὺς ἄνδρας ἐπικερτομῆσαι τὰ σεμνὰ καὶ χλευάσαι
τὰ ὀρθῶς ἔχοντα.

xxiv Lucian *Fisherman* 25

φύσει γὰρ τι τοιοῦτόν ἐστιν ὁ πολὺς λεώς, χαίρουσι
τοῖς ἀποσκώπτουσιν καὶ λοιδορουμένοις, καὶ μάλισθ'

Eupolis [F 107], and Cinesias in Platon [F 200], and Lampon in Cratinus [F 62, 125] and so on for each of the people made fun of. So our party would become a class-room or the jokes would fall on deaf and ignorant ears.

xxii With all those books of yours, which of them in par-ticular do you read? The works of Plato? Of Antisthenes? Those of Archilochus or of Hipponax? Or do you reject these, and have the orators ready at hand? Tell me, do you read the speech of Aeschines, *Against Timarchus*? Are you familiar with all of those and know each one of them? Have you dipped into Aristophanes and Eupolis?

xxiii He [Lucian] stripped me [Dialogue] of my tragic and respectable mask and gave me another, a comic and satirical one, just short of ridiculous. Then bringing me to the same place he locked in with me Jest and the Iambic and the Cynical, Eupolis and Aristophanes, men very skilled at lampooning what is decent and at making fun of what is proper.

xxiv That is what the majority of people are like by na-ture. They enjoy those who make jokes and exchange in-

THE POETS OF OLD COMEDY

ὅταν τὰ σεμνότατα εἶναι δοκοῦντα διασύρηται, ὥσπερ
ἀμέλει καὶ πάλαι ἔχαιρον Ἀριστοφάνει καὶ Εὐπόλιδι
Σωκράτη τουτονὶ ἐπὶ χλεύῃ παράγουσιν ἐπὶ τὴν σκη-
νὴν καὶ κωμῳδοῦσιν ἀλλοκότους τινὰς περὶ αὐτοῦ
κωμῳδίας.

xxv Libanius F 50 2

τί τοῦτον οὐκ ἔχει δρᾶμα; τίς οὐκ Εὔπολις; τίς οὐκ
Ἀριστοφάνης; διὰ τοῦτον εὐδοκίμησε κωμῳδία. ὅμως
δὲ καὶ κωμῳδοὶ κεκμήκασι τὰ τούτου γράφοντες.

xxvi Macrobius *Satires* 7.5.8

notus est omnibus Eupolis, inter elegantes habendus vete-
ris comoediae poetas.

xxvii Platonius *On the Distinctions among Comedians*
(Koster I)

ἐπὶ τῶν Ἀριστοφάνους καὶ Κρατίνου καὶ Εὐπόλιδος
χρόνων τὰ τῆς δημοκρατίας ἐκράτει παρ’ Ἀθηναίοις
. . . τῆς ἰσηγορίας οὖν πᾶσιν ὑπαρχούσης ἄδειαν οἱ
τὰς κωμῳδίας συγγράφοντες εἶχον τοῦ σκώπτειν καὶ
στρατηγοὺς καὶ δικαστὰς τοὺς κακῶς δικάζοντας καὶ
τῶν πολιτῶν τινας ἢ φιλαργύρους ἢ συζῶντας ἀσελ-
γείᾳ . . . ἐπὶ τοίνυν τῆς Ἀριστοφάνους καὶ Κρατίνου
καὶ Εὐπόλιδος κωμῳδίας ἀφόρητοί τινες κατὰ τῶν
ἁμαρτανόντων ἦσαν οἱ ποιηταί.

sults, especially when what is held to be most serious is being made fun of. Just as long ago they certainly enjoyed Aristophanes and Eupolis when they brought Socrates here on stage for the sake of mockery and made up all sorts of bizarre comedies about him.

xxv What play does not contain him [Alcibiades]? What Eupolis or Aristophanes ⟨did not include him in their plays⟩? He is the reason that comedy flourished. But still even the comic poets got tired of writing about his exploits.

xxvi Everyone knows Eupolis, who must be ranked among the elegant poets of Old Comedy.

xxvii In the time of Aristophanes and Cratinus and Eupolis the democracy ruled at Athens . . . because freedom of speech existed for all, those who were writing comedies had no fear of making jokes at generals and jurors who rendered bad verdicts and any of the citizens who were greedy for money or lived a life of corruption . . . so in the time of the comedy of Aristophanes and Cratinus and Eupolis the poets were an irresistible force against wrongdoers.

xxviii Platonius *On the Distinctions among Styles* (Koster II)

Εὔπολις δὲ εὐφάνταστος μὲν εἰς ὑπερβολήν ἐστι κατὰ τὰς ὑποθέσεις· τὰς γὰρ εἰσηγήσεις μεγάλας τῶν δρα-μάτων ποιεῖται καὶ ἥνπερ ἐν τῇ παραβάσει φαντα-σίαν κινοῦσιν οἱ λοιποί, ταύτην ἐκεῖνος ἐν ⟨αὐτοῖς⟩ τοῖς δράμασιν, ἀναγαγεῖν ἱκανὸς ὢν ἐξ Ἅιδου νομο-θετῶν πρόσωπα καὶ δι' αὐτῶν εἰσηγούμενος ἢ περὶ θέσεως νόμων ἢ καταλύσεως. ὥσπερ δέ ἐστιν ὑψηλός, οὕτω καὶ ἐπίχαρις καὶ περὶ τὰ σκώμματα λίαν εὔ-στοχος. ὁ δὲ Ἀριστοφάνης τὸν μέσον ἐλήλακε τῶν ἀνδρῶν χαρακτῆρα· οὔτε γὰρ πικρὸς λίαν ἐστίν, ὥσπερ ὁ Κρατῖνος, οὔτε χαρίεις, ὥσπερ ὁ Εὔπολις, ἀλλ' ἔχει καὶ πρὸς τοὺς ἁμαρτάνοντας τὸ σφοδρὸν τοῦ Κρατίνου καὶ τὸ τῆς ἐπιτρεχούσης χάριτος Εὐ-πόλιδος.

xxix Diomedes (Koster XXIV.2.46)

secunda aetate fuerunt Aristophanes, Eupolis et Crati-nus, qui et principum vitia sectati acerbissimas comoedias composuerunt.

xxviii Eupolis is exceedingly imaginative in his comic plots, for he brings important topics into his plays, and the sort of *phantasia* which the others employ in the parabasis he uses throughout his plays, being able to bring back as characters lawgivers from Hades and through them discussing the passing and repealing of laws. Just as he is lofty, so too is he charming and spot on the mark with his jokes. Aristophanes has attained a character balanced between these two [Cratinus, Eupolis], since he is not too bitter, like Cratinus, nor ‹too› charming, like Eupolis, but possesses both the power of Cratinus against wrongdoers and the pervasive charm of Eupolis.

xxix To the second age [of comedy] belonged Aristophanes, Eupolis, and Cratinus, who wrote very fierce comedies attacking the vices of the leading men.

45

THE POETS OF OLD COMEDY

XXX

(a) Tzetzes *Distinctions among Poets* (Koster XXIa.82–84)

τῆς δευτέρας ἦν ὁ ψόγος κεκρυμμένος,
ἧς ἦν Κρατῖνος, Εὔπολις, Φερεκράτης,
Ἀριστοφάνης, Ἕρμιππός τε καὶ Πλάτων.

(b) Tzetzes Proem (Koster XIaI)

οὕτως ἡ πρώτη κωμῳδία τὸ σκῶμμα εἶχεν ἀπαρα-
κάλυπτον· ἐξήρκεσε δὲ τὸ ἀπαρακαλύπτως οὑτωσὶ
κωμῳδεῖν μέχρις Εὐπόλιδος . . . ἀλλὰ ψήφισμα θέν-
τος Ἀλκιβιάδου κωμῳδεῖν ἐσχηματισμένως καὶ μὴ
προδήλως αὐτός τε ὁ Εὔπολις Κρατῖνός τε καὶ Φερε-
κράτης καὶ Πλάτων, οὐχ ὁ φιλόσοφος, Ἀριστοφάνης
τε σὺν ἑτέροις τὰ συμβολικὰ μετεχειρίσαντο σκώμ-
ματα, καὶ ἡ δευτέρα κωμῳδία τῇ Ἀττικῇ ἀνεσκίρ-
τησεν.

(c) Tzetzes *Prolegomena to Lycophron* (Koster XXIIb)

κωμῳδοὶ πραττόμενοί εἰσιν οὗτοι οἷοι Ἀριστοφάνης,
Κρατῖνος, Πλάτων, Εὔπολις, Φερεκράτης καὶ ἕτεροι.

(d) Tzetzes, *Prolegomena to Hesiod*

τῶν ποιητῶν οἱ μέν εἰσι λυρικοί, οἱ δὲ μονῳδοί, οἱ δὲ
κωμικοί, καὶ ἕτεροι τραγικοί . . . κωμικῶν δὲ ὁ γέλως

xxx

(a) Indirect insult was characteristic of second ‹comedy›, of which there were Cratinus, Eupolis, Pherecrates, Aristophanes, Hermippus, and Platon.

(b) In this way First Comedy had unrestricted jokes, and this unrestricted humour prevailed until the time of Eupolis . . . but when Alcibiades passed a law to make fun of people indirectly and not plainly, Eupolis himself and Cratinus and Pherecrates and Platon (not the philosopher) and Aristophanes along with the rest fashioned their jokes allusively and so second comedy was at its height.

(c) Comic poets that are studied are those such as Aristophanes, Cratinus, Platon, Eupolis, Pherecrates, and the others

(d) There are lyric poets, writers of monody, comic poets, and tragedians . . . ‹characteristic› of comic poets is laugh-

μετὰ χορευτῶν καὶ προσώπων, οἷος Ἀριστοφάνης, Εὔπολις, Φερεκράτης.

xxxi *Life of Aristophanes* (Koster XXVIII.2–5)

ὃς πρῶτος δοκεῖ τὴν κωμῳδίαν ἔτι πλανωμένην τῇ ἀρχαίᾳ ἀγωγῇ ἐπὶ τὸ χρησιμώτερον καὶ σεμνότερον μεταγαγεῖν, πικρότερόν τε καὶ αἰσχρότερον Κρατίνου καὶ Εὐπόλιδος βλασφημούντων ἢ ἔδει.

xxxii

(a) Σ Aristophanes *Peace* 763c

αἰνίττεται εἰς Εὔπολιν καὶ τοὺς περὶ αὐτὸν ὡς παίδων ἐρῶντας καὶ παλαίστρας περιερχομένους.

(b) Σ Aristophanes *Peace* 740b

ῥακοφοροῦντας. αἰνίττεται δὲ καὶ εἰς Εὔπολιν.

(c) Σ Aristophanes *Peace* 741b

αἰνίττεται ταῦτα εἰς Εὔπολιν, ὃς ἐποίησε τὸν Ἡρακλέα πεινῶντα καὶ Διόνυσον δειλὸν καὶ Δία μοιχὸν καὶ δοῦλον κλαίοντα.

Εὐριπίδην codd., Εὔπολιν Dobree.

ter along with dancers and masks, for example Aristophanes, Eupolis, Pherecrates.

xxxi [Aristophanes] who seems to have been the first to steer comedy, which was wandering about in the old style, to something more useful and more serious, since Cratinus and Eupolis were using insulting people more bitterly and more shamelessly than they needed to.

xxxii

(a) He is alluding to Eupolis and those around him as being in love with boys and cruising the wrestling grounds.

(b) "Wearing rags": he is alluding again to Eupolis.

(c) This alludes to Eupolis [MS: "Euripides"], who created a starving Heracles and a cowardly Dionysus and an adulterous Zeus and a wailing slave.

THE POETS OF OLD COMEDY

(d) Σ Aristophanes *Clouds* 296c

οἱ τρυγοδαίμονες οὗτοι· οἱ ἄλλοι κωμικοὶ ἐν τοῖς ποιήμασιν αὐτῶν ἀνθρώπους εἰσῆγον χέζοντάς τε καὶ ἔτερα αἰσχρὰ ποιοῦντας. λέγει δὲ δι᾽ Εὔπολιν καὶ Κρατῖνον καὶ τοὺς ἄλλους.

xxxiii Σ Aelius Aristides 3.43

εἰς τοὺς κωμικούς· ὧν εἷς ἐστιν ὁ Εὔπολις.

xxxiv Σ Thucydides 1.30.1

ἡ παλαιὰ Ἀτθίς, ἧς ἔστιν Εὔπολις, Κρατῖνος, Ἀριστοφάνης, Θουκυδίδης.

xxxv Σ Lucian *Tragic Zeus* 1

τὸ δραματουργεῖν τοῦ ὑποδραματουργεῖν ταύτῃ διαφέρει· δραματουργεῖ μὲν γὰρ ὁ ποιητὴς καὶ τῆς ὑποθέσεως ὅλης καὶ τῶν ἐπῶν, ὡς Εὐριπίδης, Εὔπολις, Ἀριστοφάνης καὶ εἴ τις τοιοῦτος.

xxxvi Rufinus *On the Metres of Terence* (*GrL* VI 564.7)

ad Probum de metris comoediarum sic dicit: "nam quod de metris comoediarum requisisti, et ego scio plurimos existimare Terentianas vel maxime fabulas metrum non habere comoediae graecae, id est Menandri Philemonos Diphili et ceterorum, quae trimetris versibus constat.

(d) "These gods of comedy": the other comic poets in their plays would bring on men shitting and doing other shameful things. He says this because of Eupolis and Cratinus and the others.

xxxiii ⟨He is alluding⟩ to the comic poets, one of whom is Eupolis.

xxxiv The Old Attic, to which belong Eupolis, Cratinus, Aristophanes, Thucydides.

xxxv "To create drama" differs from "take part in drama" in this way. The poet creates the whole of the plot and the dialogue, such as Euripides, Eupolis, Aristophanes, and any other such a one.

xxxvi He [Firmianus] writes to Probus as follows about comic metres: "Now about what you have asked about the metres of comedy, I do know that very many people believe that Terence's plays in particular do not employ the metre of Greek Comedy, that is the comedy of Menander, Philemon, Diphilus and others, which consists of verses in

nostri enim veteris comediae scriptores in modulandis fa-
bulis sequi maluerunt, Eupolis Cratinum Aristophanem."

xxxvii Hephaestion *Handbook* 16.5

καὶ τὸ Εὐπολίδειον [τὸ] καλούμενον ἐπιχοριαμβικὸν
πολυσχημάτιστόν ἐστιν, ἐν ᾧ τὰς τροχαϊκὰς παρὰ
τάξιν ποιοῦσι δέχεσθαι τὸν σπονδεῖον· ἐνίοτε δὲ καὶ
ἀντισπαστικὸν καθαρὸν ποιοῦσιν.

xxxviii Marius Plotius Sacerdos *Art of Grammar* 3.7
(*GrL* VI 536.10)

choriambicum eupolidium tetrametrum catalecticum fit
primo pede ditrochaeo, secundo choriambo, tertio ditro-
chaeo, quarto, id est novissimo, amphimacro.

xxxix Marius Victorinus (Aphthonius) *Art of Grammar* 4
(*GrL* VI 144.6)

trochaicum tetrametrum catalecticum quartum iambum
habens, quod eupolidion vocatur.

xl Galen *On his own Books* 17

τῶν παρ' Εὐπόλιδι πολιτικῶν ὀνομάτων τρία· τῶν
παρ' Ἀριστοφάνει πολιτικῶν ὀνομάτων πέντε· τῶν
παρὰ Κρατίνῳ πολιτικῶν ὀνομάτων δύο· τῶν ἰδίων
κωμικῶν ὀνομάτων παραδείγματα, ἔν· 'εἰ χρήσιμον
ἀνάγνωσμα τοῖς παιδευομένοις ἡ παλαιὰ κωμῳδία'

trimeters. For in composing their verse our writers pre-
ferred to follow the poets of Old Comedy, such as Eupolis,
Cratinus, and Aristophanes."

xxxvii The epichoriambic called "the Eupolidean" is also
multiform, in which they make the trochaic ‹syzygies› ad-
mit the spondee against the order and sometimes they
compose a pure anapaest.

xxxviii The "eupolidean" choriambic tetrameter catalec-
tic would be: in the first metron two trochees [– ∪ – ∪], in
the second a choriamb [– ∪ ∪ –], in the third again two tro-
chees [– ∪ – ∪], and in the fourth and last an amphima-
crum [– ∪ –].

xxxix The trochaic tetrameter catalectic having an iamb
in the fourth foot, which is called the "eupolidean."

xl Three books of political terms in Eupolis, five books of
political terms in Aristophanes, and two books of political
terms in Cratinus. Examples of particular comic expres-
sions, one book. *Is Old Comedy Useful Reading for
Educated Men*?

ΑΙΓΕΣ

The references to goats in the extant fragments (F 3, 12, 19, 22) and their own description of their favourite foods (F 13) show that we have an animal chorus of the type familiar from other old comedies (Beasts, Birds, Fishes, etc.). F 1 may refer to a ram and leader of the flock.

An intriguing aspect of this lost comedy is its relationship to Aristophanes' Clouds. F 17–18 show that one character, called Prodamus in F 17, was a teacher of both grammatikē *and* mousikē. *In one scene he was teaching a man from the country how to dance, and that countryman was performing badly—cf. the teaching scene at Clouds 627–804. In light of the rustic allusions at F 1, 3, 12, 13, 15, 19, 22, 24, the overall theme of the comedy may have been*

Fragments

1 Erotianus σ 55

† ὡς ἡ ποτ᾽ αὐτὸν ἦν κάμῃ τις, εὐθέως
ἐρεῖ πρὸς αὐτόν, "πρίω μοι σελάχιον"· τί δὲ ἦν
   λύκον †
κεκράξεται φράσει τε πρὸς τὸν αἰπόλον.

1 ὡς ἡ ποτ᾽ αὐτὸν ἦν codd., ὡς ἦν ποτ᾽ αὐτῶν δὴ Austin.

2 Athenaeus 106b

                    πλὴν
ἅπαξ ποτ᾽ ἐν Φαίακος ἔφαγον καρίδας.

NANNY-GOATS

the ever-popular opposition of town and country. Has the farmer been evacuated to the city, bringing with him his flock of goats?

F 20 mentions Hipponicus, father of Callias, who was dead by 421 when Callias had come into his inheritance. Thus Nanny-Goats *could belong at any festival between 429 and 422 (not L-425, L-424, D-423). I would suggest D-424, perhaps Eupolis' first victory at the Dionysia. Thus* Nanny-Goats *would be earlier than the first version of* Clouds, *a date that has consequences for the relationship between the poets.*

Recent bibliography: J. Wilkins, in Rivals *341–54; M. Telò, SemRom 9 (2006) 63–67; Rothwell 130–32, 200–204.*

Fragments

1 (A) If one gets sick, immediately he says to them, "buy some shark meat for me."
 (B) What if ⟨he spots⟩ a wolf?
 (A) He will shout and tell the goatherd.

2 Except that I once ate shrimps at Phaeax's house.[1]

[1] Phaeax (*PAA* 911410) was a well-known political figure of the 420s and 410s, who was involved in the ostracism of Hyperbolus in 416. At F 116 and at *Knights* 1375–83 he is made fun of for his pretentious rhetoric.

THE POETS OF OLD COMEDY

3 Photius (b, z) α 506

σὺ δ᾽ αἰγιάζεις ἐνθαδὶ καθήμενος.

4 Photius p. 564.17

καὶ ζῆν μαθόντι μηδὲ τάγυρι μουσικῆς.

5 Photius p. 47.6

καὶ τῆς λοπάδος· ἔνεισι δ᾽ ἑψητοί τινες.

6 Athenaeus 426f

Διόνυσε χαῖρε. μή τι πέντε καὶ δύο;

7 Priscian *Institutes of Grammar* 18.252

προσένεγκέ μούγγυς τὸ στόμ᾽ ὀσφρέσθαι τὸ σόν.

8 Photius (S^z) α 2839

ταύτην ἐγὼ ᾽ζήτουν πάλαι τὴν ἁρμογήν.

9 Σ Aristophanes *Wasps* 902b

τὴν πανδοκεύτριαν γὰρ ὁ γλάμων ἔχει.

10 Athenaeus 380e

τοῦδε νῦν γεῦσαι λαβών.

3 And you sit here and talk of goats.

4 And to live without having learned even a scrap of *mousikē*.

5 And on the plate. And there are some boiled fish on it.

6 Greetings, Dionysus, the five and two perhaps?[1]

> [1] A normal ratio for wine drinking was five parts water to two parts wine (see Athenaeus 426e).

7 Bring your mouth here and let me smell it.

8 I have been seeking this modulation for a long time.

9 The bleary-eyed man is married to the tap woman.

10 Now, you [masc.] take some of this and taste it.

11 Photius (z) ined., *Suda* χ 471

ἐγὼ τελῶ τὸν μισθὸν ὅντιν᾽ ἂν χρῇ.

12 Photius p. 290.20

ἐπίσταμαι γὰρ αἰπολεῖν, σκάπτειν, νεᾶν, φυτεύειν.

13 Plutarch *Table-Talk* 662d

βοσκόμεθ᾽ ὕλης ἀπὸ παντοδαπῆς, ἐλάτης, πρίνου
   κομάρου τε
πτόρθους ἁπαλοὺς ἀποτρώγουσαι, καὶ πρὸς
   τούτοισίν ἔτ᾽ ἄνθην,
κύτισόν τ᾽ ἠδὲ σφάκον εὐώδη, καὶ σμίλακα τὴν
   πολύφυλλον,
κότινον, σχῖνον, μελίαν, λεύκην, ἀρίαν, δρῦν, κιττόν,
   ἐρίκην,
5   πρόμαλον, ῥάμνον, φλόμον, ἀνθέρικον, κισθόν,
   φηγόν, θύμα, θύμβραν.

14 Athenaeus 409b

αὐτοῦ τὴν χερνίβα παύσεις.

15 Σ Aristophanes *Peace* 790–91a

σφυράδων πολλῶν ἀναμέστη

16 Athenaeus 301a

ὦ Χάριτες, αἷσι μέλουσιν ἑψητοί.

11 I will pay whatever fee is necessary.

12 I know how to herd goats, to dig, to plough, to plant.

13 We feed off every sort of tree: fir tree, prickly oak, and strawberry tree, munching on their tender shoots and also the foliage: the medick tree and fragrant sage, and leafy bindweed, wild olive, lentisk, ash tree, poplar, holm oak, oak tree, ivy, heather, willow, thornbush, mullein, asphodel, rockrose, deciduous oak, thyme, and savory.[1]

[1] The translations in the catalogue are based on Wilkins & Rackham.

14 You will keep the water for washing from him.

15 Crammed with sheep droppings.

16 O Graces, who care about boiled fish.

17

(a) Quintilian 1.10.17

grammatice quondam ac musice iunctae fuerunt . . . eosdem utriusque rei praeceptores fuisse cum Sophron ostendit . . . tum Eupolis, apud quem Prodamus et musicen et litteras docet

(b) Σ Dionysius Thrax, *GrGr* I 3 p. 490.25

πάλαι τοὺς αὐτοὺς γραμματικῆς καὶ μουσικῆς εἶναι διαδασκάλους, ὡς Εὔπολις εἰσάγει ἐν Αἰξί.

18 P. Oxy. 2738 col. ii

πυρριχίζων, ἐν δὲ Αἰξὶν Εὐπόλ[ιδος] τὸ μαλακὴν κε[λ]εύ[ειν] τὴν Ἀθηνᾶν ποεῖν. σκλη[ρ]ῶς ποιοῦντο[ς] τοῦ ἀγροίκου τὸ σχῆμα τῆς Ἀθηνᾶς ὁ διδ[ά]σκαλος ἐκέλευσεν μαλακῶς αὐτὸ ποεῖν.

19 The Antiatticist p. 84.19

βουκολεῖσθαι αἶγας

20

(a) Hesychius ι 292

ἱερεὺς Διονύσου· Εὔπολις Αἰξὶν Ἱππόνικον σκώπτων ὡς ἐρυθρὸν τῇ ὄψει.

17

(a) Grammar and music were once combined . . . that the same people were teachers of both subjects is shown not only by Sophron [F 155], but also by Eupolis in whom Prodamus teaches both grammar and music.

(b) Long ago the same people were teachers of grammar and music, as Eupolis brings on stage in *Nanny-Goats*.

18 "Doing the Pyrrhic dance": in Eupolis' *Nanny-Goats* there is the command to perform the Athena dance smoothly. When the farmer performed the Athena dance awkwardly, the teacher ordered him to do it smoothly.

19 To herd goats.

20

(a) "Priest of Dionysos": Eupolis in his *Nanny-Goats* making fun of Hipponicus for being red-faced.

(b) Σ Aristophanes *Frogs* 308

ὁδὶ δὲ δείσας· ὁ τοῦ Διονύσου ἱερεύς. πυρρὸς γὰρ ἦν
κατὰ φύσιν. . . . Εὔπολις δὲ "τὸν τοῦ Διονύσου ἱερέα
νομίζετ᾽ αἰγίπυρρον" ἀντὶ τοῦ πυρρόν. τὸ γὰρ ἄνθος
ἔχειν φησὶ Δημήτριος ἱκανῶς ἐρυθρόν.

νομίζετ᾽ codd., ὀνομάζει Hemsterhuis.

21 Pollux 10.102

νεόκοπον κάρδοπον

22 Σ Homer *Iliad* 16.353b

καὶ Εὔπολις "προβατικὸν χορόν" φησι τὸν ἐξ αἰγῶν.

ΑΣΤΡΑΤΕΥΤΟΙ Η ΑΝΔΡΟΓΥΝΑΙ

*The titles suggest that the play turned on the portrayal of
the* astrateutos *("one who avoided military service") as a
woman—cf. the joke at Amynias at* Clouds *691–92 and also
at Cratinus F 60, where the female runaways of the title
may be effeminate males. Men appear on stage as women
in Aristophanes'* Thesmophoriazusae, *Eupolis'* Dyers, *and
Cratinus'* Poofters. *There may also have been an allusion
to Achilles, who to avoid the Trojan War was disguised as a
woman on Scyrus.*

(b) "This one was afraid": the priest of Dionysos. For he was red-haired in appearance . . . Eupolis "consider the priest of Dionysos to be *aigipyrrhos*," instead of "red-haired" (*pyrrhos*). Demetrius [F 34] says that this flower has quite a reddish colour.[1]

1 Or with Hemsterhuis "Eupolis calls the priest of Dionysus 'aigipyyrhos.'"

21 A newly carved trough.

22 Eupolis uses *"probatikos* chorus" of goats.[1]

1 The point being that *probatikos* technically applies to sheep.

Brief fragments: (F 23) "incurable," (F 24) "leaping up" [fem.], (F 25) "little pouches," (F 26) "livelihood," (F 27) "pitiful," (F 28) "they had escaped notice," (F 29) "on horseback," (F 30) "little girl," (F 31) "anchovies," (F 32) "he behaves like a young man," (F 33) "whinny," (F 34) "sausages."

DRAFT-DODGERS OR MEN-WOMEN

Some have assumed that Eupolis was writing an anti-war play like those of Aristophanes, but "men-women" would be an odd chorus to attract the sympathies of the spectators—Plato Symposium 189e reveals that androgynos *has always been an insult at Athens. We may wonder also if the chorus was "converted" to a more manly form of behaviour during the play.*

The play could have been performed during any period of combat. Scholars have rather too confidently dated the

63

play to 426 or 423–421, but the kōmōidoumenoi *in the fragments do not allow of any certain date. Peisander (F 35) was active until 411, and Melanthius (F 43) during the 420s and 410s. Phormion is best known for his exploits during the early years of the War (431–428), but F 44 does not have to belong to that period. The mention of Pactolus*

Fragments

35 Σ Aristophanes *Birds* 1556

Πείσανδρος εἰς Πακτωλὸν ἐστρατεύετο,
κἀνταῦθα τῆς στρατιᾶς κάκιστος ἦν ἀνήρ.

36 Diogenes Laertius 3.7

ἐν εὐσκίοις δρόμοισιν Ἑκαδήμου θεοῦ.

37 Choeroboscus On Hephaestion *Handbook* 1.6

Ἀθηναίων εἰ βούλεταί τις ἐγγράφειν

38 Orus *On Orthography* fol. 280ᵛ 1

ὡς ἦρξε περὶ Μίνωαν αὐτὸς οὑτοσί.

39 Photius (b, z) α 551

ὅμοιον ᾄδειν· οὐ γὰρ ἔστ᾽ ἄλλως ἔχον.

(F 35) has been taken to refer to the military action at Spartolus (429) and Minoa to the occupation there in 427 (Thucydides 3.51). But neither reference need not be to a recent event. I would suggest 414–412.

Recent bibliography: M. Christ, CQ 54 (2004) 33–57.

Fragments

35 Peisander served at Pactolus, and there he was the most cowardly soldier in the army.[1]

 [1] Pactolus was a fabled river of gold in Lydia (Sophocles *Philoctetes* 394). Hanow read "Spartolus" here, relating the fragment to the expedition in 429 recorded at Thucydides 2.79.

36 At the shady running tracks of the divine Hecademus.[1]

 [1] A gymnasium was located in the sacred grove of the hero Hecademus, in which was located the site of Plato's school (Academy).

37 If any of the Athenians wishes to put on the roll.

38 That (when?) this man here was in charge at Minoa.

39 Sing all you want—it won't be any different.

THE POETS OF OLD COMEDY

40 Photius (z) α 3453

οἳ πεπείρους ἀχράδας ἐσθίουσιν

41 Athenaeus 397b

μήποτε θρέψω
παρὰ Περσεφόνῃ τοιόνδε ταῶν, ὃς τοὺς εὕδοντας ἐγεί-
ρει.

42 Hephaestion *Handbook* 15.22

ἄνδρες ἑταῖροι, δεῦρο ἤδη τὴν γνώμην προσίσχετε,
εἰ δυνατόν, καὶ μή τι μεῖζον πράττουσα τυγχάνει.
καὶ ξυνεγιγνόμην ἀεὶ τοῖς ἀγαθοῖς φάγροισιν.

43 Σ Aristophanes *Peace* 808b

ὅτι γὰρ ὁ Μελάνθιος ὀψοφάγος, προείρηται. καὶ παρ᾽
Εὐπόλιδι ἐν Ἀστρατεύτοις.

44 Σ Aristophanes *Peace* 348e

αὐτοῦ μέμνηται . . . Εὔπολις Ἀστρατεύτοις.

45 Σ Lucian *Alexander* 4

καὶ ὁ Φρυνώνδας ἐπὶ πονηρίᾳ βοᾶται Εὐπόλιδι ἐν
Ἀστρατεύτοις, Δήμοις.

46 Photius (b, z) α 1764

ἀνδρογύνον ἄθυρμα

66

40 Those who eat ripe pears.

41 So that I won't raise in Persephone's house such a pea-cock that wakes sleepers.

42 Comrades, now direct your attention here
    If possible, and unless < > happens to be doing some-thing more important
    And I always got together with good sea bream.[1]

[1] The first two lines are cratineans, a metre of the parabasis; Hephaestion 16.6 says that the whole parabasis of *Draft-Dogers* was in this metre. The third line is in trochaics, used in the *epir-rhemata* of parabases.

43 That Melanthios was a glutton has already been stated. And also in Eupolis' *Draft-Dodgers*.

44 Eupolis mentions him [Phormion] in *Draft-Dodgers*.

45 Phrynondas is notorious for wickedness—Eupolis in *Draft-Dodgers* and *Demes* [F 139].

46 An androgynous plaything.

Brief fragment: (F 47) "knuckle bones of deer."

ΑΥΤΟΛΥΚΟΣ Α ΚΑΙ Β

This play is unusual for two reasons. First it was produced "through Demostratus." Aristophanes used producers all through his career (Philonides, Callistratus, Araros), but this is the only documented instance for Eupolis—but see the plural at T 14. The other is that the comedy was revised and presumably performed a second time, although the extent of the revision seems not to be that extensive (see T 2 below). The date of one version is fixed by the reference in Athenaeus (T 1) to 420. This is more likely the first version, since we know from Xenophon that Autolycus' victory was at the Panathenaea—422 was a year of the most recent Panathenaea.

Two problems bedevil the student of this comedy. First is whether there is any connection with the myths of Autolycus, grandfather of Odysseus and the greatest thief in ancient lore. Euripides wrote two satyr plays called "Autolycus," one of which portrayed the story of Autolycus' ability to disguise his thefts. F 282a contains an impressive denunciation of the athlete in modern society.

The other problem is what sort of comedy could be constructed around a teenaged athlete. The boy's father was made fun of at F 61 and the boy's victory at F 63. Apsines' rhetorical example (T 3) may suggest a plotline, on which Eupolis presented himself in the prologue as being sold as a slave to Lycon, who "handed his son over to him." On this

AUTOLYCUS

line Eupolis would have found himself in charge of a not
too bright young athlete. The story of Eupolis and the dog
in Aelian (T 12) may allow one to go farther. Eupolis is de-
scribed as a "fellow slave" of Ephialtes, who had stolen
some of his plays. Can we imagine a pair of comic poets,
portrayed as slaves, competing for the tutorship of the
young Autolycus? The obvious person to lurk beneath
"Ephialtes" is, of course, Aristophanes.

    The comedy makes a nice pair with Spongers, produced
the previous year, in that both will have had something to
do with Callias, son of Hipponicus, richest man in Athens
and known to us for Plato's entertaining description in
Protagoras as one who welcomed sophists into his house
and as the lover (erastēs) of the young Autolycus in Xeno-
phon's Symposium. While nothing in the fragments must
refer to Callias, it is very likely that he had a role in this
comedy, which may have influenced Xenophon's descrip-
tion of a symposium at Callias' home following the youth's
victory in the pancration at the Panathenaea. F 58, 61, and
63 show that the family of Autolycus was made fun of in
the comedy. It has often been assumed that Lycon's wife
and mother of Autolycus was named Rhodia, but in F 58
and 61 the Greek may just mean "a Rhodian woman," with
whom Lycon was associated—cf. F 50a for Leogoras and
Myrrhine.

THE POETS OF OLD COMEDY

Testimonia

i Athenaeus 216cd

πάντ᾽ οὖν ψεύδονται οἱ φιλόσοφοι καὶ πολλὰ παρὰ
τοὺς χρόνους γράφοντες οὐκ αἰσθάνονται, καθάπερ
οὐδ᾽ ὁ καλὸς Ξενοφῶν, ὃς ἐν τῷ Συμποσίῳ ὑποτίθεται
Καλλίαν τὸν Ἱππονίκου Αὐτολύκου τοῦ Λύκωνος
ἐρῶντα καὶ νενικηκότος αὐτοῦ παγκράτιον ἑστίασιν
ποιούμενον καὶ σὺν τοῖς ἄλλοις δαιτυμόσι παρόντα
<αὐτὸν> τὸν ἴσως μηδὲ γεννηθέντα ἢ περὶ τὴν παιδι-
κὴν ἡλικίαν ὑπάρχοντα. ἐστὶν δὲ οὗτος ὁ καιρὸς καθ᾽
ὃν Ἀριστίων ἄρχων ἦν. ἐπὶ τούτου γὰρ Εὔπολις τὸν
Αὐτόλυκον διδάξας διὰ Δημοστράτου χλευάζει τὴν
νίκην τοῦ Αὐτολύκου.

ii Galen *On Hippocrates' Regimen of Life* 1.4

ἐπιδιεσκευάσθαι λέγεται βιβλίον ἐπὶ τῷ προτέρῳ γε-
γραμμένῳ τὸ δεύτερον γραφέν, ὅταν τὴν ὑπόθεσιν
ἔχον τὴν αὐτὴν καὶ τὰς πλείστας τῶν ῥήσεων τὰς
αὐτάς, τινὰ μὲν ἀφῃρημένα τῶν ἐκ τοῦ προτέρου
συγγράμματος ἔχῃ, τινὰ δὲ προσκείμενα, τινὰ δ᾽
ὑπηλλαγμένα· παράδειγμα δ᾽ εἰ βούλει τούτου σαφη-
νείας ἕνεκα, τὸν δεύτερον Αὐτόλυκον Εὐπόλιδος ἔχεις
ἐκ τοῦ προτέρου διεσκευασμένον.

EUPOLIS

Testimonia

i Philosophers make all sorts of mistakes and do not real-ise that they are committing many chronological errors, like the marvellous Xenophon, who in his *Symposium* por-trays Callias the son of Hipponicus in love with Autolycus the son of Lycon and holding a feast after Autolycus had won the pancration, with himself [Xenophon] present along with the other guests, when he had either not yet been born or was just in childhood. This was the time when Aristion was archon [421/0]. In that year Eupolis put on his *Autolycus* through Demostratus and makes fun of the victory of Autolycus.

ii "To be a revision": a work is so called when it is rewrit-ten from the original version. It has the same plot and most of the same text, but will have some things removed from the previous version, some things added, and some things revised. If for the sake of clarity you need an exam-ple of this, you have the second *Autolycus* "revised" from its previous version.

iii Apsines *Rhetoric* 3

ἐν ταῖς προσαγγελίαις ἁρμόσει σοι ἐκεῖνο τὸ θεώ-
ρημα, ὅταν ὃ βούλει ὡς ἀναιρῶν τιθῇς, οἷον ὡς ἐπ᾽
ἐκείνης τῆς ὑποθέσεως· Εὔπολις ἁλοὺς ξενίας δημο-
σίᾳ ἐπράθη. πριάμενος αὐτὸν ὁ Λύκων ἐγχειρίζει τὸν
παῖδα, ὁ δὲ ἑαυτὸν προσαγγέλλει . . . "οὔτε ἐλευθερίαν
πράξων ἐμαυτῷ, οὔτε ὅπως ἂν ἀπαλλαγείην τῆς παρ-
ούσης ταύτης δουλείας, ὥς τις ἴσως τῶν ἀκουόντων
ὑμῶν ὑπολαμβάνει, παρελήλυθα, ἀλλὰ θανάτου δεό-
μενος."

Fragments

48 Pollux 10.161

οἰκοῦσι δ᾽ ἐνθάδ᾽ ἐν τρισὶν καλιδίοις,
οἴκημ᾽ ἔχων ἕκαστος.

49 Σ Homer *Iliad* 13.353

ἤδη γὰρ Ἀρίσταρχον στρατηγοῦντ᾽ ἄχθομαι.

50

(a) Zonaras p. 548

ὅτιὴ τὰ πατρῷα πρὸς σὲ καταδιέφθορα.

iii In denunciations this technique will work for you, presenting what you want as if rejecting it, e.g., as from this situation: Eupolis was convicted of *xenia* and sold at a public sale. Lycon bought him and handed his son over to him. Eupolis denounces himself . . . "Not to gain freedom for myself have I come nor that I might be delivered from this present slavery, as perhaps one of you listening might suppose, but to ask for death."

Fragments

48 They live here in three shacks, each one having his own home.[1]

[1] This fragment has been often cited as evidence for a three-door *skene* in the 5th c. See Revermann 209.

49 I already hate Aristarchus as general.[1]

[1] An Aristarchus (*PAA* 164155) is known as general in 411.

50

(a) Because I have wasted all my inheritance on you.[1]

[1] Many have followed Runkel in identifying the speaker of F 50a as Leogoras, based on the evidence of Σ *Clouds* 109d. I would identify the speaker of F 50a as Callias (to Autolycus or a hetaera?) and regard the reference in the Aristophanic scholia as a separate fragment.

(b) Σ Aristophanes *Clouds* 109d

Εὔπολις ἐν Αὐτολύκῳ βʹ ὡς καὶ διὰ Μυρρίνην ἑταίραν τὰ χρήματα ἀποβεβληκότα.

51 *Epimerismi Homerici* ω 21

ἆρα σφόδρ᾽ ἐνεούρησεν οὐξώλης γέρων;

52 Photius (b, z) α 1197

τί δῆτ᾽ ἄν, εἰ μὴ τὴν ἀμίδα καθεῦδ᾽ ἔχων;

53 Pollux 10.44–45

τί δῆτ᾽ ἄν, εἰ μὴ τὸ σκάφιον αὐτῇ παρῆν;

54 Athenaeus 368d

σκέλη δὲ καὶ κωλῆνες εὐθὺ τοὐρόφου.

55 Pollux 9.30

ἐλλιμένιον δοῦναι πρὶν εἰσβῆναί σε δεῖ.

56 Photius p. 650.10

ἀτὰρ ἤγαγες καινόν <τι> φῖτυ τῶν βοῶν.

57 Photius (b, z) α 1797

ἀνεκάς τ᾽ ἐπαίρω καὶ βδελυρὸς σὺ τὸ σκέλος.

(b) Eupolis in his *Second Autolycus* <makes fun of him [Leogoras]> for having thrown his money away on a *hetaera* Myrrhine.

51 Has that cursed old man pissed in it?

52 What then, if he hadn't been sleeping with a chamber pot?

53 What then, if she hadn't had the basin?

54 Legs and buttocks hanging straight to the roof.

55 You must pay the harbour tax before you enter.

56 Indeed you brought a new planting of cattle.

57 You raised your leg upwards, you disgusting man.

THE POETS OF OLD COMEDY

58 Photius β 12

Ῥοδίαν γυναῖκα βακκάριδα μεμιγμένην

59 Σ Aristophanes *Clouds* 252b

καπνοὺς ἀποφαίνει καὶ σκιάς.

60 Erotianus α 103

{A.} ἐπὶ καινοτέρας ἰδέας ἀσεβῆ βίον, ὦ μοχθηρός,
ἔτριβες.
{B.} πῶς ὦ πολλῶν ἤδη λοπάδων τοὺς ἄμβωνας περι-
λείξας;

61 Σ (Arethas) Plato *Apology* 23e

Εὔπολις δ᾽ ἐν Φίλοις καὶ ἐπὶ τῇ γυναικὶ Ῥοδίᾳ κωμῳ-
δεῖ αὐτόν, ἐν δὲ τῷ πρώτῳ Αὐτολύκῳ εἰς ξένον.

62 Σ (Arethas) Plato *Apology* 19c

κωμῳδεῖται δὲ καὶ <ὅτι> τὸ τῆς εἰρήνης κολοσσικὸν
ἐξῆρεν ἄγαλμα. Εὔπολις Αὐτολύκῳ.

63 Athenaeus 216d

Εὔπολις τὸν Αὐτόλυκον διδάξας διὰ Δημοστράτου
χλευάζει τὴν νίκην τοῦ Αὐτολύκου.

58 A Rhodian woman smeared with perfume.

59 He is just showing smoke and shadows.

60 (A) Wretch, you lived an unholy life with your novel ideas.
   (B) How so, you who have licked the lips of many dishes?[1]

   [1] An exchange between two comic poets speaking metaphorically about their work?

61 Eupolis makes fun of him [Lykon] also for his wife Rhodia in *Friends* [F 295], and as a foreigner in his first *Autolycus*.

62 Aristophanes was made fun of because he set up the statue of Peace. Eupolis in his *Autolycus*.

63 Eupolis put on his *Autolykos* through Demostratus, poking fun at the victory of Autolycus.

64 Photius (z) ε 2356

Εὐτρήσιος· παρὰ τὸ τετρῆσθαι. τὸν Αὐτόλυκον ὁ Εὔ-
πολις σκώπτει. Εὔτρησις δὲ πόλις Ἀρκαδική.

65 Σ Aristophanes *Wasps* 1025b

δι᾽ Εὔπολιν· ἐν Αὐτολύκῳ δὲ τοιαῦτά φησιν ὅτι περιῄει
τὰς παλαίστρας σεμνυννόμενος καὶ τοῖς παισὶν ἑαυτὸν
δῆλον ποιῶν τῆς νίκης ἕνεκα.

66 Pollux 10.47

δίφρος Θετταλικὸς τετράπους

ΒΑΠΤΑΙ

The noun Baptae *occurs only in reference to this comedy.
The verb* baptein *has often been taken as equivalent to*
baptizesthai *(to be immersed) and the chorus as a group
initiated into the mysteries of Cotyto (see below) by immer-
sion or "baptism." But a noun ending in* –tēs/–tai *suggests
rather men doing something active, hence the frequent
translation "dippers." But in fifth-century Athenian texts,*
baptein *means "to dye" rather than "to dip." What then did
this chorus of effeminate males dye, their hair or their
robes? Probably the latter, since dyeing the hair was to
feign youth rather than display effeminacy. For choruses
with effeminate males we may compare Cratinus'* Poofters,
Run-Aways, *and Eupolis'* Draft-Dodgers.

*The testimonia reveal that the Thracian goddess Cotyto
had a role in the comedy, very likely as a character. Cotyto*

64 "Eutresian" instead of "to be drilled." Eupolis pokes fun at Autolycus. Eutresis is a city in Arcadia.

65 Because of Eupolis. He says something of the sort in *Autolycus*, that he [Aristophanes] would go around the wrestling grounds putting on airs and parading himself in front of boys on account of his victory.

66 A four-footed Thessalian chair

Brief fragments: (F 67) "to entertain," (F 68) "nettles," (F 69) "masturbation," (F 70) "lack of buyers," (F 71) "feeble," (F 72) "violence," (F 73) "interest at a fifth," (F 74) "warning," (F 75) "to be a whore."

was both a fertility goddess, whose rites were practised in Sicily in the fifth century, and a Thracian goddess, whose worship resembled that of the Mother Goddess. What Eupolis seems to have done is create a comic version, whereby Cotyto's rites at Athens were conducted by gender-challenged males. The references in both the testimonia and the fragments to lyre players might imply that Cotyto appeared in the guise of a lyre player (cf. the disguised Dionysus in Bacchae*).*

The comedy was associated strongly with Alcibiades, and elaborate stories were created to connect Alcibiades' alleged reprisal against Eupolis with a larger restriction on the freedom of Old Comedy. Ancient critics were constantly seeking evidence for the state's curtailment of the licence of the comic poets. The witty rejoinder attributed to

*Alcibiades may be historical—it does suit everything we
know about the enfant terrible of Athenian politics. But
was the entire comedy a large-scale attack on Alcibiades,
as is often assumed without sufficient evidence, or (more
probably) was he made fun of in some memorable scene,
perhaps in the latter part of the comedy and involving a vat
of dye?*

*The comedy is usually dated to 415, the year of the Sicil-
ian Expedition and of the scandals over the Herms and the
Mysteries. Critics have been quick to connect a comedy in-
volving Alcibiades and the rites of a new goddess with the
profanation of the Mysteries which would lead to his self-*

Testimonia

i Lucian *To the Uneducated Man* 27

ἀνέγνως καὶ τοὺς Βάπτας, τὸ δρᾶμα ὅλον; εἶτ᾿ οὐδέν
σου τἀκεῖ καθίκετο, οὐδ᾿ ἠρυθρίασας γνωρίσας αὐτά;

ii

(a) Juvenal 2.91–92

talia secreta coluerunt orgia taeda
Cecropiam soliti Baptae lassare Cotyto.

(b) Σ (π) ad loc

Baptae titulus libri, quo inpudici describuntur ab Eupo-
lide, qui inducit viros ad imitationem feminarum sal-

imposed exile, but on a 415 date, the comedy would have been produced before the scandal was made public. A date of 414 or 413 would have the play produced when Alcibiades was in exile and perhaps a less likely comic target. It is not unreasonable that Alcibiades' disregard for religious propriety was not a one-off activity in 416/5, had perhaps gone on for several years, and was not as much of a secret as has been assumed. I would prefer a date of 416.

Recent bibliography: A. M. Velardi, AION (fil.) *4–5 (1982–1983) 4–5, 65–74; E. C. Kopff*, AJPh *111 (1990) 318–29; V. Lozanova, in* Colloquia Pontica *I (1995) 31–40; I. C. Storey*, AJPh *114 (1993) 71–84.*

Testimonia

i Have you read *Dyers*, the whole play? And did nothing there get through to you? Did you not blush on realising it?

ii

(a) The Baptae observed such rites with secret torches, used to wearing out an Athenian Cotyto.

(b) "Baptae" is the title of a work in which Eupolis portrays immoral men; he brings on stage men dancing in the

ταντεσ. Βαπταε αυτεμ μολλεσ· Ϙυο τιτυλο Ευπολισ
ξομοεδιαμ σξριπσιτ, οβ Ϙυαμ αβ Αλξιβιαδε, Ϙυεμ
πραεξιπυε περστρινχερατ, νεξατυσ εστ.

(c) Σ (Z) ad loc

Baptae: quo titulo scripsit Eupolis comoediam, in qua in-
ducit viros Athenienses ad imitationem feminarum lassare
⟨p⟩saltriam.

(d) Σ (φ) ad loc

Baptae dicuntur molles et effeminati, quo titulo Eupolis
et Aristophanes comediam scripserunt, in qua inducunt
Athenienses viros ad imitationem feminarum colere Coty-
ton, id est psaltriam deam Atheniensium, quam effeminati
colebant.

iii "Probus" *ad* Juvenal 2.91–92

quo titulo Eupolis comoediam scripsit, ob quam Alcibia-
des, quem praecipue perstinxerat, necuit ipsum pergit in
mare praecipitando, dicens "ut tu me in theatris madefe-
cisti, nunc ego te in mari madefaciam."

iv Σ Aelius Aristides 3.8

ἄλλοι δὲ λέγουσιν ὅτι ἐκωμῴδουν ὀνομαστὶ τοὺς ἄν-
δρας μέχρις Εὐπόλιδος. περιεῖλε δὲ τοῦτο Ἀλκιβιάδης
ὁ στρατηγὸς καὶ ῥήτωρ. κωμῳδηθεὶς γὰρ παρὰ Εὐ-

guise of women. Moreover, "Baptae" are effeminates. Eupolis wrote a comedy with this title, because of which he was killed by Alcibiades, whom he had especially attacked.

(c) "Baptae"—Eupolis wrote a comedy with this title, in which he brings on stage Athenian men in the guise of women wearing out a female lyre player.

(d) By "Baptae" are meant delicate and effeminate males; Eupolis and Aristophanes wrote a comedy of this title, in which they bring on stage Athenian men in the guise of women worshipping Cotyto, that is a lyre-playing goddess of the Athenians whom effeminate men worshipped.

iii Eupolis wrote a comedy with this title, because of which Alcibiades, whom he had especially attacked, killed him by pitching him headfirst into the sea with these words: "You have drenched me in the theatre, now I will drench you in the sea."

iv Others say that they made fun of men until the time of Eupolis. Alcibiades, the general and politician, did away with this. After being made fun of by Eupolis he pitched

πόλιδος ἔρριψεν αὐτὸν ἐν τῇ θαλάττῃ ἐν Σικελίᾳ
συστρατευόμενον εἰπὼν "βάπτες με ἐν θυμέλῃσιν,
ἐγὼ δέ σε κύμασι πόντου / βαπτίζων ὀλέσω νάμασι
πικροτάτοις."

v Platonius On the Distinctions among Comedians
  (Koster I.19–21)

ἴσμεν γοῦν τὸν Εὔπολιν ἐπὶ τῷ διδάξαι τοὺς Βάπτας
ἀποπνιγέντα εἰς τὴν θάλασσαν ὑπ᾽ ἐκείνου εἰς ὃν
καθῆκε τοὺς Βάπτας.

vi Themistius 8 p. 110AB

Ἀλκιβιάδης δὲ ὁ Κλεινίου, καὶ ταῦτα στρατηγὸς ὢν
αἱρετός, οὐχ οὕτως ἀπεμνημόνευσεν Εὐπόλιδι τῷ κω-
μῳδοδιδασκάλῳ τοὺς Βάπτας, καίτοι τῆς τέχνης αὐτῷ
διδούσης τοῦ σκώπτειν τὴν ἄδειαν ἐκ τῶν νόμων;

vii Cicero ad Atticum 6.1.18

quis . . . non dixit Εὔπολιν τὸν τῆς ἀρχαίας ab Alcibiade
navigante in Siciliam deiectum in mare? redarguit Eratos-
thenes; adfert enim quas ille post id tempus fabulas do-
cuerit.

viii Tzetzes Proem (Koster XIaI.88–97)

ἐπεὶ δ᾽ οὗτος εἰς Ἀλκιβιάδην τὸν στρατηγὸν ἀπέρριψε
σκῶμμα καὶ φανερῶς τὴν τραυλότητα τούτου διελοι-

him into the sea when he was serving with him in Sicily saying: "You dyed me in the theatre, but I'll destroy you with very bitter waters, by plunging you in the waves of the sea."

v We know at any rate that Eupolis after producing *Dyers* was drowned in the sea by the man against whom he had written *Dyers*.

vi Did Alcibiades the son of Clinias, an elected general in fact, not hold *Dyers* against Eupolis the comic poet, even though Eupolis' occupation gave him freedom under the law to make jokes?

vii Everyone says that Eupolis of Old ⟨Comedy⟩ was thrown into the sea by Alcibiades as he was sailing to Sicily? Eratosthenes [*FGrHist* 241 F 19] refuted this, for he pointed out plays which Eupolis produced after that time.

viii When he [Eupolis] launched a joke against the general Alcibiades and openly made fun of his speech de-

δόρησεν—ἔτυχον δὲ τότε καὶ ταῖς τριήρεσιν ὄντες
ὡς ναυμαχίας προσδοκωμένης—κελεύει τοῖς στρατιώ-
ταις, καὶ ἢ ἅπαξ ἐκβράττουσιν αὐτὸν εἰς τὴν θάλατ-
ταν καὶ ἀπώλετο, ἢ σχοίνῳ δεδεμένον ἀνάγοντες καὶ
κατάγοντες ἦσαν εἰς θάλατταν καὶ τέλος περιέσωσαν
τοῦτον τοῦ Ἀλκιβιάδου εἰπόντος αὐτῷ· "βάπτε με σὺ
θυμέλαις, ἐγὼ δέ σε κατακλύσω ὕδασιν ἁλμυρω-
τάτοις."

Fragments

76 Hephaestion *Handbook* 4.6

ἀλλ᾽ οὐχὶ δυνατόν ἐστιν· οὐ γὰρ ἀλλὰ προ-
βούλευμα βαστάζουσι τῆς πόλεως μέγα.

77 Photius (b, z) α 989

ἀναρίστητος ὢν
κοὐδὲν βεβρωκώς, ἀλλὰ γὰρ στέφανον ἔχων.

78 Photius (z) α 3123

ὅτι οὐκ ἀτρύφερος οὐδ᾽ ἄωρός ἐστ᾽ ἀνήρ.

79 Herodian *On Singular Vocabulary* II p. 911.15

ἀλλ᾽ ἐξαπολεῖς με ναὶ μὰ τὴν ἀμυγδαλῆν.

fect—they happened at that time to be at sea with a battle imminent—Alcibiades gave an order to his men. Either they pitched him once into the sea and he died, or tying a rope around him they raised and lowered him into the sea, finally sparing his life when Alcibiades said to him: "So, dye me in the theatre, but I will soak you in very bitter waters."

Fragments

76 But that's not possible. No way because they are considering a council proposal, an important one for the city.

77 Without breakfast and having eaten nothing, but still wearing a garland.

78 That he is not an unluxurious or unattractive man.

79 You will destroy me, yes by the almond tree.

80 Σ Aristophanes *Frogs* 418

ἐπιχώριος δ᾽ ἔστ᾽ ἢ ξένης ἀπὸ χθονός;

81 Photius (b, z) α 1413

αὔλησον αὕτη κύκλιον ἀναβολήν τινα.

82 Photius (b, z) α 1901

οὐκ ἀνέχομ᾽ αὐτόν· ἀντιπράττει παρὰ μέλος.

83 Σ Apollonius of Rhodes 4.143–44

ὦ ῥύμβε μαστίξας ἐμέ

84 Priscian *On the Metres of Terence* 23

{A.} ἀνόσια πάσχω ταῦτα ναὶ μὰ τὰς Νύμφας.
{B.} πολλοῦ μὲν οὖν δίκαια ναὶ μὰ τὰς κράμβας.

85 Σ Aristophanes *Birds* 129

ἐκεῖ γὰρ ἕξεις ἀγαθὰ πολλὰ δὴ πρῴ.

86 Pollux 10.91

ἀλλὰ τὰς κοίτας γ᾽ ἔχουσι πλουσίως σεσαγμένας.

87 Ammonius *On the Difference between Related Words* 488

σὺ δ᾽ ὕπαγ᾽ εἰς τοὔμπροσθεν

88

80 Is he [Archedemus] a local or from some foreign land?[1]

> [1] Archedemus (*PAA* 208855) was a demagogue of the late 5th c. (see *Frogs* 416–21), who was made fun of for alleged irregularity about his citizenship and for impaired eyesight (*Frogs* 588).

81 You there [fem.], play some cyclic prelude.

82 I can't bear him; he plays against the tune.

83 O rhombus, that has whipped me.

84 (A) The treatment I am receiving is unholy, by the Nymphs.
  (B) Long deserved, by the cabbages.

85 Tomorrow you will have many fine things there.

86 Their boxes are richly crammed full, at any rate.

87 And you, go in front.

88 Athenaeus 183f (ll. 1–2), Erotianus F 17 (ll. 1, 3–4)

ὃς καλῶς μὲν τυμπανίζεις
καὶ διαψάλλεις τριγώνοις
κἀπικινεῖ ταῖς κοχώναις
καὶ † πείθεις † ἄνω σκέλη.

4 καὶ πείθεις ἄνω Erot., καὶ τίθεις ἄνω Schneidewin, κἀνα-
τείνεις τὼ Fritzsche.

89 Σ Aristophanes *Clouds* 554a

† κἀκεῖνος † τοὺς Ἱππέας
συνεποίησα τῷ φαλακρῷ <– ∪> κἀδωρησάμην.

κἀκείνους Hermann, κἀκείνῳ Kaibel.

90 Σ Aristophanes *Wasps* 687c

τὸν γὰρ Χαιρέαν Εὔπολις ἐν Βάπταις ὡς ξένον
κωμῳδεῖ.

91 Hesychius β 311

Βάστας ὁ Χῖος· Δημοκρίτου ἐπώνυμον, καθὰ καὶ Εὔ-
πολις ἐν Βάπταις.

92

(a) Harpocration p. 72.3

Βάταλος· Αἰσχίνης ἐν τῷ παραπρεσβείας. κεκωμῴδη-

88 You're the one who beats the drum so well, who strums the triangle harp, swings his ass, and kicks (?) his legs on high.

89 And as for the *Knights* I collaborated with the bald one on them and made him a present of them.[1]

1 There is a minor problem in the text—read either "those *Knights*" or "that bald man," the bald man being Aristophanes.

90 Eupolis in his *Dyers* makes fun of Chaireas as a foreigner.

91 "Bastas the Chian": a nickname for Democritus, so Eupolis in *Dyers*.

92

(a) "Batalus": Aischines in *On the Embassy* [2.99]. He is

THE POETS OF OLD COMEDY

ται δὲ ἐπὶ μαλακίᾳ. Εὔπολις δὲ τὸν πρωκτὸν βάταλον
λέγει. μήποτε οὖν ἔνθεν τοὺς κιναίδους βατάλους
καλοῦσι.

(b) Σ Aischines 1.126

εἰσὶ δ᾽ οἱ βάταλον προσηγόρευον τὸν πρωκτόν· καὶ
Δημοσθένην ἐκ μεταφορᾶς διὰ μαλακίαν βάταλον
ἐκάλεσαν . . . δοκεῖ δέ μοι λελέχθαι Βάταλος παρὰ τὸ
Εὐπόλιδος σκῶμμα· ἐκεῖνος γὰρ ὑπὸ τῶν βαπτῶν
ὀνόματα κεῖσθαι τοῖς αἰσχροῖς καὶ τὸν πρωκτὸν βά-
ταλον ὑπ᾽ αὐτῶν καλεῖσθαι.

93 Hesychius κ 3820

Κοτυτώ· ὁ μὲν Εὔπολις κατ᾽ ἔχθος τὸ πρὸς τοὺς
Κορινθίους φορτικόν τινα δαίμονα διατίθεται.

94 John of Alexandria *On Accent* p. 36.12

εὐαῖ σαβαῖ

95 Σ Aristophanes *Peace* 1244c

χαλκῷ περὶ κοττάβῳ

96 Σ Aristophanes *Wealth* 883

δακτύλιον φαρμακίτην.

made fun of for effeminacy. Eupolis calls the anus "Bata-
lus." Perhaps that is why they call queers "bataloi."

(b) Some people used to call the anus "Batalus" [stam-
merer] and they called Demosthenes "Batalus" because of
his effeminacy [Aeschines 2.99] . . . Demosthenes seems
to me to have been called "Batalus" from the joke of
Eupolis, for ⟨he has made⟩ names applied by the Baptae
to shameless men and the anus to be called "Batalus" by
them.

93 Cotyto: out of hatred for the Corinthians Eupolis por-
trayed ⟨her as⟩ a certain vulgar deity.

94 Hurrah, Sabae.

95 Around a bronze *cottabus* bowl.

96 A ring of protection.

98 Harpocration p. 231.7

ὅτι γὰρ τοὺς τοιούτους ἐκάλουν παλιναιρέτους, καὶ
τοὺς ἀποχειροτονηθέντας τὴν ἀρχὴν καὶ πάλιν χειρο-
τονηθέντας, Εὔπολίς τε ἐν Βάπταις δηλοῖ καὶ Ἄρχιπ-
πος ἐν τοῖς Ἰχθύσι.

ΔΗΜΟΙ

*Demes was the best known and most cited of the lost plays
of Old Comedy. The Cairo papyrus (F 99) shows that it
was still being copied (and read) in the fourth century AD.
The theme was certainly familiar to both the literary and
the scholarly traditions, and the allusion to Pericles (F 102)
was cited or alluded to by nearly thirty ancient and medi-
aeval writers.*

*The plot is clear: four dead leaders of Athens (Solon,
Miltiades, Aristides, Pericles) returned from the dead to
Athens, and presumably put things right in that city. The
character responsible for their return was called "Pyron-
ides," who was not meant, as had been thought for many
decades, to stand for the general Myronides from the 450s
and 440s. Rather it is a comic nom parlant and means ei-
ther "the fiery one" (i.e., in temperament) or "the purifier."
A figure labelled "Pyronides" is shown on a fourth-century
Paestan vase by Assteas (V 7) engaging in an altercation
with the musician Phrynis.*

*The publication of three papyrus pages, about 120
lines, from the play (F 99) in 1911 was a very welcome ad-
dition to our knowledge of Old Comedy, but unfortunately*

98 That they called men whose election had been over-turned and subsequently reversed "second catch" is revealed by Eupolis in *Dyers* and Archippus in *Fishes* [F 14].

Brief fragment: (F 97) "chimney."

DEMES

they do not tell us all that much about the larger structure of the play. One major matter of debate is whether the first part of the comedy was played in the Underworld, where the need for an embassy from the dead and its composition would have been played out before the spectators. Using Frogs as a template, although much the later play, critics have had Pyronides descend into the Underworld, obtain Hades' consent to release the dead leaders, and then preside over an agon to select them. But nothing in the fragments that we possess requires a scene in the Underworld, and I would prefer to see Pyronides conducting a necromancy or raising of the dead in the first part of the comedy. This would be the "great idea" at the heart of Eupolis' play.

On this reading the agon would not have had anything to do with the sending or raising of the Four, but would have occurred at Athens in the second part of the comedy, and would have turned on handing the state over to the Four, presumably on the grounds that the dead could only be an improvement upon the living. The parallels of Clouds, Lysistrata, and Wealth are instructive here. Certain of the fragments reveal that the comedy turned, as *often in Eupolis and Aristophanes, on the opposition of old = better and modern = inferior (F 99.40–47, 103–4, 106, 111–12, 116, 119, 127, 129–30, 132).*

F 99 presents other problems for the structure of Demes. *The first twenty lines in iambic dimeter, followed by a section in trochaics, look very much like a parabasis, but at lines 60–77 it seems that the chorus is only recognising the Four for the first time. Were they not present for the raising of the Four? If not, then we might regard F 99.1–34 as part of their initial entry* (parodos), *but with parabasis-like features, for which there are parallels in Cratinus and also at* Frogs *354–71. The difficulty is made worse if we postulate a scene in the Underworld, for what would a chorus of Athenian demes be doing there? Certain earlier critics were driven to imagine two distinct choruses, first a chorus of "dead demes" in the Underworld, and then a chorus of modern (inferior) entities in the present city.*

The plural dēmoi *(demes) at Athens in the fifth century meant either the plural of democracy, or the 139 demes established by Clisthenes in the late sixth century, or "country towns," as opposed to the "city." This last is the most frequent use, but either "demes" in the technical sense or as "country towns" would make a suitable comic chorus. On the parallel of* Cities *and* Birds, *they may have been individually identified. We need to consider also whether they maintained some sort of metaphorical identity or were just treated as "country folk," as in the choruses of Aristophanes'* Peace, Wealth, *and* Farmers. *It is worth noting at F 99.12–14 that they are hostile to those living within the Long Walls of the city, "for they eat better than we do."*

The third page from the Cairo papyrus reveals an encounter between a man who claims to be "a just man," very probably Aristides "the Just" and an informer (syco-

phantēs). This is very much in the spirit of the "intruder episodes," where outsiders to the ideal community are dismissed in a physically humiliating fashion. We may conclude that each of the Four had his own scene and his own appropriate opponent: Miltiades v. an incompetent general, Solon v. a lawgiver (or perhaps a philosopher or a poet), and Pericles v. a political leader, whom it would be nice to identify with Alcibiades. Finally F 131 shows that the play ended with the Four successful and honoured by the state.

The play was universally dated to 412, partly because a serious political comedy requires a serious political background, and what was more serious than the crisis following the defeat in Sicily in 413? Also F 99.10–12 refers to "those in the Long Walls," who, it is argued, returned there after the Spartan occupation of Decelia in 413, and the business at F 99.78–120 about the Epidaurian and the Mysteries must postdate the scandal of 415. None of these stands up to scrutiny. We do not ask what was so critical about the late 390s that the "salvation" (sōteria) could be achieved only by handing the state over to women. It is just a good comic fantasy. Andocides 1.45 shows that in 415 there were enough people living in the Long Walls to form a separate population to be marshalled in a crisis, and not all allusions to the Mysteries must follow the breaking of the great scandal involving Alcibiades in 415. Hints of his irreligious behaviour may well have been in the air for years. I suggest 417 because it makes the mention of the campaign at Mantineia in the summer of 418 (F 99.30–32), an allusion to a recent event and allows the demagogue of F 99.23–34 to be Hyperbolus, certainly the most likely target. Hyperbolus was ostracised in 416.

Testimonia

i

(a) Aelius Aristides 3.365

τῶν κωμικῶν τις ἐποίησεν τέτταρας τῶν προστατῶν
ἀνεστῶτας, ἐν οἷς δύο τούτων ἔνεισιν.

(b) Σ ad loc

Εὔπολις ἐποίησεν ἀναστάντα τὸν Μιλτιάδην καὶ Ἀρι-
στείδην καὶ Σόλωνα καὶ Περικλέα. ἐν τούτοις οὖν
ἔνεισιν δύο, φησί, Περικλῆς καὶ Μιλτιάδης.

ii Aelius Aristides 3.487

οὐδεὶς ἦν ὅστις οὐκ ἂν εὔξαιτο ἀναστῆναι, ὥστε κἂν
δράμασιν ὡς ἀνεστῶτα ὁρῶντες εὐφραίνοντο.

Recent bibliography: S. Beta, ZPE 101 (1994) 25–26; T. Braun, *in* Rivals 191–231; I. C. Storey, *in* Rivals 173–90; B. Zimmermann, *in* Rivals 273–84; I. Ruffell, *in* Rivals 488–90; M. Telò and L. Porciani, QUCC 72 (2002) 23–40; M. Telò, Philologus 147 (2003) 13–43; ZPE 146 (2004) 1–12; SemRom 7 (2004) 31–50, *in* ΚΩΜΩΙΔΟΤΡΑΓΩΙΔΙΑ 263–306; Eupolidis Demi (2007); Revermann 311–19.

Testimonia

i

(a) One of the comic poets made four leaders return from the dead, among which are two of these.

(b) Eupolis made Miltiades and Aristides and Solon and Pericles return from the dead. Among these are two, he says, Pericles and Miltiades.

ii There was no one who would not pray that he [Pericles] might return from the dead, just as they were pleased to see him return in plays.

iii

(a) Aphthonius *Progymnasmata* 11

εἰδωλοποιία δὲ ἡ πρόσωπον μὲν ἔχουσα γνώριμον, τεθνεὸς δὲ καὶ τοῦ λέγειν παυσάμενον, ὡς ἐν Δήμοις Εὔπολις ἔπλασε καὶ Ἀριστείδης ἐν τῷ Ὑπὲρ τῶν τεσσάρων.

(b) Σ ad loc

πολλὰ περὶ δημοκρατίας δημηγορεῖ. ταὐτὸ δὲ τοῦτο καὶ ὁ Εὔπολις περὶ παλαιῶν δήμων γράφων πεποίηκε.

iv John Doxapatres on Aphthonios' *Progymnasmata*, p. 142.16

ἐν τῷ Ὑπὲρ τῶν τεσσάρων τὸν Ἀριστείδην ποιῆσαι εἰδωλοποιίαν καὶ τὸν Εὔπολιν ἐν Δήμοις ποιῆσαι προσωποποιίαν

v Platonius *On the Difference in Styles* (Koster II)

ἀναγαγεῖν ἱκανὸς ὢν ἐξ Ἅιδου νομοθετῶν πρόσωπα καὶ δι' αὐτῶν εἰσηγούμενος ἢ περὶ θέσεως νόμων ἢ καταλύσεως.

vi Hypothesis to Sophocles *Oedipus at Colonus* p. 2.4

Ἀριστοφάνης ἐν τοῖς Βατράχοις . . . ἀνάγει τοὺς στρατηγοὺς ὑπὲρ γῆς.

iii

(a) "Ghost-making": having a known person, but one who is dead and thus past speaking, as Eupolis created in *Demes* and Aelius Aristides in *On the Four*.

(b) He [Aelius Aristides] says much about democracy. Eupolis has done much the same thing writing about the demes of old.

iv That in his *On the Four* Aelius Aristides employs "ghost-making" and Eupolis in *Demes* "character-making."

v Being able to bring the figures of lawgivers out of Hades and through them discoursing on the passage and repealing of laws.

vi Aristophanes in *Frogs* . . . brings leaders back up above ground.

vii Valerius Maximus 7.2 (ext.9.5)

qui in comoedia introduxit remissum ab inferis † Atheniensium Periclen uaticinantem non oportere in urbe nutriri leonem, sin autem sit altus, obsequi ei conuenire.

Fragments

99 *Pap.Cair.* 43227

καὶ δὴ δὲ Πείσανδρ[ο]ν διε-
στράφθαι χθὲς ἀριστῶντά φα-
σ᾽, † ἐπιξένοιν τιν᾽ οντ᾽ αυτου †
    οὐκ ἔφασκε θρέψειν.
5 Παύσων δὲ προσστὰς Θεογένει
δειπνοῦντι πρὸς τὴν καρδίαν
    τῶν ὁλκάδων τιν᾽ αὑτοῦ
λέψας ἅπαξ διέστρεφεν·
λ]υτὸς δ᾽ ἔκειθ᾽ ὁ Θεογένης
10   τ]ὴν νύχθ᾽ ὅλην πεπορδώς.
δια]στρέφειν οὖν πρῶτα μὲν
χρὴ Καλλίαν τοὺς ἐν μακροῖν
τειχοῖν θ᾽ ἅμ᾽, ἀ[ρ]ιστητικώ-
    τεροι γάρ εἰσιν ἡμῶν,
15 Νικήρατόν τ᾽ Ἀχαρνέα

---

1 The text of l. 3 is corrupt. I have translated the text suggested by Hartman and van Leeuwen, which does restore the iambic metre in l. 4: ἐπεὶ ξένον τιν᾽ ὄντ᾽ ἄσι/τον.

vii [Aristophanes] who in a comedy brought Pericles, the Athenian leader, on stage declaring that one should not bring up a lion in a city, but ⟨if one did⟩, one should learn to cater to it.

viii A Paestan bell-crater by Assteas, dated to the middle of the fourth century, shows two comic figures, a youthful figure holding a lyre and labelled as "Phrynis," being rough-handled by a vigorous old man labelled "Pyronides." See V 7.

Fragments

99 *This fragment consists of three leaves of the Cairo codex, first published in 1911 and recognized by Körte as belonging to* Demes.

(a) *The first leaf contains part of a parabasis-like section, in which the chorus complain in iambic dimeter (1–22) about certain notorious Athenians and then in trochaic tetrameters (23–34) about a certain political leader.*

Recto

And indeed they say that Peisander was screwed yesterday while having breakfast, after he said he wouldn't feed a hungry stranger.[1] And Pauson, standing beside Theogenes dining to his heart's content off one of his merchant ships, thrashed and screwed him good, and the beaten Theogenes lay there, farting all night long. First of all, they ought to screw Callias and those in the Long Walls, for they eat better than we do. And Niceratus of Acharnae . . . giving

103

```
....]. ιν διδόντα χοίνικας
........]εον ἑκάστωι
............]. ιη
τῶν χρημάτων [.........]
```
20   οὐ]δ᾽ ἂν τριχὸς πριαίμην.
```
                              ]ν
                              ]. ος
```

– – – –

desunt versus 12

                      κἀξιοῖ δημηγορεῖν,
χθὲς δὲ καὶ πρώην παρ᾽ ἡμῖν φρατέρων ἔρημ[ος ἦν·
25 κοὐδ᾽ ἂν ἠττίκιζεν, εἰ μὴ τοὺς φίλους ἠισχύν[ετο,
τῶν ἀπραγμόνων γε πόρνων κοὐχὶ τῶν σεμνῶν [∪ –
ἀλλ᾽ ἔδει νεύσαντα χωρεῖν εἰς τὸ κινητήρ[ιον·
τῆς ἑταιρίας δὲ τούτων τοὺς φίλους ἐσκ[– ∪ –
ταῖς στρατηγίαις δ᾽ ὑφέρπει καὶ τρυγωιδο[– ∪ –
30 εἰς δὲ Μαντίνειαν ὑμᾶς οὗτος οὐ μέμ[νησθ᾽ ὅτι
τοῦ θεοῦ βροντῶντος ὑμῖν οὐκ ἐῶντ[ας ἐμβαλεῖν
εἶπε δήσειν τοὺς στρατηγοὺς πρὸς βίαν [ἐν τῶι
    ξύλωι;
ὅστις οὖν ἄρχειν τοιούτους ἄνδρας ᾳ[ἱρεῖταί ποτε
μήτε πρόβατ᾽ αὐτῶι τεκνοῖτο μήτε γῆ κ[αρπὸν
    φέροι.

quarts of grain . . . to each . . . of the goods . . . I wouldn't buy for a penny.   (1–22)

Verso

. . . and has the gall to speak before the people. In fact yesterday and the day before he was devoid of phratries with us, and wouldn't even be speaking Attic if he weren't ashamed before his friends . . . of apolitical male prostitutes and not of respectable . . . but he should have ducked his head and gone into the brothel. Of friends such as these has he . . . his political club . . . He sneaks around the generalships and . . . the comic poets. Don't you people remember that when the god was thundering and the generals were not allowing you to take the field at Mantineia, he said he would bind the generals forcibly in the stocks? May the flocks of anyone who elects such men to govern bear no offspring and may their land never bear crops.[1] (23–34)

[1] The identity of this figure is hotly disputed and the exact point of the chorus' imprecations is affected by what one chooses to read at the ends of the lines. The most likely candidates for identification are Hyperbolus (my preference), Cleophon, and Archedemus.

35 {ΑΡ.} ὦ γῆ πατρῴα χαῖρε· σὲ γὰρ ...[
πασῶν πόλεων ἐκπαγλ[οτατ
{ – } τόδε πρᾶγμα τί ἐστι; [
{ΑΡ.} χαίρειν δέ φη[μι
πάντα προ[
40 προ[

desunt versus fere 10–12

– – –

‚τὸ χαλκίον‚
‚θέρμαινέ θ᾽ ἡμῖν καὶ θύη‚ πέττειν τι‚νὰ‚
‚κέλευ᾽, ἵνα σπλάγχ‚νοισι συγγενώμεθα.
..........]ι ταῦτα καὶ πεπράξεται.
45 ....γν]ώσεσθε τοὺς δήμους ὅσωι
..........εἰ]σι νῦν διακείμενοι
........ἡνί]κ᾽ ἤρχετον σὺ καὶ Σόλων
‚ἥβης τ᾽ ἐκείνης ν‚οῦ τ᾽ ἐκείνου καὶ φρενῶν.᾽
                                    ]αν‚ηδ[...]μάτων
50   ]οι[..]α συχνή
                                    ]χεται
                                    ]τονη
                              π]ρόσθεν
                              ]μὴ προδῶις
55   ]ν προθυμίαν
                              Π]υρωνίδην
                        ]οὺς ἀνήγαγεν
                              ]ἀσπάσασθαι
                        κ]α[ραδ]οκῶ

(ARISTEIDES)
My homeland, greeting. I . . . you . . . of all cities most . . .
What is this?
(ARISTEIDES) I say . . . to greet . . .   (35–40)

(b) *The second leaf of the Cairo codex is very badly muti-*
lated and only bits of the sense can be determined; we seem
to be seeing the reception of the Four at Athens. It may well
follow directly on (a).

Recto

(41–48) Heat the bronze pot for us and tell someone to
make cakes, so that we may come to grips with sacrificial
meats . . . this will have been done . . . And you people will
recognize by how much the demes . . . they are now . . .
when you and Solon governed "that youth and heart and
mind."[1]

(49–59) sweetenings . . . frequent . . . before . . . do not be-
tray . . . enthusiasm . . . Pyronides . . . whom he has brought
up . . . to welcome . . . I wait for.

[1] The full text of 42–44 has been restored from a citation by
Athenaeus (123a). Line 48 appears to be a citation of Cratinus
F 71.

desunt versus fere 10–12

60 {ΧΟ.} .].τος γὰρ ως.[   ] ἄνδρες,
   ὧν κ[ιχόν]τες ἐν τοίαισιν
   ἡδοναῖσι κείμεθα.
   ...].ι δοκῶ τοὺς ἄνδρας ἤδη τού[σδ'] ἰ[δεῖν
65 καθ]ημένους, οὕς φασιν ἥκειν παρ[ὰ νεκρῶν
   .....]. α μὲν δὴ τῶν φίλων προστ.[
   ὡς ὀρθὸς ἑστηκὼ[ς]....στ' αὐτῶν .[
   Πυρωνίδης, ἐρώμεθ' [α]ὐτὸ[ν
       εἰπέ μοι, ὦ[ἔ-
70   μολες ετ[
       πρὸς πολιτῶ[ν
       φράσον, τί κ[
   {ΠΥ.} ὅ]δ' αὐτός εἰμ' ἐκεῖνος ὃν σ[ὺ
   ὅ]ς τὰς Ἀθήνας πόλλ' ἔτη [
75 .].αστ[' ἀ]νάνδρους ἄνδρ[ας
       {ΧΟ.} ἦ καὶ σαφῶς οιδ[
       ἡμῖν εξ[.]ηιτρ[
       – – – – – –

   ....]ιν[....]ντε προς.[.]..[
   {ΣΥ.} ....]νῦν αὐτίχ' ἁγνός εἰμ' ἐγώ
80 ....δί]καιός εἰμ' ἀνήρ. λέγ' ὅ τι λέγεις.
   {ΣΥ.} ....].ος ποτ' εἰς ἀγο[ρὰ]ν κυκεῶ πιὼν
   ......κρ]ίμνων τὴ[ν] ὑπήνην ἀνάπλεως
   ....]....ων τοῦτ' ἐννοοῦμαί πως ἐγώ.
   ἐλ]θὼν δὲ ταχέως οἴκαδ' εὐθὺ τοῦ ξένου·

Verso

(60–77) (CHORUS) . . . the men, whom we are so pleased to meet.

(CHORUS LEADER or CHARACTER) I think I see seated these man whom they say have come from the dead . . . from friends at . . . since standing upright in front of them is Pyronides, let us ask him. Tell me . . . you came . . . to the citizens' . . . tell us what . . .

(PYRONIDES) I am that very man whom you . . . Athens for many years . . . unmanly men

(CHORUS) Indeed I know well . . . for us.

(c) *Critics hesitated at first to attribute the third leaf of the Cairo codex to* Demes, *but the claim of the second speaker to be "a just man" suggests very strongly that we have here an encounter between Aristides, one of the raised Four, and an informer.*

Recto

(78–99) (INFORMER) . . . now at once, my hands are clean.

(ARISTEIDES)And I am a just man. Tell me what you mean.

(INFORMER) . . . who into the agora after drinking a broth, his upper lip coated with barley . . . I noticed this and went straight to the home of the foreigner.

109

85 {ΑΠ.} τί] ἔδρασας, ὦ πανοῦργε καὶ κυβευτὰ σύ;
   {ΣΤ.} ἔφ]ην, κελεύων τὸν ξένον μοι χρυσίου
   δοῦν]αι στατ[ῆ]ρας ἑκατόν· ἦν γὰρ πλούσιος.
   .....]ιον ἐκ[έ]λευσέ μ᾽ εἰπεῖν ὅτι πιὼν
   ......]ν[....] κᾆτ᾽ ἔλαβον τὸ χρυσίον.
90 ....ποι]είτω τις † ὅ τι ποτε βούλεται.
   {ΑΡ.} ....]τῆς δικαιοσύνης ὅση
   {ΣΤ.} ....]ητην οὔτε πω διαστολὰς
   ....]ων ἔπραξεν οὑπιδαύριος
   ....]ρφρ. νων ἀπεκλεισ< > ἐκποδών.
95 {ΑΡ.} ....]ραν κατέλυσας ἡττηθεὶς πολύ.
   {ΣΤ.} ....ἐπρ]αξάμην δὲ χρήματ᾽ οὐ λέγω.
   ....] θανόντων {ΑΡ.} ταῦτα χάριτος ἄξια
   ......μᾶ]λλον εἰ σαφῶς τις ἀποθάνοι
                    ]υσπουτ[

                    − − −

100 ....]σι[..]ι[.]αιτωχει.[...]ιι [...]σι[
    ....]μεδ᾽ ἢ ταῦτ᾽ ἂν .ποισ. χρήμα[τα
    {ΑΡ.} .᾽τί, τοὺς θανόντας ο.υ.κ ἐᾷς τεθνηκέν.αι;᾽.
    {ΣΤ.} μ]αρτύρομαι· τί δ᾽ ο[ὐ]κ ἀγωνι[ο]ύμ[εθα;
    κα]λέσας με συνδεῖς κἀδικε[ῖ]ς. {ΑΡ.} ἀλλ᾽ οὐ[κ ἐγὼ
105 ξυνέδησά σ᾽, ἀλλ᾽ ὁ ξένος ὁ τὸν κυκεῶ πιώ[ν.
    {ΣΤ.} δίκα[ι]α δῆτα ταῦτα πάσχειν ἦν ἐμέ;
    {ΑΡ.} ἐροῦ βαδίζων ἱερέα τὸν τοῦ Διός.
    {ΣΤ.} † ὕβριζε· ταῦτα δ᾽ οὖν ἔτ᾽ ὀφλήσεις ἐμοί.
    {ΑΡ.} ἔτ[ι] γὰρ σὺ τοὐφείλειν λέγεις οὕτως ἔ[χ]ων;

110

(ARISTEIDES) What did you do, you wicked cheat?

(INFORMER) I ordered the stranger to give me a hundred staters of gold—he was a rich man . . . and he told me to say that after drinking . . . and then I took the gold . . . let him do whatever he wants.

(ARISTEIDES) . . . such justice.

(INFORMER) . . . nor yet explanations . . . the Epidaurian did . . . but sneering down at me he slammed the door.

(ARISTEIDES) Coming off very badly, you settled down . . .

(INFORMER) . . . but I . . . the money, that's not what I'm saying . . . of the dead

(ARISTEIDES) This is a reason to be grateful . . . if someone clearly died . . .

Verso

(ARISTEIDES) Why do you not let the dead be dead?[1]

(INFORMER) Witnesses! Shall we not go to trial? You summon me and then beat me and tie me up.

(ARISTEIDES) But I didn't tie you up—the foreigner who drank the broth did.

(INFORMER) It is right for me to suffer in this way?

(ARISTEIDES) Go and ask the priest of Zeus.

(INFORMER) Insult me, you'll still pay me back for this.

(ARISTEIDES) The way you are, how can you still talk of paying back?

1 This appears to be a citation of Euripides F 507.

110 {ΣΥ.} καὶ ναὶ μὰ Δία κλάοντα καθέσω σ᾽ [.
    {ΑΡ.} καὶ τοῦτό μου τὸ χρέος καταψευδ[
    ...]αγετ᾽ αὐτὸν καὶ παράδοτ᾽ ο.[
    ......]αρεστιν τῶν τοιούτων δ[εσπότης.
    ἐβο[υλ]όμην δ᾽ ἂν καὶ Διόγνητον λαβ[εῖν
115 τὸν ἱερόσυλον, ὅς ποτ᾽ ἦν τῶν ἕνδεκ[α,
    ὅς τῶν πανούργων ἐ[σ]τὶ τῶν νεωτ[έρων
    πολλῶι κράτιστος, ὁπόταν εὖ τὸ σῶμ᾽ ἔχ[ῃ.
    ἐγὼ δὲ πάσῃ προσαγορεύω τῇ πόλ[ει
    εἶναι δικαίους, ὡς ὃς ἂν δίκαιος ᾖ
120   ]λσικονημ[...]χων

100 P. Oxy. 1240

{ΠΥΡΩΝΙΔ[ΗΣ].} ἆρ᾽ οὐχὶ φαν[ερόν
                ἦ που μέγ᾽ οι[
                 ζη.[
                 κόσμος .[
5   [.].[
            _ _ _

            [ἔ]μβαινε παρ[
            κώμαζ᾽ ὁποιω[
             [.......].ισ[
        _ _ _ _ _ _

{Ο]ΙΚΕΤΗΣ.} [
10   [

112

(INFORMER) By Zeus, I'll make you sorry . . .

(ARISTEIDES) You'll forfeit that debt as well. Take him away and hand him quickly over to Oineis (?) . . . he is the master (?) of such as these.[2] I would like to have gotten Diognetus the temple robber as well—the man who was one of the Eleven, by far the most powerful of the younger villains, at least when his health is good. To all the city I proclaim to be just, since whoever is just . . .

[2] Reading παράδοτ' Οἰνεῖ ταχὺ (Körte), compare F 172.15–16.

100 *This fragment consists of four scraps of text. It is assigned to* Demes *on the basis of the name,* Pyronid[es *in the left margin of the first line. Also in the left margin are the words* o]iketēs *(servant) and* cho[rus.

(PYRONIDES) Is this not clear . . . great indeed . . . world . . . Come in . . . celebrate

(SERVANT)

_ _ _

{ΧΟ(ΡΟΣ.}   ἐγὼ δὲ φιλ[
             καὶ φιλ.․[
             καὶ νῦν ․[
             το[
15 {ΟΙΚ]ΕΤΗ(Σ).} φέρ᾽ ἴδω πλακ[

                    _ _ _ _

                           ]
                        ].
                    ] ἐξιόντας

101 P. Oxy. 863

     ].․[
]δήμου[.......]ηλυσ[
]․ τοῖς ἐνερ[τέ]ροις θεοῖς
]․ κως οὐκ ἀνεβίων οὐδ᾽ ἅπαξ
5]ημοι τῆς πόλεως πλεῖστον πολύ
]αμοι διαφθείρουσι νῦν
        ]δροί τε καὶ Πάριδες ὁμοῦ
        ]των ἐνθάδε·
        ]παρέλειπον πρὸ τ[ο]ῦ
10   ]․ εἰς ἀνάκρισιν
          ]․ως μαχου․[
            ]ται․ θεν

114

(CHORUS) And I like . . . and now . . .
(SERVANT) See here, cakes . . . people going out

101 *These lines were plausibly attributed to* Demes *by Schroeder because of the mention of "deme" (2), "the lower gods" (3), and "would never have come back to life" (4). Some restore line 7 as "Peisanders and Parises together" (cf. F 99.1–4), but "Alexanders and Parises together" is equally likely, and keeps the allusion within the world of myth.*[1]

Of a deme . . . Elysion (?) . . . to the gods down below . . . I (they?) would never have come back to life . . . by far the best part of the city . . . they now destroy . . . –anders and Parises together . . . here . . . I neglected before this . . . to a decision . . . fight

1 Wright *CQ* 56 (2006) 593–95 assigns F 101 to Cratinus' *Dionysalexander* on the basis of "Parises" in V 7. Against this see Luppe *ZPE* 160 (2007) 24–26.

102 Σ Aelius Aristides 3.51 (ll. 1–5), Diodorus 12.40.6
(ll. 5–7)

{A.} κράτιστος οὗτος ἐγένετ᾽ ἀνθρώπων λέγειν·
ὁπότε παρέλθοι ⟨δ᾽⟩, ὥσπερ ἀγαθοὶ δρομῆς,
ἐκ δέκα ποδῶν ᾕρει λέγων τοὺς ῥήτορας.
{B.} ταχὺν λέγεις μέν. {A.} πρὸς δέ ⟨γ᾽⟩ αὐτοῦ τῷ
        τάχει
5 πειθώ τις ἐπεκάθιζεν ἐπὶ τοῖς χείλεσιν,
οὕτως ἐκήλει καὶ μόνος τῶν ῥητόρων
τὸ κέντρον ἐγκατέλειπε τοῖς ἀκροωμένοις.

103 Aelius Aristides 3.51

{A.} ῥήτωρ γάρ ἐστι νῦν τις; {B.} ὧν γ᾽ ἔστιν
        λέγειν;
ὁ Βουζύγης ἄριστος ἀλιτήριος.

104 Σ Aelius Aristides 3.365

καὶ μηκέτ᾽, ὦναξ Μιλτιάδη καὶ Περίκλεες,
ἐάσατ᾽ ἄρχειν μειράκια κινούμενα,
ἐν τοῖν σφυροῖν ἕλκοντα τὴν στρατηγίαν.

105 Galen *Affections and Errors of the Soul* 7.10

{A.} † ητίας ὢν † ἐγένου δίκαιος οὕτω διαπρεπῶς;
{ΑΡΙΣΤΕΙΔΗΣ.} ἡ μὲν φύσις τὸ μέγιστον ⟨ἦν⟩,
        ἔπειτα δὲ
κἀγὼ προθύμως τῇ φύσει συνελάμβανον.

116

102 (A) This man [Pericles] was the very best at speaking. Whenever he came forward, like the best runners, he'd beat the others at speaking, from more than ten feet back.

(B) You're saying he spoke quickly?

(A) Yes, but in addition to his speed a Persuasion of sorts perched upon his lips. That's how he could cast a spell, and he alone of the speakers left a sting in his audience.

103 (A) Is there any speaker now?

(B) The best of those worth a mention is that god-damned Bouzyges.[1]

1 Probably referring to Demostratus (*PAA* 319245); see also F 113 and *Lysistrata* 391–97.

104 And, lords Miltiades and Pericles, do not let these young faggots hold office any more, who drag the generalship around their ankles.

105 (A) ‹How› did you become so outstandingly just?

(ARISTEIDES) Nature was the most important factor, and then I enthusiastically helped nature along.[1]

1 The name of A is garbled in Galen's text, but does not seem to be Pyronides. Perhaps a companion, whose name Luppe has suggested was Eugeiton (Good Neighbour).

THE POETS OF OLD COMEDY

106 Longinus *On the Sublime* 16.3

οὐ γὰρ μὰ τὴν Μαραθῶνι τὴν ἐμὴν μάχην
χαίρων τις αὐτῶν τοὐμὸν ἀλγυνεῖ κέαρ.

107 Σ Aristophanes *Birds* 1569

ταδὶ δὲ τὰ δένδρα Λαισποδίας καὶ Δαμασίας
αὐταῖσι ταῖς κνήμαισιν ἀκολουθοῦσί μοι.

108 Stobaeus 3.35.2

καὶ τοῦ μὲν ⟨ἐν⟩ κύκλῳ γε παύσομαι λόγου,
φράσω δέ σοι τὸ πρᾶγμα διὰ τῶν χωρίων.

109 Photius p. 291.3

γυναῖκ᾽ ἔχοντα μάλα καλήν τε κἀγαθήν·
αὕτη νεανικοῦντος ἐπεθύμησέ μου.

110 Plutarch *Pericles* 24.10

{ΠΕΡΙΚΛΗΣ.} ὁ νόθος δέ μοι ζῇ; {ΠΥΡΩΝΙΔΗΣ.} καὶ
πάλαι γ᾽ ἂν ἦν ἀνήρ,
εἰ μὴ τὸ τῆς πόρνης ὑπωρρώδει κακόν.

111 Athenaeus 373e

οὐ δεινὸν οὖν κριοὺς μὲν ἐκγεννᾶν τέκνα,
ὄρνεις δ᾽ ὁμοίους τοὺς νεοττοὺς τῷ πατρί;

106 (MILTIADES)
No, not by my battle at Marathon, will anyone of them
grieve my heart and get away with it.

107 These trees, Damasias and Laespodias, are following
me, shins and all.[1]

   [1] Damasias (*PAA* 300930) is otherwise unknown, but Lae-
spodias (*PAA* 600730) was a general and ambassador in the late
410s, made fun of at *Birds* 1569, Phrynichus F 17, Philyllius F 8,
Strattis F 19, and Theopompus F 40. Both he and Damasias
clearly had some visible deformity of the legs.

108 I will stop this circular talk, and explain the situation
to you point by point.

109 Who had a very fine and beautiful wife; I was young,
and she wanted me.

110 (PERIKLES)
And is my bastard son still alive?
   (PYRONIDES) Yes, and he would have grown up long
ago, if he weren't so bothered about having a whore for a
mother.

111 Is it not strange that rams and birds father children
and offspring like their father?

112 Σ Aristophanes *Clouds* 1001

εἶσ᾽ Ἱπποκράτους τε παῖδες ἐκβόλιμοί τινες,
βληχητὰ τέκνα καὶ οὐδαμῶς τοῦ < - > τρόπου.

113 Σ Aristophanes *Lysistrata* 397

τί κέκραγας ὥσπερ Βουζύγης ἀδικούμενος;

114 Orion *Anthology* 6.5

τὸ γὰρ δίκαιον πανταχοῦ φυλακτέον.

115 Plutarch *Pericles* 3.7

ὅ τι περ κεφάλαιον τῶν κάτωθεν ἤγαγες.

116 Plutarch *Alcibiades* 13.2

λαλεῖν ἄριστος, ἀδυνατώτατος λέγειν.

117 Athenaeus 316c

ἀνὴρ πολίτης πουλύπους ἐς τοὺς τρόπους.

118 Tiberius *On Figures* 47

ἅπασα γὰρ ποθοῦμεν ἡ κλεινὴ πόλις.

119 *Etymologicum Genuinum* AB

ἀμβλυστονῆσαι καὶ χλοῆσαι τὴν πόλιν.

120

112 There are the abortive sons of Hippocrates, bleating offspring and hardly <worthy?> of my (?) nature.[1]

[1] Hippocrates (*PAA* 538615), the brother of Pericles, was killed at Delion in 424. His sons were made fun of in comedy for stupidity or swinish behaviour (Aristophanes *Clouds* 1001, F 116, 568), and perhaps for physical deformity.

113 Why do you shout like an injured Bouzyges?[1]

[1] In myth an Athenian called Bouzyges (ox-yoker) was the first to plough the earth. The Bouzygae were members of an Athenian priesthood and would shout curses during a ritual ploughing. Their best-known member was Demostratus (see F 103).

114 Right must always be protected.

115 You have brought up the head of the dead.[1]

[1] Of the appearance of Pericles.

116 [Phaeax] very good at chattering, totally incapable of speaking.

117 A citizen, an octopus in his ways.

118 We long for, all this famous city.

119 For the city to spring up and flourish again.

120 Athenaeus 106b

ἔχων τὸ πρόσωπον καρίδος μασθλητίνης.

121 Photius p. 300.1

τοιαῦτα μέντοι νιγλαρεύων κρούματα

122 Pollux 7.163–64

ἐνταῦθα τοίνυν ἦν ἐκείνοισιν πιθών.

123 Pollux 9.58

ἔχων στατῆρας χρυσίου τρισχιλίους.

124 *Suda* α 3789

ἐγὼ δὲ συμψήσασα τἀργυρίδιον

125 Photius (z) α 3145

λέγ᾽ ὅτου ᾽πιθυμεῖς, κοὐδὲν ἀτυχήσεις ἐμοῦ.

126 Plutarch *Aristeides* 4.3

σοφὸς γὰρ ἀνήρ, τῆς δὲ χειρὸς οὐ κρατῶν

127 Olympiodorus on Plato *Gorgias* 50.9

δίκαιον οὐδὲν οὐδαμοῦ νεοττίον

120 With the face of a leather-red shrimp.

121 Whistling, however, such melodies.

122 Yes indeed they had a wine cellar.

123 Having three thousand staters of gold.

124 (WOMAN) And scraping together a little bit of cash,
I . . .

125 Say whatever you desire, you won't lose by me.

126 For the man [Themistocles] was clever, but couldn't
control his hand.

127 Hardly a just offspring.[1]

[1] Cited in reference to Aristides "the Just."

128 *Etymologicum Genuinum* AB

ὅτῳ δ' ἂν οἶνος ᾖ πολὺς πίσει.

129 Athenaeus 408c

κἄν τις τύχῃ πρῶτος βαλών, εἴληφε χειρόνιπτρον,
ἀνὴρ δ' ὅταν τις ἀγαθὸς ᾖ καὶ χρήσιμος πολίτης,
νικᾷ τε ‹πάντας› χρηστὸς ὤν, οὐκ ἔστι
  χειρόνιπτρον.

130 Harpocration p. 200.15

τοιγαροῦν στρατηγὸς ἐξ ἐκείνου τοῦ χρόνου οὐδεὶς
δύναται ὥσπερ μειαγωγὸς ἑστιῶν τῆς τοῦδε νίκης
πλείον' ἑλκύσαι σταθμόν.

131 Photius (b, z) a 163

{A.} ἀναθῶμεν νῦν χἠμεῖς τούτοις τασδὶ τὰς εἰρεσι-
ώνας
καὶ προσαγήλωμεν ἐπελθόντες. χαίρετε πάντες. {B.}
δεχόμεσθα.

132 Harpocration p. 223.12

ὃν χρῆν ἔν ‹τε› ταῖς τριόδοις κἂν τοῖς ὀξυθυμίοις
προστρόπαιον τῆς πόλεως κάεσθαι τετριγότα.

133 Photius p. 267.18

μὴ παιδὶ τὰ κοινά.

128 Whoever has a great deal of wine will provide the drink.

129 And if someone happens to score first, he wins a washbasin; but if a man is a good and honest citizen and surpasses ‹everyone› in honesty, for him there is no washbasin.

130 For that reason, no general since that time could outweigh that man's [Miltiades] victory—it would be like offering an undersize lamb at a sacrifice.[1]

[1] This is the sense of the text as quoted by Harpocration—there have been many attempts to render it into iambic trimeters or tetrameters.

131 (A) Now let us also go forward and dedicate these wreathes in honour of these men, and offer words of praise. All hail.
(B) We accept.

132 Whom they (you? we?) should have burned squealing among the trash at the crossroads, as a propitiation for the city.

133 Matters of state are not for a child.

THE POETS OF OLD COMEDY

134 Σ Aristophanes *Clouds* 1022a

τέταρτος ὁ τραπεζίτης, οὗ μέμνηται Εὔπολις ἐν Δή-
μοις.

135 Σ Aristophanes *Birds* 822

ἐκαλεῖτο δὲ Καπνός, ὅτι πολλὰ ὑπισχνούμενος οὐδὲν
ἐτέλει. Εὔπολις ἐν Δήμοις.

136 Σ Aristophanes *Birds* 876

καὶ ἴσως ἕτερος ἂν εἴη τοῦ παρ᾽ Εὐπόλιδος ἐν Δήμοις
καὶ Κόλαξι.

137 Σ Aristophanes *Acharnians* 61a, *Suda* β 144

Εὔπολις δὲ ἐν Δήμοις εἰσάγει τὸν Πεισίστρατον βα-
σιλέα.

εἰσάγει ΣΕ, εἰσφέρει ΣΓ, καλεῖ Suda

138 Σ Aristophanes *Peace* 348e

πέμπτος ἀρχαῖος Ἀθηναῖος μετὰ Σόλωνα ἄρξας· Εὔ-
πολις ἐν Δήμοις.

139 Σ Lucian *Alexander* 4

ὁ Φρυνώνδας ἐπὶ πονηρίᾳ βοᾶται Εὐπόλιδι ἐν Ἀστρα-
τεύτοις, Δήμοις.

126

134 The fourth [Antimachos] was a banker, whom Eupolis mentions in *Demes*.

135 He [Theogenes] was called "Smoke," because he promised much but never delivered—Eupolis in *Demes*.

136 He [Cleocritus] may be different from the one mentioned by Eupolis in *Demes* and *Spongers* [F 177].

137 Eupolis in *Demes* calls ⟨Peisistratus⟩ "king."[1]

[1] One ancient source reads "brings on stage." This would add a fifth Athenian to the cast of past leaders, but how likely was a tyrant to appear among democratic leaders?

138 The fifth Phormion was an ancient Athenian who was archon after Solon—Eupolis in *Demes*.

139 Phrynondas is celebrated for wickedness—Eupolis in *Draft-Dodgers* [F 45] and *Demes*.

141 The Antiatticist p. 95.8

ἐγχώριος ἀνήρ, ἐγχώριον πρᾶγμα

ΕΙΛΩΤΕΣ

*There was some confusion over the authorship of this com-
edy. Five of the fragments (F 147, 150, 152, 154–55) are at-
tributed to* Helots *by Eupolis, and four (F 148–49, 151,
153) to "the man who wrote* Helots." *There is no contro-
versy about the play's existence—F 148 is clearly in the
style of Old Comedy—only over its authorship. On what
grounds would authorship have been questioned? Because
it was absent from the production lists? Because it was pro-
duced through someone else, as* Autolycus *was produced
"through Demostratus"? Because it was unlike anything
else that Eupolis wrote? If Eupolis did have it produced
through another man's agency, we should regard it as an
early work, in 429 or 428. This would fit the joke against
Gnesippus, who is a comic target of the 430s.*

141 Local man, local matter.

Brief fragments: (F 140) "steam baths," (F 142) "pleasure," (F 143) "beasts," (F 144) "chimney," (F 145) "to boast," (F 146) "wine offering."

HELOTS

The title suggests a chorus of helots, the Spartan serfs. This would seem to be confirmed by the Doric expressions in F 147 and 149, as well as the "starving Dorians" of F 154. The mention of the sanctuary of Poseidon (F 149) and the possibility that Knights *1225 borrows from a scene in* Helots *(T 1) might suggest that the comedy featured runaway helots taking sanctuary, perhaps at the temple of Poseidon at Sounion (F 151)—compare Heracles' family taking refuge from hostile Peloponnesians at the temple of Zeus at Marathon in Euripides'* Children of Heracles *(c. 430).*

Recent bibliography: M. Cummings, Scholia *10 (2001) 38–53; J. Davidson, in* Rivals *41–64; J. H. Hordern,* CQ *53 (2003) 608–13; L. Pranscello,* CPh *101 (2006) 52–66.*

Testimonium

i Σ *Knights* 1225

τὸ δὲ "ἐστεφάνιξα" . . . μιμεῖται δὲ τοὺς εἵλωτας, ὅταν στεφανῶσι τὸν Ποσειδῶνα.

Fragments

147 Athenaeus 138e

αἴ κα γένηται τοῦδε σάμερον κοπίς.

148 Athenaeus 638e

τὰ Στησιχόρου τε καὶ Ἀλκμᾶνος Σιμωνίδου τε
ἀρχαῖον ἀείδειν· ὁ δὲ Γνήσιππος ἔστ' ἀκούειν.
κεῖνος νυκτερίν' ηὗρε μοιχοῖς ἀείσματ' ἐκκαλεῖσθαι
γυναῖκας ἔχοντας ἰαμβύκην τε καὶ τρίγωνον.

149 Herodian *On Singular Vocabulary* II p. 917.1

τέμενος Ποτειδᾶ ποντίῳ

150 Pollux 9.74

ὀβολὸν τὸν καλλιχέλωνον

151 Herodian *On Singular Vocabulary* II p. 933.1

† αἵμην ἀλλὰ μισχοῦν καθήμενοι

EUPOLIS

Testimonium

i "I put a garland on you": he is imitating the helots when they put a garland on Poseidon.[1]

[1] The quotation from *Knights* is in Doric. Müller, followed by Sommerstein (*CQ* 30 [1980] 46–56), interprets the scholion as "he [Ar.] is imitating [Eupolis'] *Helots*, when they [in the play] put a garland on Poseidon." Sommerstein calls attention to the use of the same verb "gave a present" at Eupolis F 89, part of the intertextual "war between the poets" over *Knights*.

Fragments

147 If there be a feast here today.

148 It is old-fashioned to sing the songs of Stesichorus and Alcman, and Simonides, but Gnesippus is the one to hear. He invented the nighttime songs for adulterers to call out their women, while holding a *sambyke* and a spindle harp.[1]

[1] Gnesippus (*PAA* 279680) is a poet of mimes and light poetry, active 450–430 and the subject of frequent comic jokes about his poetry, usually in the context of love and adultery. See Chionides F 4; Cratinus F 17, 104, 276; Teleclides F 36.

149 The precinct of Poseidon, the sea god.

150 The fair-turtled obol.

151 But seated all together.

ΚΟΛΑΚΕΣ

The hypothesis to Peace *(T 1) records this play's first-place finish at the Dionysia of 421. Eupolis' principal target is Callias, son of Hipponicus, a young man who had recently come into an inheritance which made him the richest man in Athens. We know Callias from the brilliant picture drawn by Plato in* Protagoras, *the enthusiastic amateur philosopher whose home is full of sophists, and that by Xenophon in* Symposium, *where he holds a victory party to celebrate the athletic victory of his young lover, Autolycus. Autolycus will be the subject of Eupolis' comedy of that name the next year. A less attractive picture of Callias and the complications of his personal life is presented in Andocides 1 at the end of the century.*

*Callias was especially notorious for his extravagant style of living and for the women in his life, who according to Aristophanes (*Birds *286) and other comic poets had taken him for all he was worth.* Spongers *portrayed him as the opposite of his father (F 156), planning a great party (F 160, 165, 174) and pledging his possessions to finance his extravagance (F 163–65). There are hints that Callias came to grief by the end of the comedy. Comedy frequently makes fun of Callias for squandering his inheritance.* Spongers *may be the source of this tradition. F 162 and 169 show that valuable possessions are vanishing from the house, either stolen by the guests or claimed by a money lender, F 186 mentions debts, and F 167 might show Callias now forced to clean the house.*

Brief fragments: (F 152) "seasonings," (F 153) "hare," (F 154) "hungry Dorians," (F155) "frying pan."

SPONGERS

It is very likely that Protagoras was a character in the play, presented as the typical comic "expert," who is very good at looking out for his own interests (F 157–58). In the first fragment, alitērios *can mean "cursed" or "charlatan," but also "poltergeist," and Andocides 1.130–31 records a tradition that Hipponicus' house was haunted by a poltergeist, "which kept upsetting his tables." Eupolis has turned this poltergeist into Protagoras as the master of the disturbing revels in Callias' home "upsetting his tables." Alcibiades is mentioned at F 171, and it has been suggested that both he and Socrates were characters in this comedy as well.* Spongers *may have provided Plato with much of his material for* Protagoras.

The chorus was composed of kolakes, *"spongers" who depended on fawning up to rich Athenians to acquire free meals and a living in general. From the fourth century into Roman comedy and then through later antiquity these would be called "parasites," but in Old Comedy they are "spongers." F 172 is a complete epirrhema from a parabasis, where the chorus reveal their modus operandi as well as the dangers of a sponger's life. F 177–80 list several people targeted as "spongers," but it is unlikely that we have a chorus of twenty-four distinct individuals; it is more likely that these were men named as those who frequented the houses of the wealthy, including that of Callias. "Spongers" probably included a wide variety of individual types; the connecting link was that they had attached themselves to Callias.*

Testimonia

i See Eupolis T 13c.

ii

(a) Athenaeus 218b

ὁ ἐν τῷ Πρωταγόρᾳ διάλογος, μετὰ τὴν Ἱππονίκου
τελευτὴν γενόμενος παρειληφότος ἤδη τὴν οὐσίαν
Καλλίου, τοῦ Πρωταγόρου ⟨μέμνηται⟩ παραγεγονό-
τος τὸ δεύτερον οὐ πολλαῖς πρότερον ἡμέραις. ὁ δ'
Ἱππόνικος . . . τέθνηκε πρὸ τῆς ἐπ' Ἀλκαίου διδασκα-
λίας τῶν Εὐπόλιδος Κολάκων οὐ πολλῷ χρόνῳ κατὰ
τὸ εἰκός. πρόσφατον γάρ τινα τοῦ Καλλίου τὴν παρά-
ληψιν τῆς οὐσίας ἐμφαίνει τὸ δρᾶμα. ἐν οὖν τούτῳ τῷ
δράματι Εὔπολις τὸν Πρωταγόραν ὡς ἐπιδημοῦντα
εἰσάγει, Ἀμειψίας δ' ἐν τῷ Κόννῳ δύο πρότερον
ἔτεσιν διδαχθέντι οὐ καταριθμεῖ αὐτὸν ἐν τῷ τῶν
φροντιστῶν χορῷ. δῆλον οὖν ὡς μεταξὺ τούτων τῶν
χρόνων παραγέγονεν.

(b) Athenaeus 506f

ὁ δὲ καλὸς αὐτοῦ Πρωταγόρας πρὸς τῷ καταδρομὴν
ἔχειν πολλῶν ποιητῶν καὶ σοφῶν ἀνδρῶν ἐκθεατρι-
ζόμενον ἔχει καὶ τὸν Καλλίου βίον μᾶλλον τῶν Εὐπό-
λιδος Κολάκων.

134

EUPOLIS

Recent bibliography: S. Beta, QUCC *51 (1995) 93–98;* M. Dorati, QUCC *50 (1995) 87–103;* M. Napolitano, SemRom *1 (1998) 289–98;* SemRom *8 (2005) 45–66;* A. Pawlak, Eos *84.2 (1996) 277–83;* E. Tylawsky, Saturio's Inheritance *(2002) 43–57.*

Testimonia

i See Eupolis T 13c.

ii

(a) The conversation in *Protagoras*, which took place after the death of Hipponicus, when Callias has already come into his inheritance, ⟨mentions⟩ that Protagoras had arrived ⟨in Athens⟩ for the second time not many days before. Now Hipponicus . . . had died probably shortly before the production of Eupolis' *Spongers* in the archonship of Alcaeus [422/1], since the play makes it plain that Callias' acquisition of his inheritance was something recent. In this play Eupolis brings Protagoras on stage as being present ⟨in Athens⟩, while Ameipsias in his *Connus*, produced two years earlier [D-423], does not include Protagoras in his chorus of intellectuals. It is clear that he came to Athens between these two occasions.

(b) His [Plato] excellent *Protagoras* as well as containing attacks on many poets and philosophers also depicts the life of Callias more dramatically than Eupolis' *Spongers*.

THE POETS OF OLD COMEDY

iii Σ Aristophanes *Birds* 283

ὁ Ἱππονίκου Καλλίας ἐδόκει τὰ πατρῷα διεσπαρκέναι
εἰς ἀσέλγειαν· κωμῳδεῖται δὲ εἰς ἀσέλγειαν καὶ ὡς
ληφθεὶς μοιχεύων ἀπέτισε χρήματα. κεκωμῴδηκε δὲ
αὐτὸν ἱκανῶς Εὔπολις ἐν τοῖς Κόλαξι.

iv Maximus of Tyre 14.7

ἀλλὰ Καλλίαν μὲν ἐν Διονυσίοις ἐκωμῴδει Εὔπολις,
ἰδιώτην ἄνδρα ἐν συμποσίοις κολακευόμενον, ὅπου
τῆς κολακείας τὸ ἆθλον ἦν κύλικες καὶ ἑταῖραι καὶ
ἄλλαι ταπειναὶ καὶ ἀνδραποδώδεις ἡδοναί· τὸν δὲ
δῆμον αὐτόν, τὸν τῆς Εὐπόλιδος στωμυλίας θεατήν,
ποῦ τις ἐλθὼν κωμῳδήσει;

v Philostratus *Lives of the Sophists* 2.25.3

τὸν γὰρ πατρῷον οἶκον βαθὺν αὐτῷ παραδοθέντα
κατεδαπάνησεν οὐκ ἐς ἱπποτροφίας οὐδὲ ἐς λειτουρ-
γίας, ἀφ' ὧν καὶ ὄνομά ἐστιν ἄρασθαι, ἀλλ' ἐς ἄκρα-
τον καὶ ἑταίρους οἵους παρασχεῖν καὶ κωμῳδίᾳ λόγον,
οἷον παρέσχον λόγον οἱ Καλλίαν ποτὲ τὸν Ἱππονίκου
κολακεύσαντες.

vi Phrynichus *Selection* 109

παρασίτους οὐκ ἔλεγον οἱ ἀρχαῖοι ἐπ' ὀνείδους, ὡς
νῦν, ἀλλὰ κόλακας· καὶ δρᾶμα ἔστι Κόλακες τοιούτων
ἀνθρώπων.

iii Callias, the son of Hipponicus, seems to have squandered his inheritance on wanton living. He is made fun of for wanton living and that he had to pay a fine when caught in the act of adultery. Eupolis makes fun of him quite nicely in *Spongers*.

iv Eupolis would make fun of Callias at the Dionysia as a private citizen surrounded by spongers at drinking parties, where the prizes for sponging were cups and prostitutes and low-class and servile pleasures. But where will one go to make fun of the people itself, the audience for Eupolis' insults?

v He [Hermocrates of Phocis] spent the extensive inheritance from his father not on raising horses or public services, from which one may make quite a reputation, but on strong drink and companions of the sort to provide a plot for comedy, just like the one that those who once sponged off Callias the son of Hipponicus provided.

vi The ancients did not use the insulting term "parasites" as we do now, but "spongers." There is a play called "Spongers" about such men.

vii Σ Aristophanes *Lysistrata* 1189

ἀποκοπή ἐστιν τοῦ ἄλλου χοροῦ, ὡς παρ' Εὐπόλιδι ἐν
Κόλαξι.

Fragments

156 Athenaeus 328e

ἐκεῖνος ἦν φειδωλός, ὃς ἐπὶ τοῦ βίου
πρὸ τοῦ πολέμου μὲν τριχίδας ὠψώνησ' ἅπαξ,
ὅτε τὰν Σάμῳ δ' ἦν, ἡμιωβελίου κρέα.

157 Diogenes Laertius 9.50 (l. 1), Eustathius *On the
Odyssey* p. 1547.52 (ll. 2–3)

ἔνδον μέν ἐστι Πρωταγόρας ὁ Τήιος
ὃς ἀλαζονεύεται μὲν ἀλιτήριος
περὶ τῶν μετεώρων, τὰ δὲ χαμᾶθεν ἐσθίει.

158 Plutarch *Table-Talk* 699a, Macrobius *Satires* 7.15.22

πίνειν γὰρ αὐτὸν Πρωταγόρας ἐκέλευ', ἵνα
πρὸ τοῦ κυνὸς τὸν πνεύμον' ἔκπλυτον φορῇ.

159 Σ Hippocrates *Epidemics* 5.7

καὶ τὸν Κέκροπα τἄνωθεν ἀνδρός φασ' ἔχειν
μέχρι τῶν κοχωνῶν, τὰ δὲ κάτωθεν θυννίδος.

vii Interlude of the other chorus, just as in Eupolis'
Spongers.

Fragments

156 Now he was quite the tightwad, who in his life before
the War bought anchovies only once, and when the
Samian business took place, a half-obol's worth of meat.[1]

1 Very probably Hipponicus, the father of Callias.

157 Inside there is Protagoras of Teos, the *alitērios* who
goes on and on about celestial matters, but also devours
earthly things.

158 Protagoras ordered him to drink so that he have his
lungs well soaked before the rising of the Dog Star.

159 They say that Cecrops was human as far down as the
crotch, then a tunny-fish from there on down.[1]

1 In myth and art Cecrops, one of the earliest kings of Athens,
was portrayed as human to the waist and then as a serpent below.

160 Athenaeus 328b

δραχμῶν ἑκατὸν ἰχθῦς ἐώνημαι μόνον
ὀκτὼ λάβρακας, χρυσόφρυς δὲ δώδεκα.

161 Pollux 10.10

ἄκουε δὴ σκεύη τὰ κατὰ τὴν οἰκίαν.

παραπλήσιως τέ σοι γέγραπται τἄπιπλα.

162 Pollux 9.89

φοροῦσιν, ἁρπάζουσιν ἐκ τῆς οἰκίας
τὸ χρυσίον, τἀργύρια πορθεῖται.

163 Choeroboscus *On the Canons of Theodosius*, GrGr
IV 1 p. 238.30

θὲς νῦν ἀγροὺς καὶ πρόβατα καὶ βοῦς.

164 Phrynichus *Sophistic Preparation* p. 28.9

ἵππον κέλητ᾽ ἀσκοῦντα θές.

165 Pollux 9.59

x – ◡ {A.} δεῖπνον θὲς ἑκατὸν δραχμάς. {B.} ἰδού.
{A.} κόλαξιν οἶνον θὲς ἑτέραν μνᾶν.

166 Σ Aristophanes *Clouds* 52b

λαφύσσεται λαφυγμὸν ἀνδρεῖον πάνυ.

140

160 I have bought a hundred drachmas' worth of fish alone: eight sea bass and a dozen gold-heads.

161 Listen then, here are the utensils throughout the house.

You've written down most of the household goods.

162 . . . they are taking, they are stealing the gold from the house, the silver is being plundered.

163 Put down fields and flocks and cattle.

164 Put down a racehorse in training.

165 (A) For supper put down a hundred drachmas. (B) Done.
 (A) For wine for the spongers put down another mina.[1]

 [1] "For the spongers" may be part of the quotation or a citation of the play's title.

166 He wolfs down a man-sized helping.

167 Pollux 10.28

τουτὶ λαβὼν τὸ κόρημα τὴν αὐλὴν κόρει.

168 Eustathius *On the Odyssey* p. 1406.27

κατ᾽ ἀντιβολίαν δέκα τάλαντ᾽ ἀπετεισάμην.

169 Pollux 10.90

φροῦδον τὸ χειρόνιπτρον

170 Pollux 7.192

κεκρύφαλοί τε καὶ τύλη

171 Athenaeus 535a

{Α.} Ἀλκιβιάδης ἐκ τῶν γυναικῶν ἐξίτω. {Β.} τί
    ληρεῖς;
οὐκ οἴκαδ᾽ ἐλθὼν τὴν σεαυτοῦ γυμνάσεις δάμαρτα;

172 Athenaeus 236e

ἀλλὰ δίαιταν ἣν ἔχουσ᾽ οἱ κόλακες πρὸς ὑμᾶς
λέξομεν· ἀλλ᾽ ἀκούσαθ᾽ ὡς ἐσμὲν ἅπαντα κομψοὶ
ἄνδρες· ὅτοισι πρῶτα μὲν παῖς ἀκόλουθός ἐστιν
ἀλλότριος τὰ πολλά, μικρὸν δέ τι † κἀμὸν † αὐτοῦ.
ἱματίω δέ μοι δύ᾽ ἐστὸν χαρίεντε τούτοιν,
< - > μεταλαμβάνων ἀεὶ θάτερον ἐξελαύνω
εἰς ἀγοράν. ἐκεῖ δ᾽ ἐπειδὰν κατίδω τιν᾽ ἄνδρα

167 Take this broom and sweep the courtyard.

168 On appeal I came away with ten talents.

169 The hand basin is gone.

170 Hairnets and a cushion.

171 (A) Let Alcibiades leave the women.   (B) What are you saying? Won't you go home and exercise your own wife?[1]

> [1] The point here is obscure; a possibility is to read γυμνάσει in the second line, "what are you saying? Won't *he* go home and exercise *your* wife?"

172 We shall now describe to you the life which the spongers lead. Hear first that we are clever men in every way. First we have a slave attending us, mostly someone else's, but a little bit mine (?) as well. I have two good cloaks and putting on one or the other I head off to the agora. When I see some fellow there, not too bright but

ἠλίθιον, πλουτοῦντα δ', εὐθὺς περὶ τοῦτον εἰμί.
κἄν τι τύχῃ λέγων ὁ πλούταξ, πάνυ τοῦτ' ἐπαινῶ,
καὶ καταπλήττομαι δοκῶν τοῖσι λόγοισι χαίρειν.
εἶτ' ἐπὶ δεῖπνον ἐρχόμεσθ' ἄλλυδις ἄλλος ἡμῶν
μᾶζαν ἐπ' ἀλλόφυλον, οὗ δεῖ χαρίεντα πολλὰ
τὸν κόλακ' εὐθέως λέγειν, ἢ 'κφέρεται θύραζε.
οἶδα δ' Ἀκέστορ' αὐτὸ τὸν στιγματίαν παθόντα·
σκῶμμα γὰρ εἶπ' ἀσελγές, εἶτ' αὐτὸν ὁ παῖς θύραζε
ἐξαγαγὼν ἔχοντα κλοιὸν παρέδωκεν Οἰνεῖ.

173 Hephaestion *Handbook* 13.2

φημὶ δὲ βροτοῖσι πολὺ πλεῖστα παρέχειν ἐγὼ
καὶ πολὺ μέγιστ' ἀγαθά. ταῦτα δ' ἀποδείξομεν.

174 Athenaeus 286b

παρὰ τῷδε Καλλίᾳ πολλὴ θυμηδία,
ἵνα πάρα μὲν κάραβοι καὶ βατίδες καὶ λαγῴ,
καὶ γυναῖκες εἰλίποδες.

1 Καλλίᾳ codd., del. Dindorf.

175 Plutarch *Philosophers and Men in Power* 778d

οὐ πῦρ οὐδὲ σίδηρος
οὐδὲ χαλκὸς ἀπείργει
μὴ φοιτᾶν ἐπὶ δεῖπνον.

144

very rich, I am all over him. Whatever this rich man utters, I praise to the skies and I stand there awestruck, pretending to enjoy his words. Then we go our various ways to dine off another man's bread. There the sponger must come out with many witty things immediately or be chucked out the door. I know that's what happened to Acestor (used to be a slave); he made a really bad joke, and the slave took him outside with a collar round his neck, and handed him right over to Oeneus.[1]

[1] The point of "handing him over to Oeneus" is usually explained that the *barathron*, the place of execution for certain criminals, was located in a deme in the territory of the tribe Oeneis.

173 I say that we provide for mortals by far the greatest and most numerous benefits, and we shall prove this.

174 There is much cheer at this man's house, where you can get crawfish and skates and hares, and women with a rolling walk.

175 Not fire, not iron, not bronze ever prevents them from going to dinner.

176 Athenaeus 646f

ὃς χαρίτων μὲν ὄζει,
καλλαβίδας δὲ βαίνει,
σησαμίδας δὲ χέζει,
μῆλα δὲ χρέμπτεται.

177 Σ Aristophanes *Birds* 876

καὶ ἴσως ἕτερος ἂν εἴη τοῦ παρ᾽ Εὐπόλιδος ἐν Δήμοις
καὶ Κόλαξι.

178 Σ Aristophanes *Peace* 803

ὁ δὲ Μελάνθιος κωμῳδεῖται εἰς μαλακίαν καὶ ὀψο-
φαγίαν. καὶ πολὺ μᾶλλον ἐν τοῖς Κόλαξιν Εὔπολις ὡς
κίναιδον αὐτὸν διαβάλλει καὶ κόλακα.

179 *Suda* β 374

Ὀρέστης, Μαρψίας, Καλλίου τοῦ Ἀθηναίου κόλακες
σὺν ἑτέροις.

180 Σ (Arethas) Plato *Apology* 20e

Εὔπολις δ᾽ ἐν Κόλαξιν Καλλίου κόλακα λέγει.

181 Σ Aristophanes *Frogs* 407

ὅτι σύνηθες ἦν τὸ ἐπιλέγειν, ὁπότε ἐπαινοῖέν τι ἢ
συνομολογοῖεν, καὶ Εὔπολις Κόλαξι.

176 He smells of the Graces, his walk is a dance,
he shits sesame seeds, and coughs up apples.

177 Perhaps he [Cleocritus—*PAA* 576825] is different from the man in Eupolis' *Demes* [F 136] and *Spongers*.

178 Melanthius is made fun for effeminacy and gluttony. Eupolis makes much more fun of Melanthius in his *Spongers* as a faggot and a sponger.

179 Orestes and Marpsias along with others as spongers of Callias the Athenian.

180 In his *Spongers* Eupolis calls him [Chairephon] a sponger of Callias.

181 It was customary to utter when they were thanking for something or agreeing on something. Also Eupolis in *Spongers*.

Brief fragments: (F 182) "a white day," (F 183) "spit-rests made of lead," (F 184) "foot heifers" [prostitutes], (F 185) "once and for all," (F 186) "debts," (F 187) "belly god," (F 188) "centres of attention" [women surrounded and admired by men], (F 189) "fellow neighbours," (F 190) "frypan-whiff-hunters."

ΛΑΚΩΝΕΣ

Fragment

191 Erotianus μ 4

τὰ συκάρι᾽ ἐποίησε μυττωτὸν πολύν.

ΜΑΡΙΚΑΣ

Maricas *did to* Hyperbolus *what* Knights *had done to* Cleon. *Aristophanes seems to have pioneered the dema-gogue comedy with* Knights, *but as he complains in at* Clouds *551–59 (T 1), the other comic poets could not resist following his example.* Maricas *seems to have been the first of these comedies, and can be firmly dated "two years after* Clouds" *(T 3), that is to the archon year 422/1. Since we know of his* Spongers *at the Dionysia of that year, we are left with the Lenaea of 421 for the date of this comedy.*

At Peace *680 we hear that "Hyperbolus now controls the rock on the Pnyx," that is the speaker's platform in the assembly. Now that Cleon had died in the late summer of 422, Hyperbolus would have been the natural target for the comedians, although Eupolis must have been work-ing on his* Maricas *before Cleon's death became known. Hyperbolus became one of comedy's most frequent targets, made fun of as the stereotypical demagogue (of question-able birth, ill-educated and badly spoken, unprincipled, roguish, sexually deviant, etc.). All of these themes may be*

LACONIANS

A Laconians *by Eupolis is attested only by Erotianus citing*
F 191. It is likely that a confusion with Laconians *by Platon*
has occurred, or just possibly with Eupolis' own Helots, *al-*
though Erotianus does twice quote from Eupolis' Helots *by*
that name.

Fragment

191 The utensils made up a mess of savoury paste.

MARICAS

found in the fragments of Maricas. *The name "Maricas" is*
said to be Persian, with the connotations of alien origin,
cunning behaviour, youth, and sexual perversion. Cassio
proposed a fanciful reconstruction of the comedy as set in
Persia with the Demos as the Great King and Maricas-
Hyperbolus as a clever young courtier. F 192.43 does men-
tion Persians, and F 207 does parody line 65 of Aeschylus'
Persians, but the geography and allusions of the fragments
are Athenocentric, and an identification between the Athe-
nian dēmos and the Great King is hardly a flattering one.

The most controversial thing about Maricas *was its re-*
lationship with Knights *and the "war between the poets"*
that it set off. At Clouds 553–56 Aristophanes accuses Eu-
polis of "turning our Knights *inside out," as well as lifting*
an old woman out of a play by Phrynichus for a scene of
vulgar comedy. Aristophanes F 58, continuing the meta-
phor clothing, complains that someone "made three tu-
nics out of my cloak." Eupolis will reply at Dyers *F 89 that*
he in fact collaborated with Aristophanes on Knights *and*

made a gift of them to him. The extant fragments of Mari-
cas do show an astonishing similarity to Knights: *e.g., a dis-*
guised demagogue, with rough education, a master
(Demos again?), a formal assembly, some comic business
with rings, etc. But Eupolis has made three major changes
to what Aristophanes did in Knights: *(1) a double chorus,*
one of poor men (presumably supporting Maricas, and one
of rich men, (2) an antagonist to Maricas, from the ranks of
the elite (Callias?—see F 192.154), whereas in Knights *the*

Testimonia

i Aristophanes *Clouds* 551–59

οὗτοι δ᾽, ὡς ἅπαξ παρέδωκεν λαβὴν Ὑπέρβολος,
τοῦτον δείλαιον κολετρῶσ᾽ ἀεὶ καὶ τὴν μητέρα.
Εὔπολις μὲν τὸν Μαρικᾶν πρώτιστος παρείλκυσεν
ἐκστρέψας τοὺς ἡμετέρους Ἱππέας κακὸς κακῶς,
προσθεὶς αὐτῷ γραῦν μεθύσην τοῦ κόρδακος οὕνεχ᾽,
  ἣν
Φρύνιχος πάλαι πεπόηχ᾽, ἣν τὸ κῆτος ἤσθιεν.
εἶθ᾽ Ἕρμιππος αὖθις ἐποίησεν εἰς Ὑπέρβολον,
ἄλλοι τ᾽ ἤδη πάντες ἐρείδουσιν εἰς Ὑπέρβολον,
τὰς εἰκοὺς τῶν ἐγχέλεων τὰς ἐμὰς μιμούμενοι.

ii Σ Aristophanes *Clouds* 549b

ὡς περὶ ζῶντος αὐτοῦ διαλέγεται ἐν οἷς φησι "Κλέωνα
τὸν λάρον." καὶ Ἀνδροτίων δέ φησιν αὐτὸν ἐπὶ Ἀλ-
καίου τεθνάναι δυσὶν ἔτεσιν ὕστερον Ἴσαρχου, ἐφ᾽ οὗ
αἱ πρῶται Νεφέλαι ἐδιδάχθησαν. πῶς οὖν δύναται καὶ

antagonist to Paphlagon-Cleon is an even worse villain, and (3) an old woman representing the mother of Hyperbolus. The word "age-mates" at F 193.5 shows that the two choruses were distinguished by age as well as wealth.

Recent bibliography: A. C. Cassio, CQ 35 (1985) 38–42; J. D. Morgan, CQ 36 (1986) 529–31; M. Sonnino, Eikasmos 8 (1997) 43–60; ZPE 156 (2006) 39–51; A. H. Sommerstein, in Rivals 437–51.

Testimonia

i But these fellows, as soon as Hyperbolus gave them a hold, are always pummelling the poor man and his mother. First that wretched Eupolis dragged his wretched *Maricas* on stage, turning our *Knights* inside out, tacking onto it a drunken crone for the sake of a vulgar dance, the same old woman that Phrynichus portrayed once, the one whom the sea monster was eating. Then in his turn Hermippus went after Hyperbolus and then everyone starts in on Hyperbolus, copying my metaphor of the eels.

ii He is talking about Cleon being alive when he says, "Cleon the seagull" [*Clouds* 591]. Androtion [*FGrHist* 324 F 40] says that Cleon died in the archonship of Alcaeus [422/1], two years later than that of Isarchus, in which the first *Clouds* was produced. How then can he mention

τοῦ Μαρικᾶ μεμνῆσθαι, ὃς ἐδιδάχθη μὲν πρὸ τῶν
Νεφελῶν, ὡς καὶ νῦν αὐτός φησιν, ἐκεῖ δὲ ὁ Εὔπολις
ὡς τεθνηκότος Κλέωνος μέμνηται; ἤ, ἐπεὶ οὐ φέρονται
αἱ διδασκαλίαι τῶν δευτέρων Νεφελῶν, οὐδὲν δυνά-
μεθα διαρθρῶσαι· ἢ Εὔπολις ἐπλάσατο τὴν Κλέωνος
τελευτὴν ἐν τῷ Μαρικᾷ.

iii Σ Aristophanes *Clouds* 553

δῆλον ὅτι πρῶτος ὁ Μαρικᾶς ἐδιδάχθη τῶν δευτέρων
Νεφελῶν. Ἐρατοσθένης δέ φησι Καλλίμαχον ἐγκα-
λεῖν ταῖς διδασκαλίαις, ὅτι φέρουσιν ὕστερον τρίτῳ
ἔτει τὸν Μαρικᾶν τῶν Νεφελῶν, σαφῶς ἐνταῦθα εἰρη-
μένου, ὅτι πρῶτος καθεῖται. λανθάνει δὲ αὐτόν, φησίν,
ὅτι ἐν μὲν ταῖς διδαχθείσαις οὐδὲν τοιοῦτον εἴρηκεν·
ἐν δὲ ταῖς ὕστερον διασκευασθείσαις εἰ λέγεται, οὐδὲν
ἄτοπον· αἱ διδασκαλίαι δὲ δηλονότι τὰς διδαχθείσας
φέρουσιν. πῶς δ' οὐ συνεῖδεν, ὅτι καὶ ἐν τῷ Μαρικᾷ
προτετελεύτηκε Κλέων, ἐν δὲ ταῖς Νεφέλαις λέγεται
"εἰς τὸν θεοῖσιν ἐχθρὸν τὸν βυρσοδέψην";

iv

(a) Σ Aristophanes *Clouds* 591a

"Κλέωνα τὸν λάρον"· καὶ μὴν ὡς μετὰ θάνατον Κλέ-
ωνος φαίνεται γεγραφὼς τὸ δρᾶμα, ὅπου γε τοῦ Μαρι-
κᾶ Εὐπόλιδος μέμνηται, ὃ ἐδιδάχθη καθ' Ὑπερβόλου
μετὰ τὸν θάνατον Κλέωνος. ταῦτα δὲ ὡς ἔτι ζῶντος

Maricas, which was produced before *Clouds*, as he himself says here? But there Eupolis speaks of Cleon as dead [F 211]. Or, since the production date of second *Clouds* is not preserved, we are not able to see the whole picture. Or, Eupolis made up the death of Cleon in *Maricas*.

iii It is clear that *Maricas* was produced before the second *Clouds*. Eratosthenes [F 97) says that Callimachus found fault with the production lists because they recorded that *Maricas* was produced two years after *Clouds*, while it is plainly stated that it was produced before. It escaped Callimachus' notice, he says, that in the performed version Aristophanes does not say this at all. If this was said in the version revised later, there is nothing unusual here. For clearly the production lists record plays that were actually performed. How then did he not realise that Cleon is dead by the time of *Maricas* [F 211], but in *Clouds* is spoken of as "the goddamned tanner of hides" [581]?

iv

(a) "Cleon the seagull": He seems to have written the play after the death of Cleon, at least the part where he mentions *Maricas* by Eupolis, which was written against Hyperbolus after the death of Cleon. But this part is spo-

Κλέωνος λέγεται. δῆλον οὖν, ὅτι μετὰ πολλοστοὺς χρόνους διεσκεύασε τὸ δρᾶμα.

(b) Σ Aristophanes *Clouds* 591b

ταῦτα ἀπὸ τῶν προτέρων Νεφελῶν· τότε γὰρ ἔζη ὁ Κλέων, ἐπὶ δὲ τούτων τέθνηκεν. καὶ γὰρ Εὔπολις μετὰ θάνατον Κλέωνος τὸν Μαρικᾶν ἐποίησεν.

v Σ Aristophanes *Frogs* 569

Ὑπέρβολον δέ, εἰς ὃν καὶ Εὔπολις ἔγραψε τὸν Μαρικᾶν.

vi Hesychius μ 283

Μαρικᾶν· κίναιδον. οἱ δὲ ὑποκόρισμα παιδίου ἄρρενος βαρβαρικόν.

Fragments

192 P. Oxy. 2741

ΕΥΠΟ[ΛΙΔΟΣ
Μαρικᾶ[
[ὑπ(όμνημα)

Fr. 1 Aʳ col. i
  ]μηκατα[   ]αχειαν·
  ]πατ γα[   ]νικας ἐνίκα·

ken while Cleon is still alive. It is clear, therefore, that he revised the play several years later.

(b) This comes from the earlier version of *Clouds*, when Cleon was still alive, but he was dead by the time of this version. Eupolis wrote his *Maricas* after the death of Cleon.

v Hyperbolus, against whom Eupolis wrote his *Maricas*.

vi "Maricas": faggot. Some say that it is a barbarian nickname for a male child.

Fragments

192 *These fragments of a commentary to* Maricas *are dated to the second half of the second century or the first half of the third century. The title was added later on the back of the roll, and the commentary provides four known quotations from Eupolis (two attributed to* Maricas). *It is interesting that the commentator names the main character not as "Maricas" but as "Hyperbolus" (ll. 120–21, 150).*

[Commentary] to *Maricas* by Eup[olis]

(2–6) **He won victories.** He would win victories . . . this is . . . fawn . . .

```
        ]ται̣ ταρτ̣.[        νι]κας ἐνίκα
        ]υϲ[  ].....[                ]εν ταῦτ᾽ ἐστ᾽
  5     ]. νεβρον[              ]εωνος ταυτα
        ]......πα.[              ]ε̣με̣. αι·
        ]μας πάλι[ν  νοσ]ήματα ὑποτροπάζει
        ]ὑποτροπά[ζ    χ]εῖρον διατιθέασιν
        ἐπα]ν̣ερχομέ[              ]καταλαμβάνουσιν
 10     ]..[ ]μεν̣α̣[              ]. [ ]. αυτον τ[.]ο
        ]ον̣[ ].[ ]π̣.[ ]. δ̣[ ]ησθενηκυ[ι      ]νυν πάλιν
        ]φης[ι] καταπ[ο]νεῖσθαι συ[μ]βησε[
        πολὺ]ν̣ πολλοῦ χρό[ν]ον καὶ τόν̣[δ᾽] ἀφ̣εῖ̣[σθε
        ].τι.[.]παμπ[.]υν· ἡ δὲ μ[ετα]φ[ορὰ
 15     ἀπὸ τῶν γ]ραμματοδιδ[α]σκάλων .[
        ].τι· ἡ δὲ μ[ετ]αφορὰ ἀπ[ὸ τῶ]ν γρα[μ-
        ματοδιδασκά]λων "πολὺν χρόνον ἀφεῖσθε"
              ]σ̣ὺ γοῦν ἀλλ᾽ ἐξάλειφετε τοῦτο δ᾽
              ]ν ἐστιν· "λέαινε τὰς δέλτους"·
 20           ]ν[      ]ον οὕτω φθέγξεται ε-
              ].τότε δὴ μεῖζον φθε̣.ομα̣ι̣.[
              ].τοις ἐσχάτοις ενη[
              ]κη καὶ τοῖς ἐσχάτ[οις
              ]
 25     ].τεδ[      ]ο προ[σφ  ].ν̣τ̣[ε
        ]προσφ[      ].ντε[      ]ον̣δ[
        ]μεις κ[    ]νον[  ]
        ]ετον ́.ιν[.]. οπο[      ]ημα
        ]ἀπὸ τούτου ὅλος ὁ χορὸς λέγει .[
 30     ]ω τέως καὶ νῦν τὸ τέως ἀντὶ[
```

156

(7–12) **Diseases recur on us.** ⟨Diseases⟩ recur . . . coming back make him worse . . . attack . . . weakened he says that he is hard at work again . . . [1]

(13–17) **You have been dismissed for some time.** A very great deal . . . "you have been dismissed for some time" is a metaphor from schoolteaching.

(18–19) **But you [pl.] rub out.** This . . . is "clean the tablets."

(20–21) **Thus he will speak.** Then I shall speak louder.

(22–23) **To those at the end.** . . . and to those at the end.

(25–29) **Those bringing forward (?).** . . . from this point on the whole chorus is speaking.

(30) **Up to now.** Here also "up to now" instead of . . .

---

[1] This is possibly metatheatrical, Eupolis alleging that he is just now recovering from illness and able to turn his hand again to comedy.

157

```
          ]
      ]ω.[        Fr. 2   ]ἄπασι τοῖς κ[ριταῖς
      ]ους.[       ].ς[     ]ντα ἡ δ(ὲ) με[ταφορὰ
      ]ισθ.[       ]ν[           ].·εν.[
35                 ]ω[
                   ]..[            ].ιτη[
                   ]ντ.[          ]μις[
                   ]αρεικ[        – – –
                   ]ην[
40                 ]ν.[
                   ]η[
                   – – –

     Fr. 1 Aʳ col. ii
                ].α[
         καὶ ταῖς ε.[
         τοὺς Πέρσας[
45       παρεδέξαντ[
        ‾γὰρ αὐτοῖς ἐπι[
         ζητῶν γὰρ ω[
         οὐδὲν κενὸν ˌτρύπημ᾽ ⟨ἂν⟩ ἐν ταῖς οἰκίαις ἂνˌ
         εὗρες τούτων[
50       τοις ἀγαθοῖς τ[
         κενὸν τρύπη[μ
         ο]ὐδεμία κε[νὴ
        ‾ˌ]ασαι λέγει δετ[
        π‾]εριτμήματα[
55       δερμάτων η[              Fr. 1 B col. i
         τῶν περιτεμ[νομένων        – – – –
```

(32) **By all the judges** (?).

(43–47) . . . the Persians . . . they received . . . for to them . . .

(47–53) **Even if you looked, you wouldn't have found an empty hole in the houses.** Of these . . . good men (things?) . . . empty hole . . . no empty . . . he means

(54–58) **Scraps** . . . of hides . . . cut up . . . people . . . glued

```
        τοι γὰρ ἀνθρω[π                          ] ς
        κολλητεο[                               ].
       ἕτερος δε[                               ]ε
60      κακω.[                                  [ ].η
       αλλεν[              ].[                   – – –
        σωμεν αυτη.[
        ποιησωμεν.[
        ].τελευτα[
65      διδόντες τ.[
        ριανικ[ ] .[
        καὶ θεὸς[
        προσφερο[
       οἷά τ᾽ ἐσθ᾽ ἁ[
70      το τοιουτο.[
        δεύτερον[
        ι.[ ].νοι....[
        αν ἀνθρωπο[
       τί τὸ κακόν; οὐκ[
75      τοῦτο λέγει μ[
        α[ ]ρους λ.[
        ροντο ὡς ἀντι[
       ἀλλ᾽ ὦτα μὲν μ[
        παρὰ τὴν παρ[οιμίαν
80      δῆμος αυτημε.[
᾽/      κυδῶντα δ᾽ οὐ κυ[        ἐπὶ δούλ]ων λέγεται
        τῶν ἀπαρνουμέν[ων δούλων γεγονέναι ἐ]πειδὰν ἐ-
        λεύθεροι γένων[ται]
```

(59–60) **The other one** . . .

(61–68) **But in** . . . let us . . . let us do . . . end. people giving . . . and a god . . . offering

(69–73) **Such things as** . . . Such a thing . . . second . . . men . . .

(74–77) **What's the matter?** Not . . . He means this . . .

(78–80) **Ears of Midas (?).** With reference to the proverb (?) . . . the people . . .

(81–83) **Him** κυδῶντα **but not** . . . This is said of slaves who deny that they used to be slaves now that they are free.[2]

---

[2] The verb κυδῶντα is otherwise unattested and its meaning is uncertain.

ἔξαγ[ ]ε καὶ πρώιρ[α   ]αν ἀντίπρωι-
85   ρον τὴν γλῶττα[ν   ρ̣οθ]ίαζε πρὸς τὸ
      λέγειν πρῶιρα γὰ̣[ρ   ]ῦ[ ]ιάζου λέγεται·
/   καὶ ταῖς οἰκίαις α[   ]εἰρηκ[ότο]ς ἐκείνου
      τὰς οἰκίας ἐπὶ τῶ[ν ἐν α]ὐταῖς οἰκούντων
      οὗτος ἐπὶ τῶν οἰκοδομημάτων αὐτὸ τέθεικεν
90   φέρ᾽ ἴδω τί Ἀλκμέων[α.......] πρόθυρ᾽ ἐπωφελ(εῖ);
/   εὐγενής τις οὗτος [Ἀλκμέ]ων·
      εἰδὼς ἐφ᾽ οἵων ῥηγμάτ[ων κα]ὶ̣ στιγμάτων· παί̣[ζων
      ῥήγματα λέγει τ(ὰ) ὑπ(ὸ) [το]ῖς ποσί·
      ὀριβατοῦντες
      γὰρ κόπτουσι ξύλα. ἔστιν [καὶ] παρὰ Μενάνδρωι
95   τὸ τοιοῦτον
      τοῦτ᾽ ἐκδανείζει καὶ κυκᾶις [τὸ]ν ναυτικὸν α[
      ἐπὶ τῶι πέμπτωι μέρε[ι   ]τοὺς τόκ[ους οἱ
/   ναυτικοί· ἡμεῖς δ᾽ ἄρ᾽ οἴκ[αδ᾽ ἄπιμ]εν· ὁ τῶν
      πλουσίων λέγει χορός.
      καὶ γὰρ αἱ γυναῖκ[ε]ς ὅσαι μ[ὲν ἂν] νεανίαις
100   ξυνῶσ[ι
      καταγελῶνται, [ὅσαι δ᾽   ][ ] καὶ δούλοισιν
      ὠφελοῦνται· [ ].[ ]
      νεανισκο[
      ]δουλο[
105   ]ο̣νη[
                                    ]ς
                                    ]
                                    ]
                                    ].

(84–86) **Go ahead and point** . . . "point the prow of your tongue ahead" . . . means "to speak." "Prow" is used instead of . . .

(87–89) **And in the houses** . . . the one person has used the word *oikia* of those who lived in them, while the other has used it of the buildings.

(90–91) **Well then, what good are the halls of Alcmaeon?** This man was someone of good birth . . .

(92–95) **Knowing by what sort of lacerations and punctures.** In jest. By "lacerations" he means ⟨wounds⟩ on the feet. By walking in the mountains they trample down the brush. There is something similar in Menander.

(96–98) **You borrow this and upset the fleet ⟨account⟩.** Mariners ⟨pay⟩ interest at the rate of a fifth.

(98–99) **We will go home then.** The chorus of wealthy men.

(100–104) **For the women who go with young men get laughed at, and . . . with slaves benefit.** . . . young men . . . slaves . . .

Fr. 1 C col. i

]ην

110   ].α

].ας

]ξύλωι

]

]ριτωναυ

115   ].ς γνώμην

]

Fr. 1 B col. iii

   καὶ οἱ μὲν πένητε[ς

   οἱ δὲ πλούσιοι τῶι δεσ[πότηι

   κοινῶς ὅτι ἐν τοῖς [

120 οὗτος, τί κέκυφας; .[πρὸς τὸν Ὑπέρ-

   βολον λέγει τὸ ἡμιχόρι[ον

   Λακεδαιμονίους μεν.[

   τας· ἀπὸ κοινοῦ τ[.]υλε.[

   ἀπολῶ γὰρ αὐτούς· ω.[

125 ρυ προσχωροῦντασπ..[..]..[ἐπὶ

   δυεῖν τάττεται τ[.]..[ ]. υμν[

      ·τοεν.[ ].ους...[

   παραγενέσθαι δεδ[

   ους ἐφ' ἡμᾶς.[ ]α.[

130 νὴ Δία δεδοι[κ

   γεμετουτε[

   μειν πρ[

   δεπελθο.[

   κωσιν ει[

(117–19) The poor men and the rich men . . . to the master together that in the . . .

(120–21) **Hey you, why are you bending over?** The semichorus to Hyperbolus.

(122–23) **The Spartans** . . . together.

(124–36) **I shall destroy them** . . . those approaching . . . used in two ways . . . to be present . . . to us . . . **By Zeus, I**

135   Κλέων παφλ[
     <u>παφλάζειν</u>[
    ὥσπερ γενη[
    κως ἐνίκα α[
✠   οἱ χοροὶ ὅταν[
140   ἀλλοτρίοις π[
    πον στρατη[
    ελομεν στ[Fr. 1 C col. ii
    εστρατηγη[——————
    ξας ἀλλα[   ].[
145   ].ταλλα[   ]μοι ἐστιν..[
     ].οπλ[   ]ὃ μετατιθεσθ..[
    εγ.[κ]έρδους ἕνεκα σὺ νῦν· ἐγὼ γὰρ..[
    εἰς ἐκκλησίαν ἕως οὗ οἱ συνα.[
    ταί μοι, σὺ τὸ συνέδριον σκεύαζε πρὸς τ[ὸν
150   δεσπότην ὁ Ὑπέρβολος.
    ἦ μὴν ἐγώ σε σκέψομαι γὰρ ἐν.[
     ἦ μὴν ἐγώ σε ὄψομαι ἀξιοῦντα[.].[.].[
    δ' ἂν ἦσθα δεδεμένος ἐν τῶι ξύλωι·[
    τῶν γνωρίμων τινὰ καλ[
155   ἑαυτὸν λέγει τοῦ Ὑπερβόλου κε[
   <u>λύω λέσχας.</u> ὁ χορὸς πρὸς τ[ὸ θέατρον
   πρὸς τὸ θέατρον· ἐν μὲν τῶι ε[
   – – – –

    Fr. 4

                ]αιδιδωμ[
                ]γματα λέγω.[

am afraid . . . Cleon ‹is called› "Paphlagon" ‹from the verb› "to splutter" [*paphlazein*].

(137–) **Just as** . . . He would win . . . the choruses whenever . . . to others . . . was general . . .

(147–50) **And you now for your advantage, for I** . . . to a meeting of the assembly where the . . . you [s.] get the meeting set up. Hyperbolus to his master.

(151–55) **For I indeed will observe you at** . . . Indeed I will watch you getting what you deserve . . . you would have been locked up in the stocks . . . he means himself, one of the respectable sort . . . of Hyperbolus.

(156) **I cut the cackle.** The chorus to the [audience] . . .

(157) **To the audience.** In the . . . [3]

---

[3] We may have reached the parabasis of the play at this point.

160   – – –   ]νυσιν φανερα.[

        δ[   ]ων κτημ[

        οικ.[   ]να.[ ]ων.[

        φειν τας οἰκί[ας   ]αιταν[τὰ

        χρυσία τὰ ἀργυρ[ώμ]ατα καὶ τ[

165   .]υν φησιν τωσκ[ ].λ.ιὸυτωα.[

        ]' ἐκ πονηρῶν τῶι νόθωι .[

        ]Ἀσπασίας ἐπισκέψασθαι δε[

        ]ει ἢ Πάραλον· ἀμφότεροι γὰρ[

        ]ἕτερος αὐτῶν μετήλλαχεν[

170   οἰσ.νουργῶι γ' ἀνδρί, νὴ τὸν Διοκλέα[

        κ]λεα προσθεὶς Διοκλέα εἴρηκε.[

        δίδ]ωμι τῶι καλῶι. σαρκάζων α[

        ].[ ]νμ[.]ν μακρὸν ἔχει τοδ[

            ]ὑπαλλαγῆι κέχρηται τῶι[

                – – –

Fr. 5 col. i

175   ] [

                    ]σκος[..].[

                    ]και.ω

                    ].τιμην

                    ]

180   ]τινων·

                    ]ιλευς

                 ]α..ον Λακεδαι-

        μο   ]

                    ]μηνειστα

(166–69) **From wicked men to the bastard.** We must consider ⟨whether he means⟩ the son of Aspasia . . . or Paralus, for both . . . the one of them had died . . . [4]

(170–71) **For a man who plaits twigs, by Diocles.** . . . by adding "–cles" he has created "Diocles."

(172–74) **To the good man I give.** Sneeringly . . . he has employed exaggeration.

---

[4] The commentator detects an allusion to the sons of Pericles. His two legitimate sons, Xanthippus and Paralus, had died in the plague of 430. His illegitimate son by Aspasia, named Pericles, had been made an Athenian citizen by this time.

185

ἠκούσατ᾽, ὦ̣ ξυνήλικες

].ο̣ν τὸ ἡμι-

χοριον   ὑμεῖς γά]ρ, ὦ φρενοβλα-

βεῖς   ]

]....[.....]...με.·[

Fr. 5 col. ii

‒ ‒ ‒ ‒ ‒ ‒

190   πρὸς τὸ διδο.[

Κορινθίων .α[

ὅστις προδοσίας τ[

κληθήσομαι εἰς δικ[

ἀγοράων τῶν κατα[‒ ‒ ‒ ‒ ‒ ‒

195 ⁒   προτελοῦσι. προπη[αὐτοκάρδαλα   γρά-

φουσιν αὐτοκάβδα[λα   αὐτοκάβ]δαλα

λέγεται τὰ ἐπικαθα[ἅπερ ε]ἰώθασι

⁒   κάπτειν αἱ ἀλετρί[δες   ]ἐκ-

> φατνίσματα δὲ τὰ [ἐκβαλλ]όμε-

200   να, φρυά[γμ].̣.̣[να,

τρεφουσ[

θαρτοι[‒ ‒

μη.τ.[

Frr. 6–12 (= K.-A. F 192.204–74) are but scraps from which very little can be gleaned.

193 Plutarch *Nicias* 4.3 (ll. 1–8); F 192.185 (ll. 5, 7)

{ΜΑΡΙΚΑΣ.} πόσου χρόνου γὰρ συγγεγένησαι
    Νικίᾳ;

(185–88) **Did you hear that, friends?** . . . the semi-chorus. You empty-headed fools . . . [= F 193.5, 7]

(192–93) **I who shall be indicted . . . for treason.** Into court . . .

(194) **Market goers.** Those who ‹spend time› in ‹the marketplace›.

(195) **They pay (?) in advance.** They . . . in advance. Improvisations [*autokardala*]. ‹Some› write *autokabdala* ‹with a "b"›; "improvisations" means the sort of things . . . which slave girls in the mill are accustomed to gulp down.

(199) **Scraps from the manger.**

193 (MARIKAS) How long since you got together with Nicias?

{B.} οὐδ᾽ εἶδον, εἰ μὴ ᾽ναγχος ἑστὼτ᾽ ἐν ἀγορᾷ.
{ΜΑ.} ἀνὴρ ὁμολογεῖ Νικίαν ἑορακέναι.
καίτοι τί μαθὼν ἂν εἶδεν, εἰ μὴ προυδίδου;
{ΧΟΡΟΣ ΠΕΝΗΤΩΝ.} ἠκούσατ᾽, ὦ ξυνήλικες,
ἐπ᾽ αὐτοφώρῳ Νικίαν εἰλημμένον;
{ΧΟΡΟΣ ΠΛΟΥΣΙΩΝ.} ὑμεῖς γάρ, ὦ φρενοβλαβεῖς,
λάβοιτ᾽ ἂν ἄνδρ᾽ ἄριστον ἐν κακῷ τινι;

194 Σ Plato *Sophist* 239c

καὶ πόλλ᾽ ἔμαθον ἐν τοῖσι κουρείοις ἐγὼ
ἀτόπως καθίζων κοὐδὲ γιγνώσκειν δοκῶν.

195 Σ Aristophanes *Birds* 1556

{Α.} ἄκουε νῦν Πείσανδρος ὡς ἀπόλλυται.
{Β.} ὁ στρεβλός; {Α.} οὐκ ἀλλ᾽ ὁ μέγας, οὑνοκίνδιος.

196 Σ Sophocles *Oedipus at Colonus* 1600

ἀλλ᾽ εὐθὺ πόλεως εἶμι· θῦσαι γάρ με δεῖ
κριὸν Χλόῃ Δήμητρι.

197 *Epimerismi Homerici* ω 21

κρούων γε μὴν αὐτὰς ἐωνούμην ἐγώ.

198 Photius p. 270.12

τῶν γὰρ πονηρῶν μικρόν † ἐπὶ τοῦ ὀβολοῦ.

(B) I haven't seen him, except just now standing in the agora.

(MARIKAS) The fellow confesses that he has seen Nicias. Why would he have seen him, except that he was engaged in treason?

(CHORUS OF POOR MEN) Did you hear that, age-mates, Nicias caught in the act?

(CHORUS OF RICH MEN) You empty-headed fools, how would you ever convict such a good man for anything wicked?

194 I learned a great deal in the barbershops, sitting out of the way and pretending not to understand.

195 (A) Hear now how Peisander is being destroyed.
   (B) The squint-eyed man?   (A) No, the big man, the donkey driver.

196 I am on my way straight to the Acropolis, for I must sacrifice a ram to Demeter Chloe.

197 I tapped them [fem.] when I bought them.

198 Not many scoundrels for an obol.

199 Stephanus of Byzantium p. 193.15

πότερ᾽ ἦν τὸ τάριχος Φρύγιον ἢ Γαδειρικόν;

200 *Suda* α 1785

περιήλθομεν καὶ φῦλον ἀμφορεαφόρων.

201 Orus *On Orthography* fol. 281r 20

πεύσεσθε· νὼ γάρ, ἄνδρες, οὐχ ἱππεύομεν.

202 Aelian *Historical Miscellany* 12.30

ὁμολογεῖ δὲ καὶ Εὔπολις ἐν τῷ Μαρικᾷ, ὅστις αὐτῶν εὐτελέστατος, σφραγῖδας εἶχε δέκα μνῶν.

203 Eustathius *On the Iliad* p. 300.22

ἀλλ᾽ οὖν ἔγωγέ σοι λέγω Μαρικᾶντα μὴ κολάζειν.

204 Photius (z) *apud* Tsantsanoglou pp. 119–20

ἔχοντα τὴν σφραγῖδα καὶ ψάγδαν ἐρυγγάνοντα

205 Aelius Aristides 28.91

ἀφυπνίζεσθαι ‹   › χρὴ πάντα θεατήν
ἀπὸ μὲν βλεφάρων αὐθημερινὸν ποιητῶν λῆρον
   ἀφέντα

199 Was the salt-fish from Phrygia or Gadeira?

200 We went around to a tribe, the Amphora bearers.

201 You will discover, for, people, the two of us are not knights.[1]

> [1] From the prologue, where a pair of slaves explains the situation with the caveat that "we are not doing *Knights* ⟨again⟩"?

202 Eupolis agrees ⟨about the people of Cyrene⟩ in his *Maricas*—even the most ordinary person has a ring worth ten minas.

203 And I tell you not to punish Maricas.

204 Wearing a ring and belching unguent.

205 Now every spectator must wake up and wash away from their eyes today's nonsense from the poets.

206 Photius p. 657.2

ὃς θυμήνας τοῖς στρατιώταις λοιμὸν καὶ ψῶζαν
ἔπεμψεν.

207 Σ Aeschylus *Persians* 65

πεπέρακεν μὲν ὁ περσέπτολις ἤδη Μαρικᾶς.

208 Quintilian 1.10.18

Maricas, qui est Hyperbolus, nihil se ex musice scire nisi
litteras confitetur.

209 Σ Aristophanes *Wealth* 1037

κἀκεῖ γὰρ τὴν Ὑπερβόλου μητέρα τηλίᾳ εἰκάζει τῇ
πλατείᾳ σανίδι . . . εἰς ὃ τιθέασιν οἱ ἀρτοκόποι τοὺς
ἄρτους ἐπὶ τῷ ξηραίνεσθαι . . . ἐὰν δὲ καὶ τὸ ἐν
Μαρικᾷ προσέλθῃ, ἔνθα εἰς τηλίαν φησὶ τὰ τοῦ
Ὑπερβόλου ὀστᾶ ἐμβεβλῆσθαι.

210 Harpocration p. 286.15

ὅτι δὲ καὶ τοῖς τριηράρχοις παρείποντο ταμίαι δεδή-
λωκεν Εὔπολις ἐν Μαρικᾷ.

211 Σ Aristophanes *Clouds* 549b

ἐκεῖ δὲ ὁ Εὔπολις ὡς τεθνηκότος Κλέωνος μέμνηται.

206 Who in anger at the soldiers sent pestilence and itch.

207 The city-sacking Maricas has now passed over.[1]

1 A parody of Aeschylus *Persians* 65 ("the city-sacking royal army has now passed over").

208 Maricas, who is Hyperbolus, admits that he knows nothing about learning except the alphabet.

209 There [Eupolis in his *Maricas*] likens the mother of Hyperbolus to a flat board . . . on which the bread makers place loaves to dry . . . but if we go on to the passage in *Maricas* where he says that the bones of Hyperbolus have been placed on a flat board.

210 That stewards accompany trierarchs Eupolis has made clear in *Maricas*.

211 There [in *Maricas*] Eupolis mentions Cleon as dead.

Brief fragments: (F 212) "city of slaves," (F 213) "error," (F 214) "we have dressed as Thessalians," (F 215) "harvest," (F 216) "to owe," (F 217) "small wine jar."

ΝΟΥΜΗΝΙΑΙ

Were it not for the hypothesis to Acharnians, *we would not have known that this comedy existed. If the phrase "it has not been preserved" applies to Eupolis' play as well as to Cratinus', the text of* New Moons *did not survive into the period of the Alexandrian scholars. If the title refers to the chorus, then what sort of chorus would new moons comprise, and how would one costume it? The play might*

ΠΟΛΕΙΣ

The title suggests that the chorus was made up of personified cities from the Athenian archē *and is confirmed by F 245–47, where three cities are identified as they enter. Very likely this was an individuated chorus, but if each of the twenty-four choristers received its own introduction, the scene could have lasted a hundred lines or so and run the risk of tiring out its audience. In addition to Tenos, Chios, and Cyzicus, F 256 suggests that Amorgos was among the cities, perhaps also Lesbos, if in F 243 "a proper man" carries a sexual suggestion.*

Earlier critics treated Cities *in the same manner that they had regarded Aristophanes'* Babylonians, *that in each comedy the poet was presenting the allies sympathetically against the imperial power of Athens. For neither comedy does this claim hold up. In Eupolis' play the cities would hardly be pleased with their depictions in F 245–47, and*

NEW MOONS

*have had something to do with debts coming due at the
end of the month* (Clouds 740–56), *or with the secular cal-
endar and the lunar calendar being desperately out of step*
(Clouds 607–26), *or with the revels that accompanied the
new moon* (Lysias F 53). *If the last, I would suggest that the
actual title of the comedy was* Noumeniastai (*New Moon
Revellers*).

Testimonium

i See Eupolis T 13a.

CITIES

*throughout the attitude is male v. female, master v. slave,
human v. animal, and Athens v. the cities. F 250 is in the
archilochean metre, usually reserved for the chorus, and if
this is the chorus speaking, they had a "master" to whom
they owed obedience.*

   *Several fragments demonstrate the familiar opposition
of old:superior and new:inferior that operates in* Demes. *F
219 contrasts current with former leaders, F 221 praises
the old conservative Cimon with some personal reserva-
tions, F 233 mentions the heritage of Marathon, F 237 the
weakness of old men, while F 238 praises a man as not be-
ing "meddlesome," in Greek* polypragmōn, *a touchstone of
considerable debate in the late fifth century. There is a hint
also of the debate within the play. F 238 takes the side of the
quiet v. the involved life, while F 248 claims the opposite.
Euripides is exploring precisely the same territory in his*

contemporary plays, Suppliant Women *and* Antiope, *and it would be revealing to know if Eupolis allowed the champion of involvement to prevail (and thus open the possibility of irony) or the exponent of more traditional values.*

With the exception of Demes, *the fragments of this comedy contain more allusions to kōmōidoumenoi than any other comedy, testimony perhaps to the topical theme suggested by its title. A lower date is provided by the mention of Chios as an ally (F 246), as it revolted in 412, and by*

Fragments

218 Pollux 10.192

$$\text{καρδόπους τε καὶ}$$
κρατῆρας ὀκτώ, δέχ' ὑδρίας, δύο τρυβλίω,
κνέφαλλα δέκα, θέρμαυστριν, ἐξ θρόνους, χύτραν,
κάννας ἑκατόν, κόρημα, κιβωτόν, λύχνον.

219 Athenaeus 425b

οὓς δ' οὐκ ἂν εἵλεσθ' οὐδ' ἂν οἰνόπτας πρὸ τοῦ,
νυνὶ στρατηγοὺς ⟨– ◡⟩ . ὦ πόλις, πόλις,
ὡς εὐτυχὴς εἶ μᾶλλον ἢ καλῶς φρονεῖς.

220 Σ Aristophanes *Birds* 1297

Συρακόσιος δ' ἔοικεν, ἡνίκ' ἂν λέγῃ,
τοῖς κυνιδίοισι τοῖσιν ἐπὶ τῶν τειχίων·
ἀναβὰς γὰρ ἐπὶ τὸ βῆμ' ὑλακτεῖ περιτρέχων.

*the allusion to Stilbides (F 225), who died in Sicily in 413.
Several of the* kōmōidoumenoi *seem to have been in vogue
in the late 420s (Amynias—F 222, Demus—F 227, Hiero-
cles—F 231, and Philoxenus—F 249), and for that reason a
date of D-422 is often assumed as proven. This is a reason-
able conclusion, although one would not be disturbed by
discovering that it was produced in 420 or 419.*

Recent bibliography: R. Rosen, in Dobrov (City) 149–76.

Fragments

218 Troughs and eight mixing bowls, ten water pitchers, a
pair of bowls, ten pillows, tongs, six chairs, a pot, a hun-
dred mats, a broom, a chest, a lamp.

219 Men whom before now you wouldn't even have cho-
sen as wine inspectors, now you elect as generals. O my
city, my city, you are more lucky than smart.

220 Whenever he speaks, Syracosius resembles those lit-
tle dogs upon the walls. He gets up on the rostrum and
runs about howling.[1]

[1] Political figure of the 410s (*PAA* 853435)—see *Birds* 1297;
allegedly the author of a decree against personal humour in com-
edy. Seen by some as the demagogue at F 99.23–34.

221 Plutarch *Cimon* 15.3

κακὸς μὲν οὐκ ἦν, φιλοπότης δὲ κἀμελής·
κἀνίοτ᾽ ⟨ἂν⟩ ἀπεκοιμᾶτ᾽ ἂν ἐν Λακεδαίμονι,
κἂν Ἐλπινίκην τῇδε καταλιπὼν μόνην.

222 Σ Aristophanes *Wasps* 1271a

χἀμυνίας ἐκεῖνος ἀμέλει κλαύσεται,
ὅτι ⟨ὢν⟩ ἄγροικος ἵσταται πρὸς τῷ μύρῳ,
† ὅτι θεῶν εἵνεκα † ἔπλευσε κακὸς ὢν εἴσεται.

223 Bachmann's *Lexicon* p. 128.7

ὁ Φιλῖνος οὗτος, τί ἄρα πρὸς ταύτην βλέπεις;
οὐκ ἀπολιβάξεις εἰς ἀποικίαν τινά;

224 Σ Aristophanes *Frogs* 1513

οὐκ ἀργαλέα δῆτ᾽ ἐστὶ πάσχειν τοῦτ᾽ ἐμέ,
τὸν Λευκολοφίδου παῖδα τοῦ Πορθάονος;

225 Σ Aristophanes *Peace* 1031

ὡς οὖν τίν᾽ ἔλθω δῆτά σοι τῶν μάντεων;
πότερος ἀμείνων, Ἀμφότερος ἢ Στιλβίδης;

2 ἀμφοτέρων codd., Ἀμφότερος van Herwerden

221 He [Cimon] wasn't a bad man, but he was fond of drink and thoughtless. Sometimes he would spend the night in Sparta, leaving Elpinice here all alone.

222 That Amynias will squeal with good reason, because, like the rustic at the perfume stall, he will realise that he sailed there . . . [1]

1 Amynias (*PAA* 124575) was made fun of in the late 420s (*Clouds* 690–92, *Wasps* 74, 466, 1267–70; Cratinus F 227; Hermippus *Iambs* F 5 West) for avoiding military service and for living a style of life above his means.

223 Hey, Philinus, why are you looking at her? Why don't you piss off to a colony somewhere?[1]

1 Possibly *PAA* 928030, the son of the general Cleippides and brother of Cleophon (see Antiphon 6).

224 Is it not dreadful that I, Adeimantus, the son of Leucolophides the son of Porthaon, suffer things like this?[1]

1 An important figure at Athens in the last quarter of the fifth century, a character in Plato's *Protagoras*, exiled as a result of the scandal over the Mysteries in 415, and a major player in the fall of Athens in 405/4 (*PAA* 107695).

225 So in your view, to which of the seers I should go? Which one is better, Amphoterus or Stilbides?[1]

1 Stilbides was a prominent *mantis* in the late 420s and 410s, serving in that capacity on the expedition to Sicily in 415–13 (*PAA* 835500). "Amphoterus," van Herwerden's emendation, is not an attested name at Athens.

183

THE POETS OF OLD COMEDY

226 Athenaeus 392e

{A.} ὄρτυγας ἔθρεψας σύ τινας ἤδη πώποτε;
{B.} ἔγωγε μικρά γ᾽ ὀρτύγια. κἄπειτα τί;

227 Σ Aristophanes Wasps 98a

καὶ τῷ Πυριλάμπους ἆρα Δήμῳ κυψέλη
ἔνεστιν;

228 Harpocration p. 46.22

ὡς ὑμῖν ἐγὼ
πάντ᾽ ἀποκρινοῦμαι πρὸς τὰ κατηγορούμενα.

229 Pollux 7.13

κακὰ τοιάδε
πάσχουσιν, οὐδὲ πρᾶσιν αἰτῶ

2 πάσχουσιν F, S; πάσχουσα A

230 Photius (b, z) α 1286

ὤφειλ᾽ Ὑάκινθος ἀποθανεῖν ἀμυγδάλῃ.

231 Σ Aristophanes *Peace* 1046

Ἱερόκλεες βέλτιστε χρησμῳδῶν ἄναξ

232 Σ Aristophanes *Lysistrata* 270

ὥσπερ ἐπὶ τὴν Λύκωνος ἔρρει πᾶς ἀνήρ.

184

226 (A) Have you ever raised any quails?
(B) I have, some little ones. So what?

227 And is there a chest at Demus' place, son of Pyri-lampes?

228 As I shall answer all your [pl.] charges.

229 They suffer such things, but I don't ask to be sold.

230 Hyacinthus should have been killed by an almond tree.

231 Hierocles, best of soothsayers.[1]

[1] A known expert in religious matters and a character at *Peace* 1043–1126 (*PAA* 532080).

232 Just like every male goes to ruin with Lycon's wife

233 Photius p. 362.13

ὃς τὴν Μαραθῶνι κατέλιφ᾽ ἡμῖν οὐσίαν.

234 Photius (z) α 2758

τί δ᾽ ἔστ᾽ Ἀθηναίοισι πρᾶγμ᾽ ἀπώμοτον;

235 Σ Aristophanes *Clouds* 351b

ἐξ Ἡρακλείας ἀργύριον ὑφείλετο.

236 Photius (b, z) α 1905

ὃν οὐκ ἀνέῳξα πώποτ᾽ ἀνθρώποις ἐγώ.

237 Photius (b, z) α 1936

ὡς μόλις ἀνήρρησ᾽· οὐδέν ἐσμεν οἱ σαπροί.

238 Photius (z) α 2441

οὐ γὰρ πολυπράγμων ἐστίν, ἀλλ᾽ ἀπλήγιος.

239 Harpocration p. 194.7

ἄνδρες λογισταὶ τῶν ὑπευθύνων χορῶν.

240 Moeris p. 202.30

ἐμοὶ γὰρ οὐκ ἔστ᾽ οὐδὲ λάσαν᾽ ὅπου χέσω.

233 Who left us Marathon as our inheritance.

234 What deed would be sworn as impossible for Athenians?

235 He [Simon] filched money from Heracleia.[1]

1 An alleged embezzler of public funds (*PAA* 822065—see *Clouds* 351, 399).

236 Which I have never opened to men.

237 How destroyed I am—we decrepit folk are nothing.[1]

1 The first part might read "how destroyed he is," he being one of the "decrepit folk."

238 He is not a meddlesome sort, but a simple person.

239 Gentlemen, scrutineers of the choruses under review.

240 I don't even have a basin where I may shit.

241 Stephanus of Byzantium p. 432.17

καὶ Χαόνων καὶ Παιόνων καὶ Μαρδόνων

242 Pollux 7.29

ἄνευ καλαθίσκων καὶ † πόρων † καὶ πηνίων

243 *Etymologicum Genuinum* B

ἔχω γὰρ ἐπιτήδειον ἄνδρ᾽ αὐτῇ πάνυ.

244 Photius p. 654.21

πεφυτευμένη δ᾽ αὕτη 'στὶν, ἢ ψιλὴ μόνον;

245 Σ Aristophanes *Wealth* 718

                        Τῆνος αὕτη,
πολλοὺς ἔχουσα σκορπίους ἔχεις τε συκοφάντας.

  2 ἔχεις τε cod., πολλούς τε Wilamowitz.

246 Σ Aristophanes *Birds* 880

                 αὕτη Χίος, καλὴ πόλις ‹   ›
πέμπει γὰρ ὑμῖν ναῦς μακρὰς ἄνδρας θ᾽ ὅταν
   δεήσῃ,
καὶ τἆλλα πειθαρχεῖ καλῶς, ἄπληκτος ὥσπερ
   ἵππος.

241 Of the Chaonians and the Paeonians and the Mardonians

242 Without spools and wool (?) and spindles.

243 I have a very suitable man for her.

244 Is she cultivated or just bare land?

245 She is Tenos, with many scorpions and informers.

246 She is Chios, a fine city, for she sends you warships and men whenever there is need, and the rest of the time she is nicely obedient, like a horse that does not need a whip.

THE POETS OF OLD COMEDY

247 Σ Aristophanes *Peace* 1176

{A.} ἡ δ' ὑστάτη ποῦ 'σθ'; {B.} ἥδε Κύζικος πλέα
στατήρων.
{A.} ἐν τῇδε τοίνυν τῇ πόλει φρουρῶν ⟨ἐγώ⟩ ποτ᾽
αὐτὸς
γυναῖκ᾽ ἐκίνουν κολλύβου καὶ παῖδα καὶ γέροντα,
κἀξῆν ὅλην τὴν ἡμέραν τὸν κύσθον ἐκκορίζειν.

248 Photius (z) α 2989

⟨x – ◡⟩ ἄσπονδος δ᾽ ἀνὴρ σπουδαρχίδου κακίων.

249 Σ Aristophanes *Wasps* 82b

ἔστι δέ τις θήλεια Φιλόξενος ἐκ Διομείων.

250 Σ Hephaestion *Handbook* 15.3

ὦ δέσποτα, καὶ τάδε νῦν ἄκουσον, ἂν λέγω σοι.

251 Σ Aristophanes *Frogs* 970

ὅτι δοκεῖ προσγεγράφθαι τῇ πολιτείᾳ, Ἅγνωνος αὐ-
τὸν ποιησαμένου, ὡς Εὔπολις Πόλεσιν.

252 Σ Lucian *Timon* 30

Κρατῖνος δὲ ἐν Ὥραις ὡς παρελθόντος νέου τῷ βή-
ματι μέμνηται καὶ παρ' ἡλικίαν καὶ Ἀριστοφάνης
Σφηξὶ καὶ Εὔπολις Πόλεσι.

247 (A) Where is the last one?   (B) She is Cyzicus, full of staters,
(A) Indeed, on guard duty once in that city I screwed a woman, a boy, and an old man, all for a dime. I could have spent the whole day cleaning out its cunt.[1]

[1] The text as printed in K.-A. has a single speaker throughout.

248 The unambitious man is worse than the office seeker.

249 There is a certain feminine Philoxenus from the Diomeia,

250 Master, hear now these things which I shall tell you.

251 He ⟨Theramenes⟩ seems to have been enrolled into Athenian citizenship, when Hagnon adopted him— Eupolis in *Cities*.

252 Cratinus in *Seasons* [F 283] mentions that he ⟨Hyperbolus⟩ came to speak at the *bema* at an unusually early age, also Aristophanes in *Wasps* [1007] and Eupolis in *Cities*.

THE POETS OF OLD COMEDY

253 Σ (Arethas) Plato *Apology* 20e

Εὔπολις μὲν οὖν ἐν Πόλεσι διὰ τὴν χροιὰν πύξινον
αὐτὸν καλεῖ.

254 Σ Aristophanes *Acharnians* 504e

εἰς δὲ τὰ Διονύσια ἐτέτακτο Ἀθήναζε κομίζειν τὰς
πόλεις τοὺς φόρους, ὡς Εὔπολίς φησιν ἐν Πόλεσιν.

255 Photius δ 161

δέκα τοὐβολοῦ· διὰ τὸ μικρὸν εἶναι Ἀσωπόδωρον.
Εὔπολις Πόλεσιν.

ΠΡΟΣΠΑΛΤΙΟΙ

*The publication of P. Oxy. 2813 (F 259) has changed our
view of* Prospaltians *from a comedy possibly following the
dicastic theme of* Wasps *to a potentially political drama
that was the precursor of* Acharnians. *As the first part of
the commentary seems to be describing Eupolis at the start
of his career, scholars now date the comedy as Eupolis'
first, in 429, or perhaps in 428.*

*The title indicates that this was a comedy with a chorus
of men representing an Attic deme, for which* Acharnians *is
the best parallel. But Prospalta is an out-of-the-way and
not especially prominent place, unless that is the point of
the chorus, men from the backwoods. The* Suda *(T 2) re-
cords that the Prospaltians were made fun of as "fond of
litigation," which may reflect something in comedy. Dicae-*

192

253 Eupolis in *Cities* calls him [Chairephon] "boxwood-yellow" because of his complexion.

254 It was the custom for the cities to bring the tribute to Athens at the Dionysia, as Eupolis says in *Cities*.

255 Ten for an obol—because Asopodorus was a little fellow. Eupolis in *Cities*.

Brief fragments: (F 256) "made of amorgis," (F 257) "roughriders," (F 258) "stench of goats."

PROSPALTIANS

opolis' recollection of the tempers of country folk and old men at Acharnians *370–76 may be relevant here.*

Much of the discussion has focussed on F 260, a discussion between three speakers, one of whom (C) is very likely the chorus or a subchorus. One man (A) is trying to persuade a second man (B) to do something. When he refuses, A asks C to run and tell the Prospaltians to send an army (would this be an absurdity for such a small deme?) or to convey something or themselves. Goossens proposed that this scene reflected contemporary events, identifying B as Pericles and the situation as local opposition to his policy of Sitzkrieg in the first year of the War. The options for the Prospaltians in 15–16 are thus those outlined by Thucydides: go out and fight the Spartans or withdraw into the

193

city ("convey themselves"). Goossens restored the end of v. 17 to read "so that they may not say that I sit by and waste time," relating this to the criticism by the country folk, especially the Acharnians, of Pericles' tactics (Hermippus F 47, Thucydides 2.21, Plutarch Pericles 33.7). But this is unsafe ground, and missing the ends of the lines we cannot say for certain what the point of the scene was. Also a date of 429 does not suit the context of the War, since by that

Testimonia

i Σ Aristophanes *Clouds* 541a

οὐδὲ πρεσβύτης ὁ λέγων· ὡς Εὔπολις ἐν τοῖς Προσπαλτίοις.

ii *Etymologicum Genuinum* AB, *Suda* δ 1515

ἐκωμῳδοῦντο . . . Θυμοιτάδαι καὶ Προσπάλτιοι ὡς δικαστικοί.

Fragments

259 P. Oxy. 2813

time there no longer was the option of fight or flee to the city.

*The mention of "inferior and good people" (F 260.10–11), of the deme of Prospalta, the option of sending an army, yielding to reasoned argument, the citation of An-*tigone *712–15 (a scene of political debate) do suggest that* Prospaltians *was a political comedy, of the sort that Eupolis would write in* Demes *and* Cities *(and very likely, in* Golden Race*). If it was his first comedy, he began his career on his own distinctive note.*

Testimonia

i "Nor an old man speaking": like Eupolis in *Prospaltians*.

ii The Thymoedatae and the Prospaltians were made fun as fond of litigation.

Fragments

259 *A badly mutilated papyrus of the late second or early third century AD, this is almost certainly a commentary on Eupolis'* Prospaltians *(see ll. 13, 15, 17). The lack of lemmata in the first section suggests that the commentator is summarising the poet's description of the circumstances behind the writing of the play. Perhaps in the parodos or parabasis, but I wonder if Eupolis opened his first comedy with an apologia like those found in Terence.*

Fr. 1 col. i

```
              ]ωσπ[....]ανην προ
      ] (ἔστι) δη α.[ ] ἀπεστάλησαν δεη-
σόμενοι δη]μηγορῆ[σα]ι πρὸς αὐτοῦ νέ-
ον ἀρ]χ[ο]μ(έν)ου γράφ[ειν] κωμῳδίαν κ(αὶ) ταῦτα
```
5   ἐνι]αὐτ(ῶν) ὄντος [....]ειν βιασάμ(εν)οι η-
```
      ]ο μ(ὲν) τοὺς πολίτας μὴ γράφειν
ἤ]ρωας δι̣ω̣[    ]προ[...]ων παλι-
]ος αὐτο̣ὺ̣ς α[ ].ο̣τ̣[...]τους ἤρωας
]δ(ὲ) τ(ῶν) πολιτ(ῶν) ἕκασ[τ ]προσφυῶς
```
10   ]. πωναδ.αγα[   ]οι πρέσβεις
```
          ].μ[ ]ο.[ ].[                ]σ
]χ[ ].[ ].σ̣ι δ(ὲ) λο̣ι̣[ ]ρ[        ]ωφω[
η]νέχθη χορὸς δ(ὲ) Πρ[οσπ]αλτίων
]ραιει δ(ὲ) ἤχθη ι.[        ]αι μ(ὲν) ὑπ.[
```
15   ]. ι. Εὐπόλιδος[   ]αμα
```
].θυσ̣.[                    ]σθαι εκ.[
                          ]ι̣δ' Εὐπολ[ι
]φα[..]υς[                  ]ς δ' ἔνιοι
].σδ(ια)π.[                ]λυφανου.
```
20   ].. [ ]..[   ].[   ]νεσθαι
```
].ερον[          ]λ[ ].[      ].σθῆναι
].ωμ[            ]ρας[ ].[    ]υγ
].σπ[                  ]ναγ[  ]οισακρο
]και[            ]υδο[        ]γελωτ'
```
25   ]γελωτ.[   ]ιμην
```
]φειδε[                        ].ος
                              ]μεαπο
```

196

(1–23) . . . they were sent off to ask . . . to speak out in public on his [Eupolis'] behalf , who was just beginning to write comedy and in fact was . . . years (?) and . . . compelling him or . . . not to write about citizens . . . heroes . . . the heroes themselves . . . and each of the citizens suitably . . . envoys . . . a chorus of Prospaltioi was brought on stage . . . and was brought . . . by Eupolis . . . . Eupolis . . . of Aristophanes (?) . . . and some

(24–25) **laughter:** laughter.

```
                                    ]ε̣ι̣ηθη
                                  ]νπρ[ ].̣
30                                ].̣ασω
                                  ].̣ταιπροε
              εἰπεῖν μη]δενί γελοίως
                             ]τι ἠρώτησέ με
                     ]μηδενὶ [ε]ἰπεῖν ὅτι ες[
35                     ].̣σ̣.̣ος κωμῳδία[
                     ]..[.]στον χο(ρὸν) διδάσκει
                     ].̣.συκοφαντεῖ (ἔστι) δ(ὲ)[
                     ].κλοιὸν ἀπ' ὀβελίσκου[
                     ].̣η θε̣ρμ[.̣].ουμη[
40                             ]σεπει
                             - - - -
```

```
    Fr. 1 col. ii
    γάζει   [
    η κωμῳδι[                        λαμ-
    βάνειν αυ[
    μ(έν)ους η ο[
45  δομ(εν)ον τρ[
    τας ὄψεις[
    πειων μη[
    το ἆθλον[
    βοὸς τικο.̣[
50  εν τοῖς κακ.̣[
    περὶ ταδε̣[
    .[.].κατα̣[
      ]θαικ.̣[
```

198

(32–40) **to tell nobody:** jokingly . . . he asked me . . . to tell nobody . . . comedy . . . instructs the chorus . . . and he is an informer . . . collar from a spit.

(41–67) **he kneads** . . . comedy . . . to take . . . the sights . . . the prize . . . of a cow . . . among the evils . . . around this . . .

```
        ]δημ.[
55      ]λομα[
        ]αλειν[
        ]κουει.[
        ]μ(εν)ος[
     ἔφυγε δ(ιὰ) .[
60   βουλεύειν[
     κιθαρῳδὸς[
     κ(αὶ) μετοικ.[                           πρό-
     ξενον κ(αὶ) προ[στάτην                   προ-
     στάταις ἐχ[ρ-
65   πολειτης.[                               προ-
     στάτου σπ[
     κουσιμοικο[
     τῆς γῆς μ(ὲν) ἄχθο[ς                     ἄ-
     χθος μ(ὲν) ἐπεὶ καμ[
70   κουφότης δ(ὲ) ἐπεὶ.[
     ἀλλὰ κοῦφοι κ(αὶ) φ[
     Συρακόσιον η.[
     εἴην    τούτους[
     τις Ἐξήκεστον·[
75   ταλου κομίζω.[
     π(αρα)γενόμ(εν)ον ταυ[
     νειν δοκεῖ μο.[
     μηδ᾽ ὕθλει μὴ φ[λυάρει
     πεια κλωγμός.[                           ἀν-
80   θρώπων γ[
     γλώττης[
```

200

he fled through/because of . . . to plan . . . cithara player . . .
a metic . . . a *proxenos* and a leader . . . to/for leaders . . . citizen . . . of a leader.

(68–83) **burden on the earth:** . . . burden since . . . lightness . . . but lightweights and **Syrakosios** [of Syracuse?] . . .
Execestus . . . I bring in . . . showing up . . . it seems to me
. . . **do not talk blather:** do not talk nonsense . . . noise . . .

τραγικὸς η[
  ]δ‸‸παδ[
‑ ‑ ‑ ‑

Frr. 2–4 (= K.-A. F 259.85–102) are but scraps.

Fr. 5   ]‸‸‸‸[
      ]νας σχ[
105   ]ει κ(αὶ) το‸[
      εὐ]ρύκρειο[ν
      εὖ οἶ]δ’ ὅτι τι‸[
      ε]ὖ οἶδ’ ὅτι π[
      ]εχθραν πα[
110   ]ω βόσκεις
      κ]ωμῳδεῖ θ‸[
      ]ξε δ(ὲ) ἵνα κακῶς κρ[
      ]νως Φρύγα μὰ Δί‸[
      ]σ Εὐάνδρου τοῦ Ἀ[ρκάδος
115   ]ς μᾶτερ Μεγάλα [
      ]ες αὐληταὶ ἐν ταῖς[
      ἀρ]χόμ(εν)οι ἀνακρούεσ[θαι
      ]θει ξυμμαιν‸[
      ]ρο‸[ ]ν φαῦλον ‸[ ]‸‸ρ‸[
120   ]‸υβ[ ] φλαῦρον κακὸν[
      ]‸[ ]ἐπίπονον οὗ γ’ ε[
      ]‸κράτης τοιχωρυχο[
      ο]υσιν ἔνδον μετ’ ὀφέω[ν
      οἱ] ἥρωες ζωγραφοῦνται α‸[

of men . . . tongue . . . tragic.

(103–31): **wide-ruling . . . I know well that:** I know well that . . . hostility . . . you raise . . . he makes fun of . . . and so that badly . . . **a Phrygian, no by Zeus . . . of Euander of Arcadia (?) . . . Great Mother** . . . *aulos*-players in the . . . beginning to strike up the music . . . inferior nonsense . . . laborious . . . **–crates**: burglar . . . inside the heroes are depicted with serpents . . . **most reproachable** . . .

125   ]ες *κἀπικήκαστον* ε[
      Σθενέ]βοια Προίτου τοῦ Κορι[νθίου
       ]ν αὐτ(ὴν) λέγει οὗτος σ[
             ].[ ]νοντα αρ.[
             ]..κ.φι.[
130   ]...[
             ]..αι.[

Frr. 6–15 (= K.-A. F 259.132–72) are but scraps.

260 *PSI* 1213

                – –
                ]κι
                ]ερω
                ]δες
                ]ν χορόν
5   ]ηι δέος
                ]ψειεν ἄν
                ].βον
                ].εθη
                ].αρη
10 {A.} ἐ]γὼ δ' ἵν' εἰσὶν οἱ κακο[
   .]....σδε χρηστῶν μ.[
   ε]ἰ μὴ ποοίην ω....[
   {B.} βαδίζεθ' ὑμεῖς ὡς τά[χι]στ' ε[
   καὶ φράζεθ' οἷα τἀνθάδ' ἐστ[
15 Προσπαλτίοισιν ἢ στρατιὰν[

204

Sthenboea wife of Proetus of Corinth . . . this one says that she.[1]

[1] A reference to the story of Bellerophon and Stheneboea, wife of Proetus (usually king of Tiryns), which was dramatised by Euripides in his *Stheneboea* (c. 430?).

260 (A) And I where the bad ones are . . . of honest people . . . if I were not to do

(B) You people, go as quickly as you can and tell what's going on here. Order the Prospaltians either to send an

THE POETS OF OLD COMEDY

πέμπειν κελεύετ᾽ ἢ κομίζεσθ[
ἵνα μὴ καθῆσθαι φῶσ᾽ ἀναλίσκ[
ὡς οὗτος οὐδέν, ὡς ἔοικε, πείσετ[αι.
{Γ.} ἀλλ᾽ ἐρχόμεσθ᾽· ἀτὰρ τὸ δεῖνα χρὴ[
20   πόσ᾽ ἄττα σοι πέμπωσιν. {Β.} ἔξεστι[
εἰ δεῖ γε τοῦτον ἐν κύκλωι πε[
ἀλλ᾽, ὦγάθ᾽, ἔτι καὶ νῦν πιθοῦ πά[σῃ τέχνῃ.
ὁρᾷς παρὰ ῥείθροισιν ὅταν η[...]δ[
ἢν μέν τις εἴκῃ τοῖς λόγοις ἐκσῴζε[ται,
25   ὁ δ᾽ ἀντιτείνων αὐτόπρεμνος οἴχε[ται.
αὕτως δὲ ναός {Α.} ἀπό μ᾽ ὀλεῖς, ἄνθρωπ[ε, σύ.
{Γ.} ἄνθρωπος οὗτος νοῦν ἔχοντας[
{Α.} ἀλλ᾽ οὐχὶ δυνάτ᾽· εἰ γὰρ πιθοίμ[ην σοι τάδε,
τίν᾽ ἂν τ[.]χ.ην ε.....[
30   {Β.} μέγα στένοι μέντἂν ακ[
ἡμεῖς δὲ ναῶν ναυτίλο[

261 Anonymous on Aristotle's *Nichomachean Ethics* 4.6

{Α.} τὸ δεῖν᾽, ἀκούεις; {Β.} Ἡράκλεις, τοῦτ᾽ ἔστι σοι
τὸ σκῶμμ᾽ ἀσελγὲς καὶ Μεγαρικὸν καὶ σφόδρα
ψυχρόν. † γελᾷς, ὡς ὁρᾷς, τὰ παιδία.

262 Athenaeus 326a

μήτηρ τις αὐτῷ Θρᾷττα ταινιόπωλις ἦν

263 Priscian *Institutes of Grammar* 18.225

τί; κατακροᾶσθέ μου τὰ μουσοδονήματα;

206

army or to convey . . . so that they cannot say that I just sit here, wasting . . . since this person, it seems, won't be persuaded.

(C) We're going. But you must say what they are to send you.

(B) It is possible . . . if I have to . . . in a circle. But, my good fellow, by all means heed even now. You see beside the water banks when . . . , if someone yields to argument, he is saved. But he who resists perishes root and branch. Similarly of a ship,

(A) You'll be the death of me, sir.

(C) This man . . . things that make sense.

(A) It's not possible. If I were to heed . . .

(B) . . . would be quite sorry . . . we, like sailors of the ships . . .

261 (A) The whatchamacallit, do you hear?

(B) By Heracles, that joke of yours is vulgar, Megarian, and completely frigid. You see, † laughter the boys.[1]

---

[1] For Megarian humour, regarded by the Athenians as crude and primitive stuff, see *Wasps* 57; Ecphantides F 2; Aristotle *Poetics* 1448a31–32, *Ethics* 1123a34.

262 His mother was some Thracian ribbon seller.

263 What? Are you people listening closely to my musical swirls?

264 Zenobius 2.37

ὅτι χωλὸς τὴν ἑτέραν χεῖρα εὖ σφόδρα.

265 Priscian *Institutes of Grammar* 18.190

πάντα γὰρ τυχὼν ἄπει.

266 Σ Aristophanes *Birds* 839

ἢ πηλὸν ὀργάζειν τινά

267 Σ Plato *Menexenus* 235e

ἐν δὲ Προσπατλίοις Ἑλένην αὐτὴν καλεῖ.

ΤΑΞΙΑΡΧΟΙ

This play is an example of the comic subgenre that Sommerstein calls "Dionysus as antihero." In both comedy and satyr-drama there was good value in putting Dionysus in the most incongruous situation possible and then letting the natural humour of the situation work itself out. In Eupolis' comedy Dionysus joins the navy, and like all raw recruits encounters a stern taskmaster, the renowned Athenian general Phormion, known for his naval exploits in the opening years of the War.

We can glimpse how the comedy treated Dionysus. He arrives in inappropriate dress (F 272–73), complains about the food (F 271, 275), misunderstands the jargon of the military, mistaking perigraphein *(maintain a perimeter) for marking the circle for a game of knuckle-bones (F*

264 That he is well and truly crippled in his other hand.

265 You will go away with everything you [masc. sing.] wanted.

266 Or for someone to knead the mortar.

267 In *Prospaltians* he calls her [Aspasia] Helen.

OFFICERS

269), *bewails the effect of service on his appearance (F 270, 280), and fails to learn how to row properly (F 268.51–55). Why he should be joining the navy is unclear. He may have been so compelled, or if "I fled" is correctly read in F 274, was he fleeing the wrath of Hera? Or if the play belongs in 415, can we see the god swept up in the war-fever that was engulfing Athens at this time?*

Does this scenario then make Officers *an antiwar play as some have proposed? There is a difference between exploiting the humour of the incongruous recruit and criticising the military itself. The treatment of Lamachus in Aristophanes is indicative. Comic sensibility would demand that in some fashion Dionysus redeem himself and turn the tables on the military system. An* oinochoe *in the*

*British Museum, very much like the one in T 2 (V 11e),
shows a comic figure rowing a giant fish. Is this Dionysus
returning in triumph at the end of the comedy?*

*The comedy is usually set early in Eupolis' career on the
grounds that Phormion disappears from the narrative of
Thucydides in 428 (3.7.1), but Phormion is mentioned as
late as 411 (Lysistrata 804), and, even if he had died in the
early 420s, Eupolis could have raised him from the dead as*

Testimonium

i Σ *Peace* 348e

καὶ Διόνυσος ἐν Ταξιάρχοις παρ' Εὐπόλιδι μανθάνων
παρὰ τῷ Φορμίωνι τοὺς τῶν στρατηγῶν καὶ πολέμων
νόμους.

Fragments

268 P. Oxy. 2740

‒ ‒ ‒

Fr. 1
   ].. [
    πτω[
    χρω.[
    δελεγ[
5   ]δεινεστ[
    περις[
  ]τουτου Σοφοκλέο[υς προ-

*part of the humour—in which case he would be literally
"the sergeant major from Hell." The vase (T 2) showing
Phormion and Dionysus was found with material associ-
ated with the ostracism of 416, the one* kōmōidoumenos
*(Opuntius—F 284) was made fun of in 414 (Birds 1294),
and F 280 may be a parody of Euripides'* Electra *184–85
(c.420). I suggest 415, the play's theme being "Dionysus
goes to Sicily."*

Testimonia

i In *Officers* by Eupolis, Dionysus learning from Phor-
mion the ways of generals and wars, says . . . [F 274].

ii An *oinochoe*, found in material associated with the
ostracism of 416, shows two comic figures labelled
]ONYSOS and PHOR[. See V 11d.

Fragments

268 *This papyrus commentary is dated in the opinion of
the first editor "as early as the end of the first century" and
is assigned to Eupolis'* Officers *on the mention of Phor-
mion as a character in line 13.*

(1–21) . . . **of this from Sophokles abandoning him to**

```
      ].εἰς νιν εἰς φθορ[άν
      μενται τὰ δ' ἄλλα[
10      Σοφοκλέους ἐσ[τὶν ἐκ
        Τηρέως δοκῶ [
  ___οσαρκετον λόγω[ ἀν-
        τὶ τοῦ ἀμφότεροι[ οὐ-
        κ οἶσθ' Ἄρη μοι τοὔνο[μ-
15      ]α; Ἄρης ὁ Φορμίω[ν
  ___ἐπεκαλεῖτο κόκ[κην πρῶ-
        τοι ἀντὶ τοῦ πρὶν [ εἰπεῖν
  ___κόκκυ ἡδὺ στρ[
        σ]θαι πλ.ην ἐστι[
20  ___]αμισθον ἀντ[ὶ τοῦ
        προφ[
        _ _ _
        _ _
```

Fr. 2 col. i

```
                    ]μ.ν[
                    ].ο.[
perierunt lineae 4

                    ]..ατι.[
25          ]ος ἔστηκας ηδ[
            ]αι ξύνθημαν[
            ]ασον καὶ γνω[
            ]πλησίον ἀν[τὶ
    τοῦ     ].ωι πλησίον .[
30          ]ν το συνθημα[
            ]. νὴ τὸν Δί' ἀλ[-
```

212

ruin: the following . . . is from *Tereus* by Sophocles, as I be-
lieve . . . **satisfactory. A pair of words:** instead of both
⟨words⟩ . . . **Don't you know that my name is "War"?:**
Phormion was nicknamed "War." **Cuckoo first:** instead of
saying "cuckoo before." **It is pleasant to serve in the
army ⟨and earn a⟩ wage:** instead of ⟨receive⟩.

(22–43) **(A) you stand here . . . (B) Tell the password
and know . . . nearby:** instead of . . . nearby . . . that pass-

λ   ]καὶ μισῶ γε πρ[
              ]ν Φορμίωνα . . .
              ]τε πρώτην ἐλ-
35   λείπει τὸ]φυλακήν εἶτ᾽ οὐ
            ]μον δῆτ᾽ ἐγὼ πορ-
        [ ]ς ἀντὶ τοῦ χω-
       ρὶς]ης ἁπλῶς ὅπερ
      Ἀττικ]οὶ ἀτεχνῶς λέ-
40   γουσι]ς ἐγὼ κλαίειν
            ]ονι τούτου μνη-
      μονεύει] καὶ Τηλεκλεί-
          δης]ὡς λωπο-
col. ii   δύτου

- - - - -

45   γο.[
      πα..ρι[ἀν-
    τὶ τοῦ ἐμ[
    γὰρ οὐκ ἐπίσταμαι [παρὰ
    τὸ πεζῇι βαδίζω [νεῖν
50   γὰρ οὐκ ἐπίσταμα[ι οὐ
   παύσει ῥαίνων ἡμ[ᾶς, οὐκ
  πρώιρας; εἰώθασι λ[έγειν·
    ὁ ἐκ πρώιρας, μὴ ῥ[αῖνε οὐκ
   ἐκτενεῖς οὖν τὸν σ [κελί-
55 σκον ἀντὶ τοῦ τὸ σ[κέλος

Frr. 3–11 (= K.-A. F 267.56–171) are but scraps.

word . . . **Yes by Zeus, but . . . and I hate** . . . Phormion . . . **first:** he omits "watch." **Then not . . . indeed I** . . .: instead of "separately" . . . **simply:** by which the Attic Greeks mean "really." **I . . . to be sorry** . . . Teleclides mentions him [F 73] as a clothes thief.

(45–55) **for I don't know how to** . . .: for "I am going on foot, for I don't know how ‹to swim›." **You at the front, will you not stop splashing us?** They would usually say "the one at the front, do not splash us." **So will you stretch out your little leg:** instead of "leg."

269 Pollux 9.102

{ΦΟΡΜΙΩΝ.}   οὔκουν περιγράψεις ὅσον ἐναριστᾶν
   κύκλον;
{ΔΙΟΝΥΣΟΣ.}   τί δ᾽ ἔστιν; εἰς ὤμιλλαν
   ἀριστήσομεν;
ἢ κόψομεν τὴν μᾶζαν ὥσπερ ὄρτυγα;

270 Pollux 9.58

<   > ὅτ᾽ ἦν μέντοι νεώτερος, κρόκης
πέντε στατῆρας εἶχε, ναὶ μὰ τὸν Δία.
νῦν δὲ ῥύπου γε δύο τάλαντα ῥᾳδίως.

271 Athenaeus 52b

δίδου μασᾶσθαι Ναξίας ἀμυγδάλας,
οἶνόν τε πίνειν Ναξίων ἀπ᾽ ἀμπέλων.

272 Pollux 10.63

ὅστις πύελον ἥκεις ἔχων καὶ χαλκίον,
ὥσπερ λεχὼ στρατιῶτις ἐξ Ἰωνίας.

273 Photius (b, Sᶻ) α 1065

οὐ θᾶττον αὐτὴν δεῦρό μοι τῶν τοξοτῶν
ἄγων ἀποκηρύξει τις, ὅ τι ἂν ἀλφάνῃ;

269 (PHORMION) Aren't you going to mark out a site to eat?

(DIONYSOS) What? Are we going to have lunch inside the ring, or tap our bread like a quail?[1]

> 1 "Inside the ring" is a reference to a game called *omilla* (see F 314); quail-tapping (cf. *Birds* 1297) also involved a ring.

270 When it was new, it had five staters' worth of saffron dye—yes, by Zeus, it did—but now two talents' worth of dirt, easily.

271 Give me Naxian almonds to munch and wine to drink from Naxian vines.

272 You've come here with a bathtub and a brass pot, like a she-soldier from Ionia that's just given birth.

273 Won't one of the archers quickly take her away and auction her off for whatever she may fetch?

274 Σ Aristophanes *Peace* 348e, Suda φ 604

ὡς οὐκέτ᾽ ἂν φάγοιμι † στιβάδος ἐξ ὅτου ᾽φυγον.

φύγοιμι Σ Ar., φάγοιμι Suda; φύγον Suda, φάγον Σ Ar.

275 Athenaeus 170d

< > ἐπιφαγεῖν μηδὲν ἄλλ᾽ ἢ κρόμμυον
λέποντα καὶ τρεῖς ἁλμάδας < >

276 Photius p. 658.19

οὐκ ἦν φυλάττῃ γ᾽ ὧδ᾽ ἔχων τὴν ἀσπίδα.

277 Pollux 10.136

ἐγὼ δέ γε στίξω σε βελόναισιν τρισίν.

278 Photius (z) ε 867

{A.} τίς ἐνεβρόντησέ μοι;
{B.} ὦ μοχθηρέ, τίς ἐπάταξέ σε;

279 Photius p. 337.16

ὄνος ἀκροᾷ σάλπιγγος

280 Pollux 7.168

ἀντὶ ποικίλου
πιναρὸν ἔχοντ᾽ ἀλουτίᾳ
κάρα τε καὶ τρίβωνα

274 Ever since I ran away, I would never more eat sleeping-mats.[1]

[1] The text and meaning are in considerable dispute. Other suggestions are:

(1) Ever since I began to eat, I would avoid a sleeping-mat as a bed (Meineke).

(2) Ever since I ate sleeping-mats, would I eat . . . (Bergk).

(3) Ever since I began to eat, I would avoid the sleeping-mats at Phormion's (Cobet, Kaibel).

(4) I would avoid troubles, ever since I took sleeping-mats [i.e., joined the army] (Blaydes).

275 And to eat as a side dish nothing but a peeled onion and three salted olives.

276 No, not if you protect yourself by holding your shield in this way.

277 And I will brand you with three needles.

278 (DIONYSUS ?) Who thunderstruck me?
(B) You fool, who beat you?

279 The ass hears the trumpet.

280 Wearing a cloak instead of a multicoloured ⟨robe⟩ and my hair filthy from lack of washing.

281 Photius (z) *apud* Tsantsanoglou p. 121

ἐν ταῖσι γὰρ μάχαισιν ἀποθνῄσκουσι κόκκυ πρῶτοι

282 Σ Aristophanes *Birds* 1294

ὡς τοιούτου τὴν ὄψιν ὄντος μνημονεύει αὐτοῦ καὶ μέγα
ῥύγχος ἔχοντος καὶ ὁ τὰς Ἀταλάντας γράψας καὶ
Εὔπολις ἐν Ταξιάρχοις.

ΥΒΡΙΣΤΟΔΙΚΑΙ

281 For in battles those in front die, just like that.

282 The author of the *Atalantai* [Callias F 4] and Eupolis in *Officers* record that he [Opuntius] had such facial features [one eye] and a large hooked nose.

Brief fragments: (F 283) "the craft of ironworking," (F 284) "hooking the leg," (F 285) "baggage carrier."

VIGILANTES (?)

This comedy is known only from one curious reference (T 1) by Ptolemy Chennus to the works found on the death-beds of various ancient figures. The title in Greek is hybristodikai *(violence + justice) and explained (T 2) as "those who were unwilling to bring cases to court." A comedy about people wanting to avoid the law courts would be very much in the spirit of* Wasps *or* Birds *110 ("anti-jurors"), but the term should mean something like "those who get justice with violence," hence my tentative title "vigilantes." The cases of Eupolis'* New-Moons, *Cratinus'* Tempest-Tossed, *and Platon's* Security *show that we have lost almost all knowledge of certain Old comedies, and we may thus not want to reject the existence of* Vigilantes *out of hand. Was it perhaps an alternative title for another comedy, say,* Prospaltians?

Recent bibliography: P. J. Bicknell, LCM *13 (1988) 114–15.*

Testimonia

i Ptolemy Chennus (*ap.* Photius *Library* 19, p. 151a10)

ὅτι τελευτήσαντος Δημητρίου τοῦ Σκηψίου τὸ βιβλίον
Τέλλιδος πρὸς τῇ κεφαλῇ αὐτοῦ εὑρέθη· τὰς δὲ Κο-
λυμβώσας Ἀλκμάνους πρὸς τῇ κεφαλῇ Τυννίχου τοῦ
Χαλκιδέως εὑρεθῆναί φασι, τοὺς δ' Ὑβριστοδίκας
Εὐπόλιδος πρὸς εὑρεθῆναί φασι πρὸς τῇ Ἐφιάλτου,
τοὺς δὲ Εὐνείδας Κρατίνου πρὸς τῇ Ἀλεξάνδρου τοῦ
βασιλέως Μακεδόνων, τὰ δ' Ἔργα καὶ τὰς Ἡμέρας
Ἡσιόδου πρὸς τῇ τοῦ Σελεύκου τοῦ Νικάτορος κε-
φαλῇ.

ii Pollux 8.126

ὑβριστοδίκαι δὲ ἐκαλοῦντο, εἴ τι χρὴ Κρατέρῳ πι-
στεύειν τῷ τὰ ψηφίσματα συναγαγόντι, οἱ μὴ βου-
λόμενοι τὰς δίκας εἰσαγαγεῖν.

ΦΙΛΟΙ

EUPOLIS

Testimonia

i When Demetrius of Scepsis died, the book by Tellis was found by his head, and they say that the *Diving-Women* of Alcman was found by the head of Tynnichus of Chalchis, the *Vigilantes* of Eupolis by the ⟨head⟩ of Ephialtes, and *Sons of Euneus* by Cratinus by the ⟨head⟩ of Alexander, and Hesiod's *Works and Days* by the head of Seleucus son of Nicator.

ii If one may trust Craterus at all, who collected decrees, those who were unwilling to bring cases to court were called *hybristodikai*.

FRIENDS

Only thirteen fragments survive, giving little hint of what the play was about. F 293 indicates that one of the characters, perhaps one of Old Comedy's favourite old men, may have tried to join the cavalry for its financial benefits, only to find himself hopelessly out of place, like Strepsiades in the "think-shop" or Philocleon at an upper-class symposium.

The title should refer to the chorus, but what sort of "friends" would they be? Suitors have been suggested for an attractive young kalos, *such as Autolycus or Demus, but "friend" does not need to bear an erotic sense. Another suggestion is that these "friends" were spongers, but in this context the word "friend" means the victim rather than the sponger. The ineffectual door at F 293 could support either interpretation. But the natural sense of the word is like "neighbour" or "demesman," the close people in one's life,*

223

Fragments

286 Σ Aristophanes *Acharnians* 127a

νὴ τὸν Ποσειδῶ, † οὐδέποτ' ἴσχει † ἡ θύρα.

287 Ammonius *On the Differences among Related Words* 458

οὐ δεινὰ ταῦτα † δὲ Ἀργείας φέρειν
σχιστὰς ἐνεργεῖν.

288 Photius (z) ε 972

οὐδεὶς γὰρ οἶδεν ἐν Κέῳ τίς ἡμέρα.

289 Photius p. 329.2

ῥέγκειν δὲ τοὺς ὅλμους <∪> οἴμοι τῶν κακῶν.

290 Apollonius Dyscolus *Pronouns*, GrGr II 1.1

εὐφρανῶ δὲ νώ.

291 Pollux 7.133

τί μισθοῖ; ποῖ; πόση τις ἡ φορά;

*but that does not take us far with the identity or role of
these friends.*

    *A date is almost impossible to ascertain. The 420s are
mostly full, and perhaps the early 410s, or even the latest
part of Eupolis' career, 414–411.*

Fragments

286 By Poseidon, the door never keeps out.

287 Isn't this awful, to wear Argive sandals on the job?

288 No one on Chios knows what day ⟨it is⟩.

289 And the mouthpieces [of an *aulos*] squeak—oh no!

290 I will cheer you both up.

291 What does he have to hire? To where? What is the
ferry charge?

292 Pollux 10.85

τὴν δ᾽ αὐτὸς ἐκκανάξει

293 Harpocration p. 170.7

οὐκ ἐσωφρόνησας, ὦ πρεσβῦτα, τὴν κατάστασιν
τήνδε λαμβάνων ἄφνω πρὶν καὶ μαθεῖν τὴν
ἱππικήν.

294 Σ Plato *Menexenus* 235e

αὑτὴν καλεῖ . . . Εὔπολις Φίλοις.

295 Σ (Arethas) Plato *Apology* 23e

Εὔπολις δ᾽ ἐν Φίλοις καὶ ἐπὶ τῇ γυναικὶ Ῥοδίᾳ κωμῳ-
δεῖ αὐτόν.

296 Athenaeus 266f

Χῖος δεσπότην ὠνήσατο.

ΧΡΥΣΟΥΝ ΓΕΝΟΣ

*The critics have made a number of assumptions about
this lost comedy, principally over its date (usually D-424)
and its relationship to Aristophanes' Knights. But the first
thing that the title "Golden Race" brings to mind is the use
of that term in Hesiod's Works and Days (109ff.) for the
first and best age of humanity, a paradise lost. We might*

292 And the other he will gulp down himself.

293 You weren't very smart, old man, to accept this cavalry subsidy so quickly before even learning how to ride.

294 Eupolis in *Friends* calls her [Aspasia] . . . [1]

[1] It is not clear from the text of the scholion what Eupolis called Aspasia in *Friends*; in *Prospaltians* (F 267) he calls her "Helen."

295 Eupolis in *Friends* makes fun of him [Lycon] for his wife Rhodia also.

296 A Chian has bought a master.

Brief fragment: (F 297) "to gargle."

GOLDEN RACE

want to consider whether this was an instance of Old Comedy's favourite theme of the utopian ideal, either in the past, in the future, or somewhere "out there." F 315 might support such a reading, but this is a parody of Homer, and Eupolis is not known to have employed the utopian theme elsewhere in his comedy.

THE POETS OF OLD COMEDY

The theme of the "Golden Race" is usually taken ironically and politically to apply to Athens in the 420s, which in the comedian's view was anything but a golden age, especially given the influence of Cleon (F 316). This assumes a somewhat jaundiced view of democracy "where it is possible for the inferior and ugly in appearance" to rule, be the equal of the "good and the noble." This need not be Eupolis' own view, but only that of his chorus, but if F 316 is from a parabasis, then Eupolis could be seen as voicing some of the same reservations about Athenian society as Aristophanes.

The play is usually dated to D-424, partly on the reference to Cleon "overseeing the cities," which, it is argued, means his ascendancy after Pylos in 425/4, and partly on the assumption that Eupolis followed Aristophanes in the assault on Cleon. But F 308 "sand-hundreds" seems to be

Fragments

298 Porphyry *ap.* Σ Homer *Iliad* 10.252

{A.} δωδέκατος ὁ τυφλός, τρίτος ὁ τὴν κάλην ἔχων,
ὁ στιγματίας τέταρτός ἐστιν ἐπὶ δέκα,
πέμπτος δ᾽ ὁ πυρρός, ἔκτος ὁ διεστραμμένος·
{B.} χοὗτοι μέν εἰσ᾽ ἑκκαίδεκ᾽ εἰς Ἀρχέστρατον.
5 {A.} ἐς τὸν δὲ φαλακρὸν ἑπτακαίδεκ᾽. {B.} ἴσχε δή.
{A.} ὄγδοος ὁ τὸν τριβών᾽ ἔχων.

3 πύργος cod., πυρρός Runkel.

228

topped by Aristophanes' "sand-hundred-heaps" at Achar-
nians *3 (L-425), and this would push Eupolis' play back to
426 at least. Sidwell and others have also made a good case
for Aristophanes adapting material from Eupolis in the
creation of* Knights *(see Eupolis F 89 for his claim of "col-
laboration") and for* Golden Race *as that comedy by Eu-
polis. Cleon may in fact have been a character in* Golden
Race, *the scene mentioned by Dicaeopolis at* Acharnians *5–
8? I suggest L-426 for the comedy, on which occasion
Eupolis won his first victory at the Lenaea. Cleon's pres-
ence at Thucydides 3.36–40 as the champion of an imperi-
alistic policy toward the cities in 427 shows that Cleon
could be seen as "overseeing the cities" before his success at
Pylos.*

Recent bibliography: Ruffell, in Rivals *490–92.*

Fragments

298 (A) Twelfth is the blind man, thirteenth the man with
the hump, the branded man makes fourteen, fifteenth the
redhead, next the man with the squint.

(B) Ah, that makes sixteen up to Archestratus.

(A) Seventeen to the bald man.   (B) Hold on there.

(A) The man with the tunic is eighteen.[1]

[1] I have given v. 4 to speaker B. The numbering has suggested
to some that this was an individuated chorus of "ugly Athenians,"
appropriate for an ironic "Golden Age." Some have seen "the bald
man" as Aristophanes.

299 Σ Aristophanes Wasps 925

λοιπὸς γὰρ οὐδείς· ⟨ἡ⟩ τροφαλὶς ἐκεινηὶ
ἐφ᾽ ὕδωρ βαδίζει σκῖρον ἠμφιεσμένη.

300 Pollux 10.140

ἔπειθ᾽ ὁ κουρεὺς τὰς μαχαιρίδας λαβὼν
ὑπὸ τῆς ὑπήνης κατακερεῖ τὴν εἰσφοράν.

301 Athenaeus 657a

οὐκ ἀλλ᾽ ἔθυον δέλφακ᾽ ἔνδον θῆστίᾳ
καὶ μάλα καλήν.

ωδον MS, ᾠδον K.-A., νωδόν Meineke; ἔνδον Kock, ἀπα-
λήν Blaydes.

302 Stephanus of Byzantium p. 433.5

{Α.} ὁρῶ. {Β.} θεῶ νῦν τήνδε Μαριανδυνίαν.

303 Σ Aristophanes *Thesmophoriazusae* 162

ὦλκαῖε Σικελιῶτα Πελοποννήσιε

304 Zenobius 6.2

ἀτεχνῶς μὲν οὖν τὸ λεγόμενον σκύτη βλέπει.

305 Pollux 10.63

ἀλλ᾽ ὦ φίλε Ζεῦ κατάχυτλον τὴν ῥῖν᾽ ἔχεις.

299 There's not one left. That cheese over there is heading for water, wearing its rind.

300 Then the barber will take his blades and from his lip will shear away . . . the income tax.[1]

¹ The *eisphora* was a tax on the wealthy introduced in the early 420s and connected with Cleon. We expect "hair" or "beard" and get "income tax." But who was being shaved: a wealthy victim, or perhaps Cleon himself?

301 No, but I was [they were?] sacrificing a pig inside (?) to Hestia and a very fine . . .

302 (A) I see.   (B) Now look over here at Mariandynia.[1]

¹ Mariandynia was a region on the coast of the Black Sea near Paphlagonia. Do we have a viewing scene like that at *Knights* 168–75 or a map scene as at *Clouds* 201–16?

303 Alcaeus of Sicily and from the Peloponnese.

304 As they say, he looks totally whipped.

305 O dear Zeus, you have a shower for a nose.

306 Photius (z) α 2602

{A.} τί γάρ ἐστ᾽ ἐκεῖνος; {B.} ἀποπάτημ᾽ ἀλώπεκος.

307 Σ Hephaestion *Handbook* 2.1

καὶ σκεῦος οὐδὲν εὗρον ἐν τᾠκήματι.

308 Σ Aristophanes *Acharnians* 3a

ἀριθμεῖν θεατὰς ψαμμακοσίους

309 Σ Aristophanes *Birds* 42

τίς ὁ φῶνος, ὦ ῥαψῳδέ;

310 Choreboscus *On the Canons of Theodosius, GrGr*
IV 2

εἰ μή τις αὐτὴν κατακλιεῖ

311 Σ Aristophanes *Wasps* 1278a

ὦ καλαβρὲ κιθαραοιδότατε

312 Photius p. 596.20

τοῦ Διὸς τὸ σάνδαλον

313 P. Oxy. 1803

καὶ .αρα.. ης..μ᾽ ἦλθες
ἐξυρημένος σαβύττους

306 (A) So what is he?   (B) Fox droppings.

307 I found no furniture in the house.

308 To count spectators by the sand-hundreds.

309 What's that noise, rhapsode?

310 Unless someone shuts it.

311 O foreign one, most skilled on the lyre.

312 The sandal of Zeus.

313 And . . . you [masc.] came to me with a nice haircut.

314 Σ (Arethas) Plato *Lysis* 206e

ἡ δὲ ὤμιλλα ἐστιν ὅταν περιγράψαντες κύκλον ἐπιρ-
ρίπτωσιν ἀστραγάλους ἤ τι ἄλλο, ὡς τῇ μὲν ἐντὸς
βολῇ νικώντων τῇ δὲ ἐκτὸς ἡττωμένων. Εὔπολις Χρυ-
σῷ Γένει μεταφέρων ἐπὶ τὴν ἐν κύκλῳ κατάκλισιν
τοὔνομα οὕτω φησίν·
† ἔπειτ᾿ εἴσειμι ἐνθάδε μείνας
εἰς ὤμιλλαν κἂν μὴ μετίῃ.

   2 μετίῃ codd., μεθίῃ Erbse.

315 Zenobius 1.15

αὐτόματοι δ᾿ ἀγαθοὶ δειλῶν ἐπὶ δαῖτας ἴασιν.

316 Priscian *On the Metres of Terence* 26

ὦ καλλίστη πόλι πασῶν ὅσας Κλέων ἐφορᾷ,
ὡς εὐδαίμων πρότερόν τ᾿ ἦσθα νῦν δὲ μᾶλλον ἔσῃ

ἔδει πρῶτον μὲν ὑπάρχειν πάντων ἰσηγορίαν

πῶς οὖν οὐκ ἄν τις ὁμιλῶν χαίροι τοιᾷδε πόλει
ἵν᾿ ἔξεστιν πάνυ λεπτῷ κακῷ τε τὴν ἰδέαν

317 Photius (z) α 2824

ἄρκτους, ἐλάφους, ἐλέφαντας, ὕστριχας, χελώνας

314 *Omilla*: when they draw a circle and shoot knuckle bones or some other object, those with a cast inside are the winners, and those outside the losers. In *Golden Race* Eupolis uses it in a metaphorical sense when he says:

Then I shall go in, and staying inside the *omilla*, even if he doesn't throw.[1]

[1] The text is uncertain and the application to *omilla* not immediately obvious. I take μείνας in the sense of "stay," "stick" of a successful cast, and read μεθίῃ (throw) for μετίῃ (follow).

315 The brave come uninvited to the banquets of the cowardly.

316 O fairest city of all that Cleon oversees, how fortunate you were before and now will be even more so.

First of all there had to be equal speech for all.

How would one not be happy to be part of such a city where it is possible for the inferior and ugly in appearance . . .

317 Bears, deer, elephants, boars, tortoises.

318 Σ Aristophanes *Frogs* 1036

Παντακλέης σκαιός

319 The Antiatticist p. 96.18

Λάμπων οὐξηγητής

320 Athenaeus 408e

κατὰ χειρὸς ὕδωρ

ΑΔΗΛΩΝ ΔΡΑΜΑΤΩΝ

326 Photius β 88

{Α.} ἄγε δή, πότερα βούλεσθε τὴν ⟨νῦν⟩ διάθεσιν
ᾠδῆς ἀκούειν ἢ τὸν ἀρχαῖον τρόπον;
{Β.} ἀμφότερ᾽ ἐρεῖς, ἐγὼ δ᾽ ἀκούσας τοῖν τρόποιν
ὃν ἂν δοκῇ μοι βαστάσας αἱρήσομαι.

327 Pollux 9.47

οὗ τὰ βιβλί᾽ ὤνια

περιῆλθον εἰς τὰ σκόροδα καὶ τὰ κρόμμυα
καὶ τὸν λιβανωτόν, κεὐθὺ τῶν ἀρωμάτων,
καὶ περὶ τὰ γέλγη.

328 Zonaras p. 605

τίς οὐξεγείρας μ᾽ ἐστίν; οἰμώξει μακρά,
ὁτιή μ᾽ ἀνέστησ᾽ ὠμόυπνον.

318 Pantacles <is> stupid.

319 Lampon the interpreter of oracles.

320 Water for hand washing.

Brief fragments: (F 321) "bran heap," (F 322) "settler," (F 323) "pea," (F 324) "corn bin," (F 325) "the Odeion."

UNASSIGNED FRAGMENTS

326 (A) Well now, do you people want to hear the modern style of song or the old sort?
   (B) Do both. I will listen to the two styles and upon exmination choose the one that I prefer.
                              [*Nanny-Goats, Golden Race, Demes*?]

327 Where books are for sale.

   I went around to the garlic stalls, to the onion stalls and the incense market, straight through the spice market, and then around the odds and ends.   [*Maricas*?]

328 Who is it who woke me up? He'll be very sorry, because he roused me from sleep.   [*Demes*?]

329 Pollux 3.115

ἤδη χορηγὸν πώποτε
ῥυπαρώτερον τοῦδ᾽ εἶδες;

330 Eustathius *On the Odyssey* p. 1441.11

πόλιν ‹   › θεοφιλεστάτην
οἰκοῦσιν ἀφθονεστάτην τε χρήμασιν.

331 Moeris p. 213.31

πρῶτος γὰρ ἡμᾶς, ὦ Κλέων,
χαίρειν προσεῖπας πολλὰ λυπῶν τὴν πόλιν.

332 Photius (b, z) α 1977

συνέτυχεν ἐξιόντι μοι
ἄνθρωπος ἀποφρὰς καὶ βλέπων ἀπιστίαν.

333 [Herodian] *On Figures of Speech*, *Rh.Gr.* VIII p.
     583.8

καὶ λέγουσί γε
τὰ μειράκια προϊστάμενα τοῖς ἀνδράσι.

334 Photius p. 178.17

οὐ πάνυ ταχὺ
ῥίψας ἐμοὶ τοῦτ᾽ ἀναβαλεῖς τὸ Κρητικόν;

329 Have you ever seen a more miserly *chorēgus* than him?

330 They live in a city very dear to the gods and most abundant in possessions. [*Cities*?]

331 Cleon, you were the first to say to us "Be well," while doing the city great harm. [*Golden Race*, *Demes*?]

332 As I was going out a miserable fellow met me, with falsehood all over his face.

333 And they say that youngsters stand up before the men. [*Demes*?]

334 Please, won't you quickly cast this off and put on the Cretan robe?

335 [Herodian] *Philetaerus* 231

κἂν ποίᾳ πόλει
τοσοῦτος ⟨ὢν⟩ τὸ μέγεθος ἰχθὺς τρώγεται;

336 *Etymologicum Genuinum* β 89

ὅσον
γένοιτ' ἂν αὐτῇ βελτίω τὰ πράγματα.

337 Cocondrius *On Styles*, *Rh.Gr.* VIII, p. 789.18

κατεικάζουσιν ἡμᾶς † σχάδι
βολβῷ.

338 Athenaeus 56e

ῥαφανίδες ἄπλυτοι, σηπίαι,
δρυπεπεῖς τ' ἐλᾶαι.

339 Eustathius *On the Odyssey* p. 1535.18

σὺ δὲ τὰ καλῴδια
ταῦθ' ἀρκυώρει.

340 Σ Aeschines 2.167

οὗτος ἐν τοῖς φρουρίοις κοιτάζεται

καὶ τοὺς περιπόλους ἀπιέναι 's τὰ φρούρια.

335 And in what sort of city is such a large fish eaten?

336 How much better things might be for her (it?).

337 They liken us to a fig and an onion.[1]

[1] The text is uncertain. For σχάδι Walz᾽ ἰσχάδι (fig) is a reasonable reading, but Kaibel's ἰσχαλέῳ (dried ‹onion›), based on Homer *Odyssey* 19.232 is tempting.

338 Unwashed radishes, squid, and ripe olives.

[*Cities*?]

339 You [sing.], keep a close watch on these strings.

340 This man is sleeping in the watch-posts.

‹It is necessary for› the scouts to depart to the watch-posts.

341 Eustathius *On the Odyssey* p. 1680.24

μὴ τρηχὺς ἴσθι.

ὦ δαιμόνι᾽ ἀνδρῶν, μὴ φθονερὸν ἴσθ᾽ ἀνδρίον.

342 Σ Homer *Iliad* 2.333

οἷόν γέ πού 'στι γλῶσσα κἀνθρώπου λόγος.

343 Eustathius *On the Odyssey* p. 1517.8

ἀλλ᾽ ὥσπερ ἵππῳ μοὐπιβαλεῖς τρυσίππιον;

344 Σ Homer *Odyssey* 7.104

τῇ χειρὶ νῶσαι μαλθακωτάτην κρόκην

345 Photius (z) α 2949

ὥσπερ ἀνέμου 'ξαίφνης ἀσελγοῦς γενομένου

346 *Epimerismi Homerici* π 165

καὶ μὴ πονηρούς, ὦ πονήρα, προξένει.

347 Bachmann's *Lexicon* 164.4

ἐγὼ δ᾽ ἄδειπνος ἑσπέρας ἠυλιζόμην.

348 [Herodian] *Philetaerus* 52

οὐ γὰρ κατάξει τῆς κεφαλῆς τὰ ῥήματα.

341 Don't be harsh.

Best of men, don't be a spiteful fellow.   [*Spongers*?]

342 So what a thing is a tongue, and also human speech.
                                                    [*Demes*?]

343 But will you put a brand on me as if I were a retired
horse?   [*Officers*?]

344 Women spinning the softest thread with their hands.

345 Just as if a violent wind had suddenly arisen.

346 (DEMOS) Do not recommend such wretched lov-
ers, you wretched woman.   [*Friends*?]

347 I spent last night without having had dinner.
                                                    [*Officers*?]

348 Words will not break my head.

349 [Herodian] *Philetaerus* 137

ἄγαμαι κεραμέως αἴθωνος ἐστεφανωμένου.

350 [Herodian] *Philetaerus* 229

ἱμάντας ἥξω δεῦρο πυκτικοὺς ἔχων.

351 Σ Dionysius Thrax 20

μῶν μὴ παρ' αὐτῇ Νικίας ἀναπαύεται;

352 Σ Homer *Iliad* 7.86

ῥιψάσπιδόν τε χεῖρα τὴν Κλεωνύμου

353 Pollux 2.90

† ἀνωροθεῖα ἡ † παρὰ τὰ χείλη τῆς νεώς.

354 Pollux 2.159

ὅταν δὲ δὴ πίνωσι τὴν ἐπιδέξια

355 Pollux 6.65

οἴνου παρόντος ὄξος ἠράσθη πιεῖν.

356 Photius p. 369.11

ἐγὼ δὲ χαίρω † πρὸς τοῖς σοῖς παιδικοῖς.

349 Hooray for the fiery potter wearing a garland.

[*Maricas*?]

350 I shall come here with boxing straps.

[*Prospaltians*?]

351 Nicias isn't staying with her, is he?   [*Maricas*?]

352 The shield-throwing hand of Cleonymus.

353 Raise your oar up (?) to the lips of the ship.

[*Officers*?]

354 Whenever they drink to the right.

355 Even when there was wine, he loved to drink vinegar.

356 I too am happy, along with your boyfriends.

357 *Etymologicum Genuinum* AB

γυνὴ μέλαιναν δέρριν ἠμφιεσμένη.

358 *Etymologicum Genuinum* AB

ἐκ τῶν ἀγρῶν ἥκουσιν ἐβλαστηκότες.

359 Photius (b, Sᶻ) α 1984

οὐκ ἐς κόρακας, ἀνθρωπάριον, ἀποφθερῇ;

360 Eustathius *On the Odyssey* p. 1817.46

οὐ γὰρ λέλειπται τῶν ἐμῶν οὐδ᾽ ἔγκαφος.

361 *Etymologicum Genuinum* AB

ὡς οἴχεται μὲν τυρὸς ἐξεγλυμμένος.

362 *Etymologicum Genuinum* AB

εἰ μὴ κόρη δεύσειε τὸ σταῖς ἤθεος.

363 *Etymologicum Genuinum* AB

βάπτειν τὰ κάλλη τὰ περίσεμνα τῇ θεῷ.

βάπτειν codd., Βάπταις Hemsterhuis

364 *Etymologicum Genuinum* AB

αὐτοῦ δ᾽ ὄπισθεν κατέλαβεν τὸν κόντιλον.

246

357 A woman wearing a black leather coat. [*Friends*?]

358 They have come from the fields in full bloom.
[*Golden Race*?]

359 Won't you go to hell, you nasty little man?

360 There isn't even a morsel left of my things.
[*Spongers*?]

361 My cheese is gone, all hollowed out.
[*Golden Race*?]

362 Unless an unmarried girl should moisten the dough.

363 To dye the purple robes sacred to the goddess.[1]
[*Dyers*?]

1 Or "in *Dyers*: 'the purple robes sacred to the goddess.'"

364 He seized the pole behind him.

365 Athenaeus 68a

ὄψῳ πονηρῷ πολυτελῶς ἠρτυμένῳ.

366 Athenaeus 623e

καὶ μουσικὴ πρᾶγμ᾽ ἐστὶ βαθύ τι † καὶ καμπύλον.

367 Zonaras p. 548

ὃς τὸν νεανίσκον συνὼν διέφθορεν.

368 Zonaras p. 601

τὸ σῶμ᾽ ἔχουσι λεῖον ὥσπερ ἐγχέλεις.

369 Σ Theocritus 1.95–98c

λυγίζεται καὶ συστρέφει τὸν αὐχένα.

370 Σ Dionysius Thrax, *GrGr* I 3 p. 97.2

μάττει γὰρ ἤδη καὶ τὸ πῦρ ἐκκάεται.

371 Photius (b, S^z) α 2019

ἀνόητά γ᾽ εἰ τοῦτ᾽ ἦλθες ἐπιτάξων ἐμοί.

372 Σ Aristophanes *Frogs* 1400

ἀποφθαρεὶς δὲ δύο κύβω καὶ τέτταρα

365 Bad food lavishly seasoned.

366 The arts are a deep and intricate thing.

367 Who has corrupted the young man just by being with him.   [*Dyers, Demes, Spongers, Nanny-Goats*?]

368 They have smooth bodies just like eels.

369 He writhes and bends his neck.

370 He (she?) is already kneading bread and the fire is blazing up.   [*Maricas, Demes*?]

371 That's crazy if you've come to give me this order.

372 Done in by two ones and a four.   [*Helots*?]

373 Σ Aristophanes *Peace* 812a

παρὰ τῆδε < - > σὺ τῇ σοβάδι κατηγάγου;

374 Plutarch *On Distinguishing a Friend from a Sponger* 54b

τῶν περὶ τάγηνον καὶ μετ᾽ ἄριστον φίλων

375 *Etymologicum Gudianum* p. 290.18

ὅσος <δ᾽> ὁ βρυγμὸς καὶ κοπετὸς ἐν τῇ στέγῃ.

376 *Etymologicum Genuinum* AB

ἄνδρες, δοκῶ μοι νῦν ὁρᾶν ἀφαδίαν

377 Photius (z) α 2664

καὶ γὰρ αἰσχρὸν ἀλογίου 'στ᾽ ὀφλεῖν.

378 [Herodian] *On Mistaken Words* 24

τῇ νῦν καταδέχεσθε τοὺς φακούς.

379 Zenobius 2.57

ὥσπερ ἀπὸ χοὸς πεσών

380 Pollux 6.56

ζωμὸς ἀλφίτων μέτα

373 Did you stay with this whore?   [*Maricas, Friends*?]

374 [of a parasite] One of the frying-pan and after lunch
friends.   [*Spongers*?]

375 What a noise of eager eating in the house.
                                    [*Maricas, Demes*?]

376 Men, I think I see an enemy ‹ship›.
                                    [*Draft-Dodgers, Officers*?]

377 For it is a disgrace to be convicted for not submitting
accounts.   [*Officers*?]

378 Here, take these lentil beans.

379 Like falling off a wine jar.

380 Broth with barley.

381 Photius p. 460.3

πρόσισχε τὸν νοῦν τῇδε

382 Athenaeus 502b

σὺν φθοῖσι προπεπωκώς

383 Stephanus of Byzantium p. 143.5

εἰς Ἄτραγα νύκτωρ

384 Stobaeus 4.1.9

καὶ μὴν ἐγὼ πολλῶν παρόντων οὐκ ἔχω τί λέξω.
οὕτω σφόδρ᾽ ἀλγῶ τὴν πολιτείαν ὁρῶν παρ᾽ ἡμῖν.
ἡμεῖς γὰρ οὐχ οὕτω τέως ᾠκοῦμεν οἱ γέροντες,
ἀλλ᾽ ἦσαν ἡμῖν τῇ πόλει πρῶτον μὲν οἱ στρατηγοὶ
5 ἐκ τῶν μεγίστων οἰκιῶν, πλούτῳ γένει τε πρῶτοι,
οἷς ὡσπερεὶ θεοῖσιν ηὐχόμεσθα· καὶ γὰρ ἦσαν.
ὥστ᾽ ἀσφαλῶς ἐπράττομεν· νυνὶ δ᾽ ὅπῃ τύχοιμεν,
στρατευόμεσθ᾽ αἱρούμενοι καθάρματα στρατηγούς.

2 ἡμῖν codd., ὑμῖν van Herwerden.   3 ὦ codd., οἱ
Brunck.   7 τύχοιμεν codd., τύχωμεν Kaibel; ὅποι 'ν
τύχωμεν, ὅταν τύχωμεν Kock.

381 Turn your [sing.] attention here.

382 Having drunk with saucers.   [*Cities*?]

383 By night to Atrax.[1]

1 A city in Thessaly.

384 Well now, with so many possibilities I don't know what to say. I am so upset when I look at our [your?] state of government. This is not how we old men used to live. Our city had generals from the greatest families, leaders in wealth and birth, to whom we prayed as if they were gods—and gods they were to us. And so we lived in security. But now we take the field in haphazard fashion, electing as our generals the scum of the earth.[1]

[*Demes*, *Cities*, *Maricas*?]

1 In the first line the text might also be translated, "with so many people present."

385 Athenaeus 17d

{ΑΛΚΙΒΙΑΔΗΣ.} μισῶ λακωνίζειν, ταγηνίζειν δὲ
κἂν πριαίμην.
{Β.} πολλὰς δ᾽ † οἶμαι νῦν βεβινῆσθαι.
{ΑΛΚ.} <   > ὃς δὲ πρῶτος ἐξεῦρον τὸ πρῴ
’πιπίνειν;
{Β.} πολλήν γε λακκοπρωκτίαν ἡμῖν ἐπίστασ᾽
εὑρών.
5 {ΑΛΚ.} εἶἑν. τίς εἶπεν "ἀμίδα παῖ" πρῶτος μεταξὺ
πίνων;
{Β.} Παλαμηδικόν γε τοῦτο τοὐξεύρημα καὶ σοφόν
σου.

386 Asclepius On Aristotle's *Metaphysics*, CAG Vi 2, p.
135.21

μισῶ δὲ καὶ † Σωκράτην,
τὸν πτωχὸν ἀδολέσχην,
ὃς τἆλλα μὲν πεφρόντικεν,
ὁπόθεν δὲ καταφαγεῖν ἔχοι
5   τούτου κατημέληκεν.

387 *Etymologicum Genuinum* A

                              εἴ τις ἀποτέτιλται
αὐτῶν ὁ πέμπτος ὥσπερ εἰς ζήτρειον ἐμπεσών ‹ ›

388 *Etymologicum Magnum* p. 18.10

ἀλλ᾽ ἀδολεσχεῖν αὐτὸν ἐκδίδαξον, ὦ σοφιστά.

EUPOLIS

385 ALCIBIADES I don't like life Spartan-style; I'd much rather buy something to grill.

(B) I expect that many women have been screwed (?).
(ALCIBIADES) . . . I who was the first to invent early morning drinking.

(B) Realise that you invented a lot of disgusting behaviour for us.

(ALCIBIADES) Okay, who was the first to say in the middle of drinking, "Slave, a basin"?

(B) Now that was a clever invention of yours, one worthy of Palamedes.[1]   [*Dyers, Spongers*?]

[1] See S. Beta, *AFLS* 21 (2000) 33–44.

386 I also hate Sokrates, the babbling beggar. He has thought out everything; but where he might get something to eat, that he has never considered.[1]   [*Spongers*?]

[1] The metre is iambic dimeter, used in songs in the parabasis (F 99.1–22), between episodes (*Acharnians* 836–59), and in the *parodos* (*Frogs* 417–39) for a sequence of personal insults.

387 If each fifth one of them has had his hair plucked out, just as when someone lands in a slave prison.

388 Sophist, teach him to talk nonsense.   [*Spongers*?]

THE POETS OF OLD COMEDY

389 *Lexicon Vindobonense* cod. Naep. II D 29

ἄνθρωπον εὐηθέστατον καὶ πρᾶον εἰς ἅπαντα

390 Choeroboscus *On the Canons of Theodosius, GrGr*
IV I p. 145.25

ταὐτὸν ποιεῖ τό τ᾿ Ἀττικὸν τῷ ζῆλα συγκεραννύς.

391 Orion *Anthology* 8.10

ἢ πολλά γ᾿ ἐν μακρῷ χρόνῳ γίγνεται μεταλλαγῇ
⟨τῶν⟩ πραγμάτων· μένει δὲ χρῆμ᾿ οὐδὲν ἐν ταὐτῷ
ῥυθμῷ.

392 Stobaeus 3.4.32

ἀλλ᾿ ἀκούετ᾿, ὦ θεαταί, τἀμὰ καὶ ξυνίετε
ῥήματ᾿, εὐθὺ γὰρ πρὸς ὑμᾶς πρῶτον ἀπολογήσομαι.
ὅ τι μαθόντες τοὺς ξένους μὲν λέγετε ποιητὰς
    σοφούς,
ἢν δέ τις τῶν ἐνθάδ᾿ αὐτοῦ μηδὲ ἐν χεῖρον φρονῶν
5 ἐπιτιθῆται τῇ ποιήσει, πάνυ δοκεῖ κακῶς φρονεῖν,
μαίνεταί τε καὶ παραρρεῖ τῶν φρενῶν τῷ σῷ λόγῳ.
ἀλλ᾿ ἐμοὶ πείθεσθε, πάντως μεταβαλόντες τοὺς
    τρόπους
μὴ φθονεῖθ᾿ ὅταν τις ἡμῶν μουσικῇ χαίρῃ νέων.

393 Phrynichus *Sophistic Preparation* p. 75.16

ὡραζομένη καὶ θρυπτομένη

389 A very nice person and gentle in all things.

390 He does the same thing mixing Attic ‹honey?› with Thracian piss.[1]

   [1] "Piss" translates *zēla*, defined by Choeroboscus (GrGr IV 1 p. 145.25) as "how wine is called among the Thracians." Platnauer (CR 35 [1921] 150) suggests that the beverage is beer. In either case *zēla* is meant to be derogatory.

391 Indeed, many things come to be in the long course of time through a change of circumstances; nothing stays on the same beat.

392 Now listen, spectators, and understand my words, for right now I will make my first defence to you.
   How come you consider foreign poets good, but if someone from around here applies himself to poetry, with not a bad idea, he really seems to have got it all wrong, he's crazy and completely off his head, in your opinion? But listen to me, change your ways completely, and don't get upset when one of us youngsters enjoys *mousikē*.[1]

[*Autolycus, Nanny-Goats*?]

   [1] At the end the mention of "youngsters" (νέων) seems otiose and probably hides a participle to complete "enjoys."

393 Preening herself and playing coy.

394 Photius p. 200.7

ἐξεπλάγη γὰρ ἰδὼν στίλβοντα τὰ λάβδα.

395 Σ Aristophanes *Clouds* 96

δεξάμενος δὲ Σωκράτης τὴν ἐπιδείξι᾽ ⟨ᾄδων⟩
Στησιχόρου πρὸς τὴν λύραν, οἰνοχόην ἔκλεψεν.

396 Hephaestion *On Poetry* 8.2

εἰωθὸς τὸ κομμάτιον τοῦτο

397 Σ Euripides *Medea* 520

ἡ διστχία τοῦ χοροῦ ἐστι. κατὰ δὲ τοὺς χρόνους ἤδη
τὰ τῶν χορῶν ἠμαύρωτο. τὰ μὲν γὰρ ἀρχαῖα διὰ τῶν
χορῶν ἐπετελεῖτο. ὅθεν καὶ Εὔπολις φησι·

   † τί χορὸς οὗτος κλαίειν εἴπωμεν πυρανιᵈ

398 Athenaeus 2d

ὡς τὰ Πινδάρου ⟨ὁ⟩ κωμῳδιοποιὸς Εὔπολίς φησιν
ἤδη κατασεσιγασμένα ὑπὸ τῆς τῶν πολλῶν ἀφιλο-
καλίας

399 Athenaeus 667d

ὅτι δὲ ἆθλον προὔκειτο τῷ εὖ προεμένῳ τὸν κότταβον
προείρηκε μὲν καὶ ὁ Ἀντιφάνης· ᾠὰ γάρ ἐστι καὶ
πεμμάτια καὶ τραγήματα. ὁμοίως δὲ διεξέρχονται Κη-

394 Seeing the flashing Lambdas he was terrified.[1]

[1] Spartans (Lacedaemonians) had a lambda (Λ) emblazoned on their shields.

395 Socrates received the cup as it went from left to right, and while singing some Stesichorus to the lyre, stole a wine decanter.　　　　　　　　[*Spongers, Nanny-Goats*?]

396 This little song is customary.[1]

[1] Referring to the first part of the parabasis, the *kommation*.

397 These two lines [*Medea* 520–21] belong to the chorus. At this period the role of the chorus was already diminishing. In Old Comedy the chorus was essential to the plot. And so Eupolis says:

why this chorus to complain, shall we say.[1]

[1] The odd word πυρανιδ or πυρωνιδ might hide a reference to Pyronides, the main character of *Demes*.

398 As the comic poet Eupolis says that the songs of Pindar have been consigned to silence because of the decline in popular taste.　　　　　　　　[*Helots*?]

399 Antiphanes [F 57] has already been cited that there was a prize for the winner in *cottabus*, eggs and buns and

φισόδωρος ἐν Τροφωνίῳ καὶ Καλλίας ἢ Διοκλῆς ἐν Κύκλωψι καὶ Εὔπολις Ἕρμιππός τε ἐν τοῖς Ἰάμβοις.

400 Σ Aristophanes *Peace* 740b

ῥακοφοροῦντας. αἰνίττεται δὲ καὶ εἰς Εὔπολιν.

401 Σ Aristophanes *Knights* 941a

τὸν πεζὸν λόγον. ἔστι δὲ πολλὰ καὶ παρ᾽ Εὐπόλιδι σεσημειωμένα.

402 Σ Aristophanes *Thesmophoriazusae* 828

συνέχεεν καὶ οὗτος ὡς Εὔπολις πολλάκις· στρατιὰ μὲν γὰρ τὸ πλῆθος, στρατεία δὲ ἡ στράτευσις.

403 Choricus 1.4

ἐξ ὁδοῦ τινας ἀγείρας εἰς θέατρον

404 Eustathius *On The Iliad* p. 1165.15

ἀγελαίας ἰσχάδας

405 Photius (b, z) α 810

ἀκούοντα ἄριστα

406 Photius (b, z) α 1801

ἄνεμος καὶ ὄλεθρος ἄνθρωπος

cheese. Cephisodorus gives a similar list in *Trophonius* [F 5], also Callias (or Diocles) in *Cyclopes* [F 12], Eupolis, and Hermippos in his *Iambs* [F 7 West].   [*Dyers*?]

400 "Rag wearers": he is also alluding to Eupolis.

401 Prose speech: there are many passages also in Eupolis so indicated.

402 He too is confused here, as Eupolis is several times: *stratia* is the "army," and *strateia* the "expedition."

403 Gathering some people from the street into the theatre.

404 Common figs.

405 With a very good reputation.

406 A person who is wind and ruin.

THE POETS OF OLD COMEDY

407 Photius (b, z) α 1617

ἀνεπτερῶσθαι τὴν ψυχήν

408 Photius (b, z, Sᶻ) α 1978

ἄνθρωπος ἐξ ὁδοῦ.

409 Phrynichus *Sophistic Preparation* p. 4.11

ἀνωφέλητος ἄνθρωπος

410 Σ Aeschylus *Prometheus* 451a

αὐλὴ πρόσειλος

411 Diogenianus 2.15

γάλα ὀρνίθων

412 Pollux 7.40

γῆν σμηκτρίδα

413 Photius p. 29.11

εὖ ἔχειν στόμα

414 Zonaras p. 917

εὐκτότατον γάμον

407 That the soul has taken flight.

408 A person from the street.

409 A person who can't be helped.

410 A courtyard facing the sun.

411 Birds' milk.

412 Fuller's earth.

413 To hold one's tongue.

414 A very desirable marriage.

415 Pollux 10.92

μακρὸν χαλκίον

416 Hesychius o 925

ὄνου γνάθος

417 Pollux 2.233

σαρκίνη γυνή

418 Pollux 7.83

σκύτινα χηλεύειν

424 Σ Dionysius Thrax, *GrGr* I 3, p. 149.27

Ἀμφιπτολεμοπηδησίστρατος

444 Hesychius δ 181

Δαμασικόνδυλον

415 A long copper vessel [of an oil bottle].   [*Spongers*?]

416 Ass' Jaw [of a glutton].   [*Draft-Dodgers*?]

417 A corpulent woman.

418 To stitch leather.

424 Amphiptolemopedesistratos   (Double-war-leap-is-
tratos)

444 "Damasi-knuckles": Eupolis says this meaning Da-
masistratus, a Chian wrestler.

*Brief fragments: (F 419) "to be radiant," (F 420) "streets,"
(F 421) "of Adramyttium," (F 422.) "mistakenly," (F 423)
"people of Amyrus," (F 425) "he sacrifices," (F 426) "most
kidnappingly," (F 427) "blameless," (F 428) "loved in re-
turn," (F 429) "exactly," (F 430) "fatherless."*

*(F 431) "they sleep separately," (F 432) "it must be sheared
off," (F 433) "I will cut my nails," (F 434) "she-dyer,"
(F 435) "Heavy-Getas," (F 436) "large and stupid," (F 437)*

"*a strapping lad,*" (*F* 438) "*cow-eyed,*" (*F* 439) "*Galepsus,*" (*F* 440) "*to fence off.*"

(*F* 441) "*signet ring,*" (*F* 442) "*tongues*" [*of an* aulos], (*F* 443) "*damarippeus*" [*a type of fig*], (*F* 445) "*stuffing,*" (*F* 446) "*very painful,*" (*F* 447) "*to kick out,*" (*F* 448) "*vomiter*" [*of a badly spoken man*], (*F* 449) "*he wooed,*" (*F* 450) "*to take out.*"

(*F* 451) "*women in love,*" (*F* 452) "*unmixed wine,*" (*F* 453) "*wide-mouthed jar,*" (*F* 454) "*you knew,*" (*F* 455) "*wet nurse,*" (*F* 456) "*I will talk nonsense,*" (*F* 457) "*locks of hair,*" (*F* 458) "*little thief,*" (*F* 459) "*to adorn oneself,*" (*F* 460) "koroneus" [*a type of fig*].

(*F* 461) "*corn-crake*" [*of a boaster*], (*F* 462) "*dice,*" (*F* 463) "*throat,*" (*F* 464) "*I have taken,*" (*F* 465) "*he eats up,*" (*F* 466)"*water channels,*" (*F* 467) "*to need the lash,*" (*F* 468) "*dark-skinned,*" (*F* 469) "*to talk of details,*" (*F* 470) "*small pay.*"

(*F* 471) "*tail,*" (*F* 472) "*I would stick tight,*" (*F* 473) "*rotations*" [*of a pestle*], (*F* 474) "*an extra,*" (*F* 475) "*Prastillus,*" (*F* 476) "*wine that has been filtered,*" (*F* 477) "*having stuffed,*" (*F* 478) "*rotten,*" (*F* 479) "*Silens,*" (*F* 480) "*temple attendant.*"

(*F* 481) "*umbrella,*" (*F* 482) "*the scout*" [*a dance figure*], (*F* 483) "*sophist*" [*of a rhapsode*], (*F* 484) "*partners in life,*" (*F* 485) "*continually,*" (*F* 486) "*ladle,*" (*F* 487) Trageae [*city on Naxos*], (*F* 488) "*racks,*" (*F* 489) "*and Eupolis in . . .* " [*of words beginning in* "*b*"].

494 Fortune is of little assistance to wise men; rather the things which are most important and essential are controlled by the judgements of the mind and the heart. Many philosophers have said this, and no less have the poets, who wrote Greek Comedy long ago, expressed these sentiments on the stage in their verses: Eu‹polis›, Crates [F 60], Chionides [F 8], Aristophanes [F 924], and especially along with these Alexis.

ΕΥΞΕΝΙΔΗΣ

Testimonium

i *Suda* ε 2766

Ἐπίχαρμος . . . ἦν δὲ πρὸ τῶν Περσικῶν ἔτη ἕξ, διδάσκων ἐν Συρακούσαις· ἐν δὲ Ἀθήναις Εὐέτης καὶ Εὐξενίδης καὶ Μύλλος ἐπεδείκνυντο.

EUXENIDES

The sole evidence for the existence of this poet is the testimony of the Suda *(T 1), which if trustworthy places Euxenides among the very earliest comic poets, active in the 480s.*

Testimonium

i Epicharmus: he was active six years before the Persian Wars [486/5] producing plays in Syracuse. At Athens Euetes and Euxenides and Myllus were putting on plays.

ΗΓΗΜΩΝ

*Although Hegemon was best known as a writer of paro-
dies, he was assigned by some to Old Comedy (T 2–4).
Athenaeus (T 4) places him chronologically with Crati-
nus. Polemon (T 4) describes him as the first competitor in*
parōidia, *and since Hermippus, a comic poet from the 430s
onward, is also said to have written* parōidia *(T 4), we
should date Hegemon to the 430s and later. The two anec-
dotes recorded by Chamaeleon (see T 3) associate him with
persons and events of the late fifth century, but the details
are suspicious and the stories are probably later inven-
tions. The second, how Hegemon was saved from prosecu-
tion by the intervention of Alcibiades, is clearly a compan-
ion piece to the story, popular with the later critics, of
Alcibiades' attack on Eupolis. Hegemon is said to have
come from Thasos, an island associated with the early*

Testimonia

i *Suda* η 52

Ἡγήμων, ὁ Θάσιος, ὁ ἐπικληθεὶς Φακή.

HEGEMON

iambic poet Archilochus, and thus to have been active at
Athens at the same time as Cratinus the comic poet was
creating comedy strongly influenced by Archilochus, is
suggestive.

Athenaeus 699a (T 4), in addition to preserving the one
major fragment of his parodic work (twenty-one dactylic
hexameters in a low colloquial tone with constant Homeric
allusions), cites a comedy, Philinna, "in the old style."
However, the title suggests rather a hetaera play of the sort
familiar from the fourth century, and the one fragment is
very much in the culinary style of Middle Comedy. I sus-
pect that we have two Hegemons here: the parodist from
the latter half of the fifth century and a comic poet from the
fourth. The Suda (η 53) knows a Hegemon from the time of
Demosthenes, whose "plays include a Philinna."

Testimonia

i Hegemon: of Thasos, the man nicknamed "Bean-soup."

271

THE POETS OF OLD COMEDY

ii Athenaeus 5ab

δείπνων ἀναγραφὰς πεποίηνται ἄλλοι . . . καὶ Ἡγή-
μων ὁ Θάσιος ὁ ἐπικληθεὶς Φακῆ, ὃν τῇ ἀρχαίᾳ
κωμῳδίᾳ τινὲς ἐντάττουσιν.

iii Athenaeus 406e–7c

Χαμαιλέων ὁ Ποντικὸς ἐν ἕκτῳ περὶ τῆς ἀρχαίας
κωμῳδίας "Ἡγήμων" φησίν, "ὁ Θάσιος ὁ τὰς παρῳ-
δίας γράψας Φακῆ ἐπεκαλεῖτο . . . εἰσῆλθε δέ ποτε καὶ
εἰς τὸ θέατρον διδάσκων κωμῳδίαν λίθων ἔχων πλή-
ρες τὸ ἱμάτιον, οὓς βάλλων εἰς τὴν ὀρχήστραν διαπο-
ρεῖν ἐποίησε τοὺς θεατάς. καὶ ὀλίγον διαλιπὼν εἶπε·

λίθοι μὲν οἵδε· βαλλέτω δ᾽ εἴ τις θέλει·
ἀγαθὸν δὲ κἂν χειμῶνι κἂν θέρει φακῆ."

iv Athenaeus 698b–99a

Πολέμων δ᾽ ἐν τῷ δωδεκάτῳ τῶν πρὸς Τίμαιον περὶ
τῶν τὰς παρῳδίας γεγραφότων ἱστορῶν τάδε γράφει·
"κέχρηται δὲ καὶ Ἐπίχαρμος ὁ Συρακόσιος ἔν τισι
τῶν δραμάτων ἐπ᾽ ὀλίγον καὶ Κρατῖνος ὁ τῆς ἀρχαίας
κωμῳδίας ποιητὴς ἐν Εὐνείδαις καὶ τῶν κατ᾽ αὐτὸν
Ἡγήμων ὁ Θάσιος, ὃν ἐκάλουν Φακῆν . . . πεποίηκε δὲ
παρῳδίας καὶ Ἕρμιππος ὁ τῆς ἀρχαίας κωμῳδίας
ποιητής. τούτων δὲ πρῶτος εἰσῆλθεν εἰς τοὺς ἀγῶνας
τοὺς θυμελικοὺς Ἡγήμων καὶ παρ᾽ Ἀθηναίοις ἐνίκη-
σεν ἄλλαις τε παρῳδίαις καὶ τῇ Γιγαντομαχίᾳ."

ii Others have written accounts of dinner parties . . . including Hegemon of Thasos, nicknamed "Bean-soup," whom some assign to Old Comedy.

iii Chamaeleon of Pontus in Book 6 of his *On Old Comedy* writes [F 44 Wehrli], "Hegemon of Thasos, the man who wrote parodies, was nicknamed 'Bean-soup' . . . once when he was producing a comedy, he went into the theatre with his cloak full of stones, which he cast into the orchestra and made the spectators wonder. After waiting a bit he said:

> These are stones, anyone who wants can throw them.
> A good thing both in summer and in winter is bean
>   soup."

Chamaeleon goes on to relate two stories: (1) how Hegemon's "parody," *Battle of the Giants*, was so amusing that spectators remained in the theatre to hear it, even though on the same day came the news of the disaster in Sicily [413], and (2) how Hegemon was supported in a lawsuit at Athens by the "artists of Dionysus" and protected by the personal intervention of Alcibiades.

iv Polemon in Book 12 of his work *On Timaeus* writes as follows about those who have written parodies [F 45 Preller], "Epicharmus of Syracuse also uses ⟨parodies⟩ to some extent in certain of his plays, also Cratinus the poet of Old Comedy in his *Sons of Euneus*, and among those of his time Hegemon of Thasos, whom they call 'Bean-soup' . . . Hermippus, the poet of Old Comedy, also wrote parodies. But of these the first to enter theatrical contests was Hegemon, who was victorious at Athens with other parodies, but especially with *Battle of the Giants*."

THE POETS OF OLD COMEDY

ΦΙΛΙΝΝΑ

Testimonia

i Athenaeus 699a

γέγραφε δὲ καὶ κωμῳδίαν εἰς τὸν ἀρχαῖον τρόπον, ἣν ἐπιγράφουσιν Φίλινναν.

ii *Suda* η 53

Ἡγήμων· Δημοσθένης ἐν τῷ ὑπὲρ Κτησιφῶντος. εἷς ἦν τῶν Μακεδονιζόντων καὶ τῶν ἐπὶ δωροδοκίᾳ διαβεβλημένων. τῶν δραμάτων αὐτοῦ ἐστι Φιλίννα, ὡς Ἀθήναιος ἐν Δειπνοσοφισταῖς.

Fragment

1 Athenaeus 108c

μάλα ταχέως αὐτῶν πρίω <μοι> πουλύπουν,
καὶ δὸς καταφαγεῖν κἀπὸ τηγάνου γόνον.

274

HEGEMON

PHILINNA

Testimonia

i He [Hegemon] also wrote a comedy in the old style which they title "Philinna."

ii Hegemon: Demosthenes *In Defence of Ctesiphon*. He was one of those who supported Macedon and accused of taking bribes (*PAA* 480795). His plays include *Philinna*, according to Athenaeus [108c].

Fragment

1 With this ‹money› very quickly, buy ‹for me› an octopus and give it to me to eat, and also fingerlings right out of the fry pan.

ΕΡΜΙΠΠΟΣ

A *comic poet of the generation previous to Aristophanes,
Hermippus' career may be dated from the mid-430s to the
early 410s. Secure dates are a victory in 435 (T 3) and his
Bakery-Women in 420 or 419. If F 47 is from Fates, then
that comedy belongs to 430 or 429, and if F 63 is assigned
correctly to Basket-Bearers, we can infer a date of 428–425
for that play. The Suda (T 1a) gives him forty titles, but we
know of only ten, and rather than assume that the ancients
lost all record of three-quarters of his work, the figure of
"forty" should be lowered considerably.*

*Hermippus seems to have been active in other poetic
genres. He wrote iambic poems, cited explicitly, and also
parōidia, a much more shadowy genre, for which there
may have been public performances, even competitions,
in fifth-century Athens. Both genres clearly overlap with
comedy: iambic for its vigorous and coarse language, also
its essential nature of attacking targets, parōidia in that it
turned the form and language of serious epic into some-
thing humorous. One must always consider whether a
fragment attributed only "to Hermippus" might in fact
come from an iamb or a parōidia, and keep the counter-
consideration in mind that a man who wrote iambics and
parōidia might have written comedies in the same style.*

276

HERMIPPUS

He wrote mythological burlesques, his Birth of Athena *anticipating the vogue in "birth plays" by about thirty years, as well as an* Agamemnon *and a* Europa. *But a strong political strain can also be detected in his comedy. While not totally centred upon the demagogue Hyperbolus,* Bakery-Women *to some extent continued the development of the demagogue comedy, pioneered by Aristophanes in* Knights, *enough to arouse Aristophanes' complaint (T 6), while F 47 is a biting song against Pericles' conduct of the War. Critics are divided whether the story of the accusation against Aspasia (T 3) is an actual historical fact or something that Hermippus said in a comedy.*

The plural titles suggest a strong choral presence in the style of Aristophanes and Cratinus. There are a number of places where Dionysus is known or conjectured plausibly to have been a character—F 36, 77 for certain, perhaps also in Soldiers *or* Basket-Bearers. *Silenus might be the speaker of F 44–45.*

Recent bibliography: D. Braund, G&R *41 (1994) 41–48; D. Gilula, in* Rivals *75–90; B. Zimmermann, in* Rivals *273–76; Harvey, in* Rivals *280–84; Pellegrino* (Utopie) *195–225.*

THE POETS OF OLD COMEDY

Testimonia

i

(a) *Suda* ε 3044

Ἕρμιππος, Ἀθηναῖος, κωμικὸς τῆς ἀρχαίας κωμῳ-
δίας, ἑτερόφθαλμος· ἀδελφὸς δὲ Μυρτίλου τοῦ κωμι-
κοῦ, δράματα διδάξας μ΄.

(b) *Suda* μ 1460

Μυρτίλος, Ἀθηναῖος, κωμικός, υἱὸς μὲν Λύσιδος,
ἀδελφὸς δὲ τοῦ κωμικοῦ Ἑρμίππου.

ii Plutarch *Pericles* 32.1

περὶ δὲ τοῦτον τὸν χρόνον Ἀσπασία δίκην ἔφευγεν
ἀσεβείας, Ἑρμίππου τοῦ κωμῳδιοποιοῦ διώκοντος καὶ
προσκατηγοροῦντος, ὡς Περικλεῖ γυναῖκας ἐλευθέρας
εἰς τὸ αὐτὸ φοιτώσας ὑποδέχοιτο.

iii *IG* ii² 2318

    Ἰσοκράτη[ς   ἐχορήγει
    Ἕρμιππος[ἐδίδασκεν

iv *IG* ii² 2325.57

    Ἕρμ[ιππος

HERMIPPUS

Testimonia

i

(a) Hermippus: of Athens, poet of Old Comedy, a man with only one eye, brother of Myrtilus the comic poet. He produced forty plays.

(b) Myrtilus: of Athens, comic poet, son of Lysis and brother of Hermippus the comic poet.

ii About this time [at the trial of Phidias] Aspasia was the defendant on a charge of impiety, the prosecutor being Hermippus the comic poet, who added the accusation that she was arranging assignations with Pericles for freeborn women at her house.

iii [record of the dramatic contests for 435]
Isocrates [was the *chorēgus*]/Hermippus [produced]

iv [list of the victors at the Dionysia]
Herm[ippus]

v *IG* ii² 2325.123

Ἕρμιππος ΙΙΙΙ

vi Aristophanes *Clouds* 557–58

εἶθ᾽ Ἕρμιππος αὖθις ἐποίησεν εἰς Ὑπέρβολον,
ἄλλοι τ᾽ ἤδη πάντες ἐρείδουσιν εἰς Ὑπέρβολον

vii Σ Aristophanes *Clouds* 541b

τἄπη τῇ βακτηρίᾳ· ὡς εἰς τοῦτο τὸ μέρος εὐεπίφορον
ὄντα τὸν Ἕρμιππον σκώπτει.

viii Athenaeus 699a

πεποίηκε δὲ παρῳδίας καὶ Ἕρμιππος ὁ τῆς ἀρχαίας
κωμῳδίας ποιητής.

ix Aristophanes F 590.90

ταδ᾽ Ἑρμι[ππο

x Tzetzes *Distinctions among Poets* (Koster XXIa.82–84)

τῆς δευτέρας ἦν ὁ ψόγος κεκρυμμένος,
ἧς ἦν Κρατῖνος, Εὔπολις, Φερεκράτης,
Ἀριστοφάνης, Ἕρμιππός τε καὶ Πλάτων.

v [list of the comic victors at the Lenaia]

Hermippus 4

vi Then in his turn Hermippus went after Hyperbolus and then everyone starts in on Hyperbolus, copying my metaphor of the eels.

vii "Words with his stick": he is making fun of Hermippus for being prone to this sort of thing.

viii Hermippus the poet of Old Comedy also wrote parodies.

ix [from a commentary to Aristophanes]

This ⟨is⟩ from Hermi[ppus].

x Indirect insult was characteristic of second ⟨comedy⟩, to which belonged Cratinus, Eupolis, Pherecrates, Aristophanes, Hermippus, and Platon.

THE POETS OF OLD COMEDY

Fragments

ΑΓΑΜΕΜΝΩΝ

1 Orus *Orthography* fol. 283ʳ 14

κάτειπε πόθεν εἶ μηδέ < - > ψεύσῃ μάτην.

ΑΘΗΝΑΣ ΓΟΝΑΙ

2 Photius p. 61.22

ὁ Ζεὺς "δίδωμι Παλλάς" ἠσί "τοὔνομα."

3 *Etymologicum Genuinum* A, s.v. ἀρνός

τὴν μὲν διάλεκτον καὶ τὸ πρόσωπον ἀμνίου
ἔχειν δοκεῖς, τὰ δ᾽ ἔνδον οὐδὲν διαφέρεις
δράκοντος.

HERMIPPUS

Fragments

AGAMEMNON

Both Aeschylus and Ion of Chios wrote tragedies with this title. We should not assume that a play called "Agamemnon" must refer to the story as dramatised in Oresteia. *Homer provides other possibilities for a humorous treatment of Agamemnon, e.g., the dispute with Achilles over Briseis, or an encounter during the fighting. Is F 1 from a scene where two potential combatants meet?*

1 Tell me where you are from and do not tell a useless lie.

BIRTH OF ATHENA

The heyday of comedies about the birth of gods or heroes seems to lie in the early fourth century—see Nesselrath in Dobrov (BA) *1–27—but we can find earlier examples, such as this comedy by Hermippus, Cratinus'* Nemesis *(birth of Helen), and Aeschylus' satyr play* Net-Haulers *(Perseus as an infant). Homer could display the personal life of the gods in a humorous fashion (witness* Iliad *14 or* Odyssey *8), and the comic birth theme may be traced back to the* Homeric Hymn to Hermes *and ahead to the sketches by Lucian in the second century AD. The references to weaving (F 4–5) suit this traditional interest of Athena.*

2 And Zeus says, "I give ⟨you⟩ the name "Pallas."

3 You seem to have the speech and face of a lamb, but inside you are no different from a serpent.

4 Photius (z) α 3129, Bachmann's *Lexicon* p. 162.5

ἀπὸ τῆς τραπέζης τουτονὶ τὸν στήμονα
ἄττεσθ᾽ ἐπινοῶν.

    2 ἐπινοῶν Lexicon, ἐπὶ νοῶν Photius, ἐπινοῶ Valckenaer

5 Photius (b, Sᶻ) α 1956

καιροσπάθητον ἀνθέων ὕφασμα καινὸν Ὡρῶν.

λεπτοὺς διαψαίρουσα πέπλους ἀνθέων γέμοντας.

6 Σ Plato *Gorgias* 497a

τὸ ἀκκίζεσθαι ἐκ γυναικὸς εἰρῆσθαί φασιν Ἀκκοῦς
καλουμένης, ἣν οὕτως εὐήθη λέγουσιν ὡς ἀπὸ τοῦ
ἱστοῦ θοἰμάτιον καθελομένην ἡμίεργον ἀμφιέσασθαι,
εἴς τε τὸ κάτοπτρον βλέπουσαν πρὸς τὴν παρ᾽ αὐτῆς
ἔμφασιν εἰς αὐτὸ γιγνομένην ὡς ἑτέρᾳ προσλαλεῖν
γυναικί. μέμνηται ταύτης Ἕρμιππος ἐν Ἀθηνᾶς γο-
ναῖς.

ΑΡΤΟΠΩΛΙΔΕΣ

4 Having in mind ⟨to take⟩ this warp from the table ⟨and⟩ fit it in place.[1]

1 Valckenaer's reading could make Athena herself the speaker.

5 A close-woven new robe with flowers ⟨woven by⟩ the Seasons.

Gently caressing [fem.] delicate robes laden with flowers.

6 "To be an Acco" they say is taken from a woman named Acco. They record that she was so silly that she took a half-completed dress from the loom and put it on, and that she looked at her own reflection in a mirror and had a conversation with it as if it were another woman. Hermippus mentions her in *Birth of Athena*.

BAKERY-WOMEN

This is one of the comedies about which Aristophanes complains in the revised parabasis of Clouds *(c.418), that the idea of the demagogue comedy, which he pioneered in* Knights *(424), was then appropriated by other poets and used against Hyperbolus, first Eupolis with* Maricas *(L-421), then Hermippus, and "now everyone starts in on Hyperbolus" (T 6). Thus Hermippus' comedy belongs to 420 or 419. The scholia to* Clouds *557 tell us that Hermippus' comedy was* Bakery-Women, *but that the whole play was not aimed at Hyperbolus. Only certain parts of the play were intended to make fun of him. Aristophanes says that Eupolis in* Maricas *added an old woman to the comedy, whom the scholiasts identify as Hyperbolus'*

285

7 Σ Aristophanes *Birds* 1556

† ἐνέβαινε σιγῇ Πείσανδρος μέγας αὐτός †
ὥσπερ Διονυσίοισιν οὑπὶ τῶν ξύλων.
† ἐλαίης ἔρεισιν ὄνον κανθήλιον

8 Photius (b, z) α 163

φέρε νῦν ἀγήλω τοὺς θεοὺς ἰοῦσ᾽ ἐγώ,
καὶ θυμιάσω τοῦ τέκνου σεσωσμένου.

9 Pollux 7.202

ὦ σαπρὰ καὶ πασιπόρνη καὶ κάπραινα.

10 Athenaeus 119c

καὶ τάριχος πίονα

ΔΗΜΟΤΑΙ

*mother. The feminine forms in F 8–9, plus the word
"dokiko" in F 11, perhaps playing on Eupolis' name for
Hyperbolus' mother (Doko), suggest that a character in
this play also was meant to represent the demagogue's
mother. "Bakery-woman" was proverbial in ancient Greek
for a woman with a foul tongue (e.g., Frogs 858), like
"fishwife" in English.*

7 The great Peisander himself got up in silence, like the
chief usher at the Dionysia . . . pack-ass.[1]

1 The text is very uncertain, but I would prefer ἀναβαίνει or
ἀνέβαινε in the first line ("go up <to the bema>," "get up to
speak"). The words "chief usher" translate "the man in charge of
the wooden things," the last being taken as "the wooden benches
of the theatre," but it is possible that the opening of the third line
hides the name "Phales" and that it could mean "like Phales on the
poles at the Dionysia."

8 Well now, I [fem.] shall go to praise the gods and offer
incense now that my son has been saved.

9 You worn-out sow, whore to all.

10 And a fat salt fish.

*Brief fragments: (F 11) "to sell garlic," (F 12) δοκικῶ for
δοκῶ ["I think"].*

DEMESMEN

*An Athenian would regard demesmen as a group close to
him. At* Clouds *1209 Strepsiades imagines the envy of "my*

13 Pollux 9.70

οἴμοι, τί δράσω σύμβολον κεκαρμένος;

14 Athenaeus 285e

νῦν δ᾽ οὐδ᾽ ἀφύην κινεῖν δοκεῖς.

15 Pollux 10.165

ἔχοντες ἴσον ἀσπίδιον ὀγκίῳ.

16 Hesychius ο 1920

οὐ φροντὶς Ἱπποκλείδῃ

ΕΥΡΩΠΗ

friends and demesmen," and at 1322 calls for help from "neighbours, kinsmen, and demesmen." The chorus is presumably composed of demesmen of the main character. Eupolis wrote a comedy called "Friends," Crates a "Neighbours."

13 Oh dear, what shall I do with my hair half-cut [or "my face half-shaved"].

14 But now you don't even seem to be disturbing a minnow.[1]

> [1] It is possible that we have a *sensus obscenus* here, since Aphye (minnow) is the name of a prostitute (Archippus F 19), and *kinein* (disturb) means also "to have sex with."

15 Having [pl.] a little shield the size of a wicker case.

16 Hippoclides doesn't care.[1]

> [1] For the story see Herodotus 6.129.

Brief fragments: (F 17) "pump" [of a woman's shoe], (F 18) "ba!" [a shout], (F 19) "a pot with three legs," (F 20) "with a retentive memory," (F 21) "subtle talk," (F 22) "be present."

EUROPA

The title suggests a burlesque of myth, and we can imagine the comic possibilities of Zeus choosing to appear as the great bull of the myth. Lucian knows the story and describes the scene vividly (Dialogues of the Sea-Gods 15).

23 Photius p. 481.13

ῥύζων ἅπαντας ἀπέδομαι τοὺς δακτύλους.

ΘΕΟΙ

24 Athenaeus 426f

ἔπειθ᾽ ὅταν πινώμεθ᾽ ἢ διψώμεθα,
εὐχόμεθα πρὸς τοῦθ᾽ † ὁ οἶνος, ωκαιρας γενου.
οὐκ ἀστοῦ καὶ πηλουγω † φέρω παίζων ἅμα,
κανθεὶς γεγένηται τοῦτο πέντε καὶ δύο.

*The one fragment (F 23) shows someone under consider-
able stress threatening to gnaw his own fingers. The verb
"growling" is used especially of dogs. Are we watching
Zeus suffering from his lust for Europa?*

23 I [masc.] shall growl as I gnaw away at all my fingers.

GODS

*If a plural title indicates the identity of the chorus, did gods
form the chorus, and were individual identities revealed?
At the end of* Birds *barbarian gods are juxtaposed with
traditional Olympians, while in Lucian's* Assembly of the
Gods, *the point lies in a conflict between traditional deities
and more recent additions to the pantheon. Several plays
of Old Comedy had as their subject the arrival of a new
god: Cotyto in Eupolis'* Dyers, *Sabazius in Aristophanes'*
Heroes *(or* Seasons). *F 25 mentions the procession at the
Panathenaea, F 32 a celebration at Taenarum, while sev-
eral fragments suggest that a party was part of the action
(F 24, 27, 29, 31, 35).*

24 Then whenever we are drinking or whenever we are
thirsty, we pray to this †the wine . . . and I carry, joking at
the same time that when heated it became the five-and-
two.[1]

[1] The central section of this fragment is corrupt. "This" [neut.]
could be the magic horn of Amalthea, which supplied never-
ending food and drink. The "five-and-two" is a standard mixture of
water and wine. Is the speaker the errand god Hermes?

25 Σ Aristophanes *Birds* 1551

{A.} ὥσπερ αἱ κανηφόροι
λευκοῖσιν ἀλφίτοισιν ἐντετριμμένος.
{B.} ἐγὼ δ' ἐνέκαψα λανθάνων τὴν διφροφόρον.

26 Photius p. 538.21

ἐξ ἀγορᾶς δ' ἐγὼ
ὠνήσομαι λύχνον τιν' ἢ στίλβην.

27 Σ Aristophanes *Wasps* 674

καὶ πρὸς κύβους ἔστηκ' ἔχων ⟨τὸ⟩ κήθιον.

28 Phrynichus *Sophistic Preparation* p. 44.7

ἃ τόθ' ἥσθην, ταῦτα νῦν ἀνήδομαι.

29 Athenaeus 478c

τόν τε κότυλον πρῶτον ἤνεγκ' ἐνέχυρον τῶν
    γειτόνων.

30 Herodian *On Singular Vocabulary* II p. 923.5

φήμης ἱερᾶς ἐξοιγνυμένης ὥσπερ πέπονος δοθιῆνος.

31 Athenaeus 636cd

λεπάδας δὲ πετρῶν ἀποκόπτοντες κρεμβαλιάζουσι.

25 (A) Powdered with bleached barley dust, like the basket bearers.

(B) And I [masc.] grabbed the stool bearer without anyone noticing.

26 I shall buy a lamp or a candle from the market.

27 And he stood by the dice tables, box in hand.

28 What I liked then I dislike now.

29 First he took the wine cup from the neighbours as security.

30 Of a sacred tale unfolding like a ripe abscess.

31 Breaking off limpets from the rocks, they use them as castanets.

32 Stephanus of Byzantium p. 598.13

καὶ σὲ τί χρὴ παραταιναρίζειν.

ΚΕΡΚΩΠΕΣ

36 Athenaeus 551a

       νῦν γὰρ πενόμενοι
ἀνάπηρά σοι θύουσιν ἤδη βοίδια,
Λεωτροφίδου λεπτότερα καὶ Θουμάντιδος.

32 Why must you observe the celebration at Taenarum?

Brief fragments: (F 33) "small tunic," (F 34) "young man," (F 35) "to play at five stones."

CERCOPES

In the archaic period the Cercopes were part of the myths about Heracles. They were cunning dwarf-like creatures, who would steal from passersby, and are associated with both central Greece (Herodotus 7.216) and Asia Minor. On sixth-century vases and stone reliefs, a pair of these is shown as captured by Heracles and hanging head-down from a pole. Although two is the usual number in art, several names are known for them, and it is easy to imagine a comic chorus of such humorous creatures. F 38 shows that someone stole a gold cup in the comedy. Is Dionysus (see F 36) relating his experience with these creatures? Did Dionysus summon his half-brother Heracles to assist him? The two kōmōidoumenoi of F 36 belong to the period 424–414, while the Hieroclides who may lie behind the coinage in F 39, was made fun of by Phrynichus in Revellers, *a comedy also of the 410s.*

36 But now being poor, all they sacrifice to you [Dionysus] are stunted little cows, leaner than even Leotrophides and Thoumantis.[1]

---

[1] Thoumantis (*PAA* 515550) is known as a hungry person at *Knights* 1268, while Leotrophides (*PAA* 607070)) is described as being as thin as a bird at *Birds* 1406 and as "a featherweight" at Theopompus F 25.

THE POETS OF OLD COMEDY

37 Athenaeus 650e

ἤδη τεθέασαι κόκκον ἐν χιόνι ῥόας;

38 Athenaeus 502b

χρυσίδ᾽ οἴνου πανσέληνον ἐκπιὼν ὑφείλετο.

39 Hesychius κ 3309

Κολακοφωροκλείδης

MOIPAI

For the title we may compare Eumenides, *both by Aeschylus and Cratinus,* Seasons *by Aristophanes and Cratinus,* Muses *by Phrynichus. Traditionally three in number, they may have been increased to provide the requisite twenty-four for the comic chorus, or (more likely) "Fates" may not refer to the chorus at all, but perhaps to some scheme to deceive the Fates, as Apollo got them drunk (Eumenides 727–28). Some, pointing to the theme of war and arming for war in F 46–48, have suggested that the title had nothing to do with the Fates,* moirai *referring rather to divisions of the Spartan army. But as F 49–50 mention spinning and needles, can we imagine some character, like*

37 Have you [sing.] ever seen a pomegranate seed in snow?

38 After drinking down a golden full-moon cup of wine he ran off with it.

39 Suck-up—thieving—clides.[1]

1 A comic coinage based on *kolax* (suck-up) + *phoro* (rob) + *clides* (the end of the name "Hieroclides" according to Hesychius). See Phrynichus F 18.

Brief fragments: (F 40) "well water," (F 41) "have a conversation."

FATES

Trygaeus in Peace, *seeking out the Fates in an attempt to stop the War? Does the mention of "humans" in F 46.1 imply that the speaker is a god?*

Kōmōidoumenoi *in the fragments include the tragic poet Nothippus (F 46) and Diagoras (F 43), the former unknown elsewhere, and the latter probably the sophist. If F 47 does belong to this comedy, then the reference to Pericles' policy of Sitzkrieg dates the play to 430 (or less likely, 429). Some have unconvincingly argued that F 42, 43, and 46 are jokes against Pericles and his conduct of the War. The pair of songs in anapaestic dimeter (F 47–48) remind one of the antiwar sentiments in* Acharnians, *especially the sympotic context at 976–99.*

42 Athenaeus 418cd

ὁ Ζεὺς δὲ τούτων οὐδὲν ἐνθυμούμενος
μύων ξυνέπλαττε Θετταλικὴν τὴν ἔνθεσιν.

43 Σ Aristophanes *Frogs* 320

μείζων γὰρ ἢ νῦν δή 'στι, καὶ δοκεῖ γ' ἐμοί,
ἐὰν τοσοῦτον ἐπιδιδῷ τῆς ἡμέρας,
μείζων ἔσεσθαι Διαγόρου τοῦ Τερθρέως.

44 Athenaeus 476d

οἶσθά νῦν ὅ μοι ποίησον; τήνδε νῦν μή μοι δίδου,
ἐκ δὲ τοῦ κέρατος αὖ μοι δὸς πιεῖν ἅπαξ μόνον,

45 Athenaeus 486a

ἢν ἐγὼ πάθω τι τήνδε τὴν λεπαστὴν ἐκπιών,
τῷ Διονύσῳ πάντα τἀμαυτοῦ δίδωμι χρήματα.

46 Athenaeus 344c

εἰ δ' ἦν τὸ γένος τῶν ἀνθρώπων τῶν νῦν τοιόνδε
    μάχεσθαι,
καὶ βατὶς αὐτῶν ἡγεῖτ' ὀπτὴ μεγάλη καὶ πλευρὸν
    ὕειον,
τοὺς μὲν ἄρ' ἄλλους οἰκουρεῖν χρῆν, πέμπειν δὲ
    Νόθιππον ἑκόντα·
εἷς γὰρ μόνος ὢν κατεβρόχθισεν ἂν τὴν
    Πελοπόννησον ἅπασαν.

42 Zeus with no thought for any of this shut his eyes and put together a Thessalian mouthful.

43 Bigger than he is now, and in my opinion, if he grows as much today, he will be bigger than Diagoras the Quibbler's son.

44 Know what you can do for me? Do not give me this ⟨cup⟩, but just this once let me drink from the horn.

45 (SILENUS?) If anything happens to me after I down this punch bowl, I leave all my worldly goods to Dionysus.

46 If the race of men today were to fight in such a way and a great roasted skate were leading them along with a side of pork, they could keep the rest in the camp and send Nothippus as a volunteer—since he by himself could swallow down the entire Peloponnese.[1]

---

1 The first half of Nothippus means "Bastard," but the name is attested in Attic prosopography for this period. See *PAA* 720940 and *TrGF* I nr. 26, p. 144.

THE POETS OF OLD COMEDY

47 Plutarch *Pericles* 33.6

βασιλεῦ Σατύρων, τί ποτ' οὐκ ἐθέλεις
δόρυ βαστάζειν, ἀλλὰ λόγους μὲν
περὶ τοῦ πολέμου δεινοὺς παρέχῃ,
    ψυχὴν δὲ Τέλητος ὕπεστιν;
5 κἀγχειριδίου δ' ἀκόνῃ σκληρᾷ
παραθηγομένης βρύχεις κοπίδος,
    δηχθεὶς αἴθωνι Κλέωνι.

48 Athenaeus 668a

χλανίδες δ' οὖλαι καταβέβληνται,
θώρακα δ' ἅπας ἐμπερονᾶται,
κνημὶς δὲ περὶ σφυρὸν ἀρθροῦται,
βλαύτης δ' οὐδεὶς ἔτ' ἔρως λευκῆς,
5 ῥάβδον δ' ὄψει τὴν κοτταβικὴν
ἐν τοῖς ἀχύροισι κυλινδομένην,
Μανῆς δ' οὐδὲν λατάγων ἀίει,
τὴν δὲ τάλαιναν πλάστιγγ' ἂν ἴδοις
παρὰ τὸν στροφέα τῆς κηπαίας
10   ἐν τοῖσι κορήμασιν οὖσαν.

49 Pollux 10.136

ῥάμμ' ἐπέκλωσας

47 King of the satyrs, why are you so unwilling to wield the spear? You do deliver fearsome speeches about the war, but inside lurks the heart of a Teles. At the sound of a dagger being sharpened on a hard whetstone you grind your teeth, bitten by fierce Cleon.[1]

1 Plutarch makes it clear that this song is directed against Pericles. For the disquiet over his reluctance to prosecute the war actively, see Thucydides 2.20–22, 59–65. Some have wanted to take "king of the satyrs" as an intertextual reference to the supposed portrayal of Dionysus as Pericles in Cratinus' *Dionysalexander*, but "king of the satyrs" may just allude to the cowardly nature of satyrs in drama (see *Cyclops* 590–653). This fragment shows Cleon as an active opponent of Pericles c. 430.

48 Woollen cloaks are cast aside, everyone is putting on his breastplate, greaves are being fastened about the shins, no one wants the white slipper any more. You will see the *cottabus* stick rolling among the bran husks, Manes no longer hears the drops of wine, and you might see the sorry basin lying among the sweepings behind the kitchen door.

49 You spun a thread.

Brief fragment: (F 50) "*needles.*"

ΣΤΡΑΤΙΩΤΑΙ (ΣΤΡΑΤΙΩΤΙΔΕΣ?)

The comedy is cited as "Soldiers" (Stratiōtai) on all but one occasion (F 52), where it is cited as "She-Soldiers" (Stratiōtides). The best explanation of the confusion of titles and of F 54 and 57 is that the chorus is composed of soldiers from Ionia, a region celebrated not just in comedy for its effeminate and luxurious mode of dress and behaviour. Harvey suggests that "that fellow from Abydus" (F 57) could indicate an individuated chorus of men from different Ionian cities. The humour would have turned on the

51 Athenaeus 649c

οἴμοι τάλας, δάκνει, δάκνει,
ἀπεσθίει μου τὴν ἀκοήν.

52 *Epimerismi Homerici* π 141

{A.} τίς ἐσθ᾽ ὁ πωλῶν τἀνδράποδ᾽; {B.} ὅδ᾽ ἐγὼ
πάρα.

53 Athenaeus 77a

τῶν φιβάλεων μάλιστ᾽ ἂν ἦ τῶν κοράκεων.

54 Hesychius π 355

{A.} ὥρα τοίνυν μετ᾽ ἐμοῦ χωρεῖν ‹τὸν› κωπητῆρα
λαβόντα
καὶ προσκεφάλαιον, ἵν᾽ ἐς τὴν ναῦν ἐμπηδήσας
ῥοθιάζῃς.

SOLDIERS (OR SHE-SOLDIERS)

*unmilitary appearance and performance of these soldiers
(see F 56–58). Here we may compare Cratinus'* Poofters,
Eupolis' Draft-Dodgers *or* Men-Women, *or Dionysus in
both* Frogs *and Eupolis'* Officers, *where at F 272 Dionysus
is compared to a "she-soldier* (stratiōtis) *from Ionia who
has just given birth." On the basis of F 52, 54, 55–56, Dio-
nysus may have been a character in the comedy (cf. F 36 of*
Cercopes *and F 77, spoken by him). If so, then F 54 may
have been the original of the rowing scenes in* Officers *and*
Frogs.

51 Oh no, oh dear, it's [he's/she's] biting, biting, chewing
my ear off.

52 (A) Who is it that's selling slaves?   (B) Here I am, at
your service.

53 Of Philabean figs especially, or of raven-black ones.

54 (A) Well then it is time for you to pick up your oarlock
and a cushion and come with me, so that you may leap onto
the ship and start rowing.

{B.} ἀλλ' οὐ δέομαι πανικτὸν ἔχων τὸν πρωκτόν.

55 Athenaeus 480e

Χία δὲ κύλιξ ὑψοῦ κρέμαται
περὶ πασσαλόφιν.

56 Pollux 10.182

νικᾷ δ' ᾦα λιθίνην μάκτραν.

57 Athenaeus 524f

{A.} χαῖρ', ὦ διαπόντιον
στράτευμα, τί πράττομεν;
† τὰ μὲν πρὸς ὄψιν μαλακῶς
ἔχειν ἀπὸ σώματος †
5   κόμῃ τε νεανικῇ
σφρίγει τε βραχιόνων.
{B.} ἤσθου τὸν Ἄβυδον ὡς
ἀνὴρ γεγένηται;

58 Zenobius 1.72

ἀνερίναστος εἶ

(B) I don't need ‹a cushion›, my butt's so covered with boils [?].[1]

[1] The meaning of the adjective, *panikton* describing the speaker's butt, is not clear.

55 A Chian cup hangs high on its peg.

56 A sheepskin beats a stone trough.

57 (A) Greetings, army from across the sea, how are we doing? Now to look at . . . the body is soft with youthful hair and plump arms.
(B) Have you [sing.] heard that fellow from Abydos has become a man?[1]

[1] The metre is telesilleans, and likely comes from an exchange with the chorus leader (B) during the parodos. Zimmermann follows the earlier (unlikely) identification of "that fellow from Abydus" with Alcibiades; Harvey prefers it as a straightforward ethnic.

58 You are uncaprified.[1]

[1] Refers to a process described by Theophrastus (*Enquiry into Plants* 2.3.8) where insects (*erinea*) from wild fig trees are applied to the fruits of domestic figs in order to make the fruit firm and ripe. Hesychius ((5086) says that the word is used of a man who is "effeminate and without offspring."

Brief fragments: (F 59) "rows of pegs," (F 60) "to have had breakfast."

THE POETS OF OLD COMEDY

ΦΟΡΜΟΦΟΡΟΙ

The title suggests a chorus of "baggage bearers," perhaps the ancient equivalent of our "stevedores," and if F 63 does belong to this play and not to a parōidia by Hermippos, then the comedy may have turned on matters of trade, perhaps even with Dionysus as a character (see F 63.2). Most of the sources that cite all or part of F 63 either give no attribution or just "Hermippus." Hesychius (δ 1922) cites Hermippus' Basket-Bearers for "hazel nuts," and Photius (α 1286) and the Antiatticist (p. 82.19) for "almonds" (F 63.20). Are these three references sufficient to tie the whole fragment to this comedy? The metre of F 63 is dactylic hexameter, rare for comedy, but the metre of epic and of parōidia, which Hermippus is alleged to have written also.

61 Pollux 9.70

παρὰ τῶν καπήλων λήψομαι τὸ σύμβολον.

62 Athenaeus 700d

τῇδ᾽ ἐξιόντι † δεξιᾷ, ὦ λυχνίδιον.

63 Athenaeus 27de

ἔσπετε νῦν μοι Μοῦσαι Ὀλύμπια δώματ᾽ ἔχουσαι,
ἐξ οὗ ναυκληρεῖ Διόνυσος ἐπ᾽ οἴνοπα πόντον,
ὅσσ᾽ ἀγάθ᾽ ἀνθρώποις δεῦρ᾽ ἤγαγε νηὶ μελαίνῃ.
ἐκ μὲν Κυρήνης καυλὸν καὶ δέρμα βόειον,

306

BASKET-BEARERS

Given the serious engagement with Homer in F 63, one may wonder if this is really a fragment of parōidia *that has got mixed in with comedy. However, the personal mention of Sitalces and Perdiccas (F 63.7–8) and the possibility that a second speaker interjects at lines 7–8 (or just 8) and 10–11 do suggest the mood and the form of comedy,*

If F 63 does come from Basket-Bearers, *a date before 424 is assured by the mention of Sitalces, who died in 424, and after 431 in view of the "mange for the Spartans," much more likely in wartime, and the situation in Corcyra which blew up into open civil war in 427 (Thucydides 3.80). To this we may add F 64, the mention of Phrynichus the comic poet, whose debut belongs in 429. Thus a date of 428–425 seems reasonable.*

61 I shall take the token from the shopkeepers.

62 Little lamp, to the one going out on the right.[1]

  [1] The text is very uncertain and might read "show the way to one going out."

63 Tell now for me, Muses who have your home on Olympus, all the good things that Dionysus brought for people here, ever since he sailed as a trader over the wine-dark sea in his black ship. From Cyrene stalks of silphium and

5 ἐκ δ' Ἑλλησπόντου σκόμβρους καὶ πάντα ταρίχη·
 ἐκ δ' αὖ Ἰταλίας χόνδρον καὶ πλευρὰ βόεια·
 καὶ παρὰ Σιτάλκου ψώραν Λακεδαιμονίοισι
 καὶ παρὰ Περδίκκου ψεύδη ναυσὶν πάνυ πολλαῖς.
 αἱ δὲ Συράκουσαι σῦς καὶ τυρὸν παρέχουσι.
10 καὶ Κερκυραίους ὁ Ποσειδῶν ἐξολέσειεν
 ναυσὶν ἐπὶ γλαφυραῖς, ὁτιὴ δίχα θυμὸν ἔχουσιν.
 ταῦτα μὲν ἐντεῦθεν. ἐκ δ' Αἰγύπτου τὰ κρεμαστὰ
 ἱστία καὶ βίβλους, ἀπὸ δ' αὖ Συρίας λιβανωτόν.
 ἡ δὲ καλὴ Κρήτη κυπάριττον τοῖσι θεοῖσιν,
15 ἡ Λιβύη δ' ἐλέφαντα πολὺν παρέχει κατὰ πρᾶσιν·
 ἡ Ῥόδος ἀσταφίδας ⟨τε⟩ καὶ ἰσχάδας ἡδυονείρους.
 αὐτὰρ ἀπ' Εὐβοίας ἀπίους καὶ ἴφια μῆλα·
 ἀνδράποδ' ἐκ Φρυγίας, ἀπὸ δ' Ἀρκαδίας ἐπικούρους.
 αἱ Παγασαὶ δούλους καὶ στιγματίας παρέχουσι.
20 τὰς δὲ Διὸς βαλάνους καὶ ἀμύγδαλα σιγαλόεντα
 Παφλαγόνες παρέχουσι· τὰ γάρ ⟨τ'⟩ ἀναθήματα
  δαιτός.
 † Φοινίκη δ' αὖ † καρπὸν φοίνικος καὶ σεμίδαλιν·
 Καρχηδὼν δάπιδας καὶ ποικίλα προσκεφάλαια.

 6 Ἰταλίας codd., Θετταλίας Kock. 9 σῦς . . . παρ-
έχουσαι Athenaeus CE, σῖτον . . . παρέχουσι Eustathius. If the
participle is to be kept, Kaibel indicated a lacuna after l. 9.

64 Σ Aristophanes *Birds* 749

τρίτος, Φρύνιχος ὁ κωμικός, οὗ μέμνηται Ἕρμιππος

ox hides, from the Hellespont mackerel and salted fish of all sorts, from Italy [Thessaly?] grain and sides of beef. From Sitalces, mange for the Spartans; from Perdiccas many ships full of lies. Syracuse exports pork and cheese, and may Poseidon destroy the people of Corcyra with their hollow ships, because their hearts are divided. That's from those places. From Egypt hanging gear, sails, and papyrus cables, from Syria frankincense. The beautiful land of Crete exports cypress wood for the gods' statues, Libya much ivory for sale, and Rhodes raisins and figs that give good dreams. Then from Euboea pears and plump apples, slaves from Phrygia, mercenaries from Arcadia. Pagasae exports slaves and branded men, the Paphlagonians hazel nuts and shiny almonds, the crowning touches to a feast. Phoenicia ⟨exports⟩ dates of the palm tree and hard wheat, Carthage rugs and multicoloured cushions.

64 There is a third Phrynichus, the comic poet, whom

THE POETS OF OLD COMEDY

ἐν Φορμοφόροις ὡς ἀλλότρια ὑποβαλλομένου ποιή-
ματα.

65 Pollux 10.122

Ἕρμιππος ἐν Φορμοφόροις τὸν κύαθον καὶ τὴν οἰνο-
χόην καὶ τὸ λύχνιον καὶ τὰ τοιαῦτα σκεύη "χαλκίδια
καὶ χαλκία" καλεῖ ὡς ἐκ χαλκοῦ πεποιημένα.

ΑΔΗΛΩΝ ΔΡΑΜΑΤΩΝ

68 Athenaeus 18c

μὰ ⟨τὸν⟩ Δί' οὐ μέντοι μεθύειν τὸν ἄνδρα χρὴ
τὸν ἀγαθὸν οὐδὲ θερμολουτεῖν, ἃ σὺ ποιεῖς.

69 Athenaeus 59c

           τὴν κεφαλὴν ὅσην ἔχει.
ὅσην κολοκύντην.

70 Phrynichus *Sophistic Preparation* p. 12.4

σὺ δὲ τὴν κεφαλὴν ψάθαλλέ μου.

71 Zonaras p. 1556

ἀλλ' ἐκεῖσε θεῖ

72 Zonaras p. 1556

δεῖ τοῦτον

310

Hermippus mentions in *Basket-Bearers* for passing other people's work off as his own.

65 Hermippus in *Basket-Bearers* uses the terms "bronze" and "bronze-ware" for a cup and a wine ladle and a lamp stand and such implements since they are made of bronze.

Brief fragments: (F 66) "living abroad," (F 67) "with seven straps" [of sandals].

UNASSIGNED FRAGMENTS

68 No by Zeus, there is no way that a good man should be getting drunk and taking hot baths, as you are doing.

69 What a size of head he has—as big as a pumpkin.

70 You [sing.], scratch my head.

71 But run over there.

72 Bind him.

73 Stobaeus 1.8.36

ἐκεῖνός ἐστι στρογγύλος τὴν ὄψιν, ὦ πονηρέ,
ἐντὸς δ᾽ ἔχων περιέρχεται κύκλῳ τὰ πάντ᾽ ἐν αὑτῷ,
ἡμᾶς δὲ τίκτει περιτρέχων τὴν γῆν ἀπαξάπασαν·
ὀνομάζεται δ᾽ Ἐνιαυτός, ὢν δὲ περιφερὴς τελευτὴν
5 οὐδεμίαν οὐδ᾽ ἀρχὴν ‹ἔχει›, κυκλῶν δ᾽ ἀεὶ τὸ σῶμα
οὐ παύσεται δι᾽ ἡμέρας ὁσημέραι τροχάζων.

74 Photius (b, z) α 624

                    ἐγώ σου τήμερον
τύπτων τὸ πρόσωπον ‹νὴ Δί᾽› αἱ-
μορρυγχιᾶν ποιήσω.

75 Athenaeus 45c

ὥστε Μαραθῶνος τὸ λοιπὸν ἐπ᾽ ἀγαθῷ μεμνημένοι
πάντες ἐμβάλλουσιν ἀεὶ μάραθον ἐς τὰς ἁλμάδας.

76 Eustathius *On the Odyssey* p. 1828.56

ὥρα μάττειν ἐπὶ τοῖς ἱεροῖς καὶ τὴν ᾤαν
    περιδεῖσθαι
περὶ τὴν ὀσφύν

77 Athenaeus 29e

† Μενδαίῳ μὲν ἐνουροῦσιν καὶ † θεοὶ αὐτοὶ
στρώμασιν ἐν μαλακοῖς. Μάγνητα δὲ μειλιχόδωρον

312

73 You wretched man, he is spherical in appearance, and having everything inside within himself he runs round in a circle. As he races over the whole earth he gives birth to us.[1] He is called "The Year," and being round he has no beginning nor end, and as he is ever circular in form will never stop going round, all day every day.

  [1] The identity of "us" is unclear, but some subdivision of the year might be suggested: days or months or seasons—see F 6, plus the play titles "Seasons" of Cratinus and Aristophanes.

74 Today I am going to hit you and give you a bloody nose ⟨by Zeus⟩.

75 And so for all time all men honour the name of Marathon by always adding fennel to salted olives.[1]

  [1] The joke turns on the similar words: Marathón (the battle of 490) and márathon (fennel).

76 Now is the time to start kneading ⟨bread⟩ for the sacrifices and to wrap the sheepskin around one's loins.

77 (DIONYSUS) The gods themselves piss Mendaean ⟨wine⟩ in their soft beds. Now as for the sweet gift from

καὶ Θάσιον, τῷ δὴ μήλων ἐπιδέδρομεν ὀδμή,
τοῦτον ἐγὼ κρίνω πολὺ πάντων εἶναι ἄριστον
5 τῶν ἄλλων οἴνων, μετ' ἀμύμονα Χῖον ἄλυπον.
ἔστι δέ τις οἶνος, τὸν δὴ σαπρίαν καλέουσιν,
οὗ καὶ ἀπὸ στόματος στάμνων ὑπανοιγομενάων
ὄζει ἴων, ὄζει δὲ ῥόδων, ὄζει δ' ὑακίνθου
ὀσμὴ θεσπεσία, κατὰ πᾶν δ' ἔχει ὑψερεφὲς δῶ,
10 ἀμβροσία καὶ νέκταρ ὁμοῦ. τοῦτ' ἐστὶ τὸ νέκταρ.
τούτου χρὴ παρέχειν πίνειν ἐν δαιτὶ θαλείῃ
τοῖσιν ἐμοῖσι φίλοις, τοῖς δ' ἐχθροῖς ἐκ Πεπαρήθου.

78 Pollux 7.194

προδόσει πίνειν

Magnesia and the wine from Thasos, from which wafts a
scent of apples, these two I judge to be much the best of all
other wines, after the blameless Chian, destroyer of grief.
But there is a wine, which men call "Full Mellow." When
the jar is opened, from the mouth drifts the heavenly scent
of violets, of roses, and hyacinths, a heavenly bouquet,
which fills that high-roofed hall, ambrosia mixed with nec-
tar. This is nectar, and this is what I must serve for my
friends to drink at a grand banquet—for my enemies
⟨wine⟩ from Preparethus.[1]

[1] The metre is dactylic hexameter, the same as F 63. Critics
have wanted to assign this fragment also to *Basket-Bearers*, but
the metre and the clear engagement with Homer in a number of
places give one pause to consider whether one or both fragments
might belong to the *parōidiai* which Hermippos is said to have
written. However, Dionysus is a familiar comic character, and it is
perhaps safer to retain this fragment for comedy.

78 To drink on one's tab.

*Brief fragments: (F 79) "to be a glutton," (F 80) "what must
not be done," (F 81) "a pair of women following," (F 82)
"first cousin's son," (F 83) "feet of sheepskin," (F 84) "they
sent away," (F 85) "having cheated," (F 86) "Lollo,", (F 87)
"one who speaks insincerely," (F 88) "sour" [of wine], (F
89) "to talk on and on," (F 90) "sales woman," (F 91) "of
moths," (F 92) "to keep a lookout for," (F 93) "towel," (F 94)
"chill."*

ΙΩΝ

Testimonia

i Σ *Peace* 835

Ἴων ὁ Χῖος· διθυράμβων ποιητὴς καὶ τραγῳδίας καὶ μελῶν . . . περιβόητος δὲ ἐγένετο. ἔγραψε δὲ καὶ κωμῳδίας καὶ ἐπιγράμματα καὶ παιᾶνας καὶ ὕμνους καὶ σκολιὰ καὶ ἐγκώμια καὶ ἐλεγεῖα.

ii *Suda* δ 1029

διθυραμβοδιδάσκαλοι, περὶ μετεώρων καὶ περὶ τῶν νεφελῶν λέγουσι πολλὰ καὶ συνθέτους δὲ λέξεις ἐποί-ουν καὶ ἔλεγον ἐνδιαεριαιερινηχέτους· οἷος ἦν Ἴων ὁ Χῖος, ὁ ποιητής . . . περιβόητος δὲ ἐγένετο. ἔγραψε δὲ κωμῳδίας καὶ ἐπιγράμματα.

316

ION OF CHIOS

Ion was a poet of considerable versatility, credited with having written tragedies, dithyrambs, lyric poetry, philosophy, prose anecdotes, and, according to the Suda *and an Aristophanic scholiast (T 1, 2), comedies. This would be unusual, especially in view of Socrates' claim at the end of Plato's* Symposium *(223d) that a comic poet should be able to write tragedy and vice versa, the implication being that such is not the case. At TrGF 19 T 1, Snell suggests that his satyr plays were mistaken for comedies in the later tradition.*

Testimonia

i Ion of Chios: a poet of dithyrambs and tragedies and lyric poems . . . he was celebrated, and also wrote comedies and epigrams and paeans and hymns and drinking songs and praise songs and elegies.

ii "Dithyrambic poets": they write a great deal about things celestial and about clouds, and they would create compound words and say things like "air-haunting-swiftly-soaring"—Ion of Chios was one such poet . . . and was very well-known. He wrote comedies and epigrams.

iii Aristophanes *Peace* 832–37

{ΟΙ.} οὐκ ἦν ἄρ᾽ ἃ λέγουσι, κατὰ τὸν ἀέρα
ὡς ἀστέρες γιγνόμεθ᾽, ὅταν τις ἀποθάνῃ;
{ΤΡ.} μάλιστα. {ΟΙ.} καὶ τίς ἐστιν ἀστὴρ νῦν ἐκεῖ;
{ΤΡ.} Ἴων ὁ Χῖος, ὅσπερ ἐπόησεν πάλαι
ἐνθάδε τὸν Ἀοῖόν ποθ᾽· ὡς δ᾽ ἦλθ᾽, εὐθέως
Ἀοῖον αὐτὸν πάντες ἐκάλουν ἀστέρα.

iii (SERVANT) Is it true then what they say, that when somebody dies, we become stars in the sky?

(TRYGAEUS) Yes indeed.

(SERVANT) Who is a star there now?

(TRYGAEUS) Ion of Chios, who once long ago wrote "The Dawn Star." So when he arrived, immediately everyone started calling him "Dawn Star."

ΛΕΥΚΩΝ

Testimonia

i *Suda* λ 340

Λεύκων· † Ἀγνώς, † γεγονὼς ἐν τοῖς Πελοποννησια-
κοῖς. τῶν δραμάτων αὐτοῦ ἐστι ταῦτα· Ὄνος ἀσκο-
φόρος, Φράτορες.

    ἀγνώς codd., Ἄγνωνος Toup, Ἀγνούσιος Wolf.

ii *IG* ii² 2325.66

    Λεύ[κων

iii Hypothesis I *Wasps*

ἐδιδάχθη ἐπὶ ἄρχοντος Ἀμεινίου διὰ Φιλωνίδου . . . β′
ἦν εἰς Λήναια. καὶ ἐνίκα πρῶτος Φιλωνίδης Προ-
άγωνι. Λεύκων Πρέσβεσι.

LEUCON

One of the lesser figures of Old Comedy, Leucon competed against Aristophanes in 422 (with Envoys) *and 421 (with* Phratry-Members), *finishing third on both occasions. Only* Phratry-Members *is ever cited; it may have been the only one available to the writers of antiquity. Leucon did win a victory at the Dionysia (T 2), but some years later, c. 410.*

Testimonia

i Leucon, son of Hagnon (?) [or "of Hagnous," an Attic deme], lived during the Peloponnesian War. His plays include: *Bag-Bearing Donkey*, *Phratry-Members*.

ii [on the list of victors at the Dionysia, c. 410]

Leu[con

iii [*Wasps*] was produced in the archonship of Ameinias [423/2] through Philonides . . . it was second at the Lenaea. Philonides won first prize with *Preview*, Leucon ⟨was third⟩ with *Envoys*.

iv Hypothesis III *Peace*

ἐνίκησε δὲ τῷ δράματι ὁ ποιητὴς ἐπὶ ἄρχοντος Ἀλκαίου ἐν ἄστει. πρῶτος Εὔπολις Κόλαξι, δεύτερος Ἀριστοφάνης Εἰρήνῃ, τρίτος Λεύκων Φράτερσιν.

ΟΝΟΣ ΑΣΚΟΦΟΡΟΣ

ΠΡΕΣΒΕΙΣ

iv The poet won a prize with his play [*Peace*] at the City Dionysia in the archonship of Alcaeus [422/1]. Eupolis came first with *Spongers*, Aristophanes second with *Peace*, and Leucon third with *Phratry-Members*.

BAG-BEARING DONKEY

Donkeys seem to have been good comic material, witness the parody of Odyssey 9 *in* Wasps *and the opening scene of* Frogs *as well as Archippus'* Donkey's Shadow *and Plautus' later* Asinaria. *The play is known only from the record of the* Suda *(T 1). Boeckh ingeniously recreated the plot of the comedy from an anecdote in Zenobius (1.74) about a man named Leucon—the tradition has also "the Laconian"—whose donkey fell, revealing the contraband he was hiding in* askoi *(leather bags).*

ENVOYS [OR OLD MEN]

The word presbeis *can mean "old men" or "envoys," and we cannot tell which meaning applied (presumably) to the chorus. Athenians usually sent out embassies of three or five or ten members, but increasing the number to twenty-four may have made their excesses more pointed. See* Acharnians *61–128. For the suggestion that a vase depicting Heracles pursuing a slave with two cakes belongs to this play, see V 25.*

ΦΡΑΤΕΡΕΣ

For the title, which suggests a chorus of people supporting the principal character, we may compare Eupolis' Friends, Crates' Neighbours, and Hermippus' Demesmen. The ancient Greek institution of the phratria *does not correspond easily with any modern institution. It was a mixture of an extended kinship group, neighbours, social club, or fraternity. Membership in one's traditional phratry was essential*

Testimonia

i

(a) Hephaestion *Handbook* 32.13

δίμετρον δὲ ἀκατάληκτον τὸ καλούμενον Γλυκώνειον, αὐτοῦ Γλύκωνος εὑρόντος αὐτό.

(b) Choeroboscus *On Hephaestion* p. 240.12

τὸ καλούμενον Γλυκώνειον—κωμικὸς δὲ ἦν ὁ Γλύκων, οὗ καὶ δρᾶμα φέρεται κωμικὸν οἱ Φράτορες.

Fragments

1 Hesychius π 2

ἀτάρ, ὦ Μεγάκλεες, οἶσθά που Παάπιδος
Ὑπέρβολος τἀκπώματα κατεδήδοκεν.

324

LEUCON

PHRATRY-MEMBERS

*for Athenian citizen status, and boys were traditionally in-
troduced to their father's phratry at a young age. Jokes
in comedy mock those who allegedly lacked membership
in a phratry (Birds 764–65, 1669; Frogs 417–18; Eupolis
F 99.24). Comedy regularly made fun of demagogues as
aliens (xenoi)—see Frogs 416–21 of Archedemus, "who has
not yet grown his phratry teeth." Was Hyperbolus (F 1)
made fun of in this way here?*

Testimonia

i

(a) There is also the acatalectic dimeter called the "gly-
conean," from Glycon, who invented it.

(b) "Called the glyconean": Glycon was a comic poet,
whose comedy *Phratry-Members* is preserved.[1]

   [1] "Leucon" seems at some point to have been corrupted into
"Glycon."

Fragments

1 Megakles, do you know about Paapis' drinking cups
which Hyperbolus has devoured?[1]

   [1] Megakles is a common Athenian name, best known in the
family of the Alcmaeonidae, but it could be a suitable name of a
character in comedy. Heyschius adds that Paapis "had sent these
cups as a gift for the Athenians." A Paapis (*PAA* 760730) dedicated
a gold vessel in 406/5 (*IG* ii² 1383).

325

THE POETS OF OLD COMEDY

2 P. Oxy. 1087.52 (= Σ Homer *Iliad* 7.76)

δμ[ῶ]ον ἀλλ᾽ οὐκ οἰκέτην

3 Athenaeus 343c

κωμῳδοῦσι δ᾽ αὐτὸν ἐπὶ ὀψοφαγίᾳ Λεύκων ἐν Φράτερσιν, Ἀριστοφάνης ἐν Εἰρήνῃ, Φερεκράτης ἐν Πετάλῃ. ἐν δὲ τοῖς Ἰχθύσιν Ἄρχιππος τῷ δράματι ὡς ὀψοφάγον δήσας παραδίδωσι τοῖς ἰχθύσιν ἀντιβρωθησόμενον.

4 Photius p. 587.18

Τίβιοι

5 Photius (z) ε 24 (Tsantsanoglou p. 127)

ἐγγεγορτυνωμένος· οἷον εὐτελής. ἐσκώπτοντο γὰρ εἰς εὐτέλειαν οἱ Κρῆτες. κέχρηται δὲ Λεύκων ἐν Φράτορσι τῷ ὀνόματι.

ΑΔΗΛΩΝ ΔΡΑΜΑΤΩΝ

6 Photius (z) α 2491

ἀποζέσαι τὸν θυμόν

7 Photius (z) α 3139

ἀττικουμένη

326

2 ‹Having› a slave but not a house servant.

3 The following make fun of him [Melanthius] for glut-
tony: Leucon in *Phratry-Members*, Aristophanes in *Peace*
[804], Pherecrates in *Petale* [F 148], and in his play *Fishes*
Archippus ties him up as a glutton and hands him over to
the fishes to be eaten in his turn [F 28].

4 The Tibians.

5 "Gortynified": that is "mean," for Cretans were made
fun of for being mean and stingy. Leucon employs the
term in *Phratry-Members*.

UNASSIGNED FRAGMENTS

6 To settle down one's heart.

7 Acting Attic [fem. sing.].

ΛΥΚΙΣ

Testimonia

i *IG* ii² 2325.65

Λύκ[ις

ii Aristophanes *Frogs* 12–15

{ΞΑ.} τί δῆτ᾽ ἔδει με ταῦτα τὰ σκεύη φέρειν,
εἴπερ ποήσω μηδὲν ὧνπερ Φρύνιχος
εἴωθε ποιεῖν καὶ Λύκις κἀμειψίας
σκεύη φέρουσ᾽ ἑκάστοτ᾽ ἐν κωμῳδίᾳ;

iii Σ Aristophanes *Frogs* 14

Λύκις· κωμῳδίας ποιητής. ὡς ψυχρὸς κωμῳδεῖται·
λέγει δὲ αὐτὸν καὶ Λύκον· οὗ οὐδὲν φέρεται.

iv *Suda* λ 808

Λύκις· λέγεται καὶ Λύκος. κωμῳδεῖται δὲ ὡς ψυχρὸς
ποιητής. Ἀριστοφάνης· τί δῆτ᾽ ἔδει με ταῦτα τὰ σκεύη
φέρειν, εἴπερ ποιήσω μηδὲν ὧνπερ Φρύνιχος πεποίηκε
καὶ Λύκις κἀμειψίας. οὗτοι οὖν οἱ τρεῖς κωμικοὶ ὑπό-
ψυχροι.

328

LYCIS

We know very little about this poet, whom Aristophanes thought worth disparaging in Frogs *(T 2). He won a victory in the late 410s (T 1) and was active into the next decade. No play titles or fragments have survived.*

Testimonia

i [on the list of victors at the Dionysia]

Lyc[is]

ii (XANTHIAS) So why did I have to carry this baggage if I'm not going to be making any of the jokes that Phrynichus is used to doing, and Lycis and Ameipsias, carrying baggage in every comedy?

iii Lycis: a comic poet, made fun of for being frigid. He also calls him "Lycus." Nothing of his is preserved.

iv Lycis: he is also called "Lycus." He is made fun of for being a frigid poet. Aristophanes: "Why did I have to carry this baggage, if I'm not going to be making any of the jokes that Phrynichus does, and Lycis and Ameipsias?" These then are three very frigid comic poets.

ΛΥΣΙΠΠΟΣ

Testimonia

i *Suda* λ 863

Λύσιππος· τῶν δραμάτων αὐτοῦ ἐστι Βάκχαι, ὡς
Ἀθήναιος λέγει ἐν γ΄ Δειπνοσοφιστῶν καὶ ἐν τῷ η΄·
καὶ ἕτερα αὐτοῦ δράματα· Θυρσοκόμος.

ii *IG* ii² 2325.56

Λύ[σιππος

LYSIPPUS

*This poet seems to have had a long career with not all that many productions, and only one play (*Bacchae*) that was available to the ancient scholars (see T 3). If his name is correctly restored on the victors' list at the Dionysia (T 2), then he won his first victory around 440. On the Roman inscription (T 3), he appears with Callias and Aristomenes, whose careers began also around this time. But* Mockeries *was produced in the archonship of a man whose name ended in –pus, the only possibility being Glaucippus (410/ 09). The* Suda *knows of two titles, one through Athenaeus, and with* Mockeries *we now know of three. The details of Lysippus' career and other plays, clearly more than those we have, were quickly lost.*

Testimonia

i Lysippus: his plays include *Bacchae*, as Athenaeus records in Book 3 of his *Learned Banqueters* [124d] and also in Book 8 [344e]. There are other plays by him: *Thyrsus-Keeper*.

ii [from the list of victors at the Dionysia—around 440]

Ly[sippus.

iii *IG Urb.Rom.* 216.7–9

———Λ]ύσιππος ἐνίκα μὲν [———
———ἐπὶ Γλαυκίπ]που Καταχήναις
———Βάκχ]αις· αὗται μόναι σῶ[αι

Fragments

BAKXAI

1 Athenaeus 124cd

{Α.} Ἕρμων. {ΕΡΜ.} τί ἔστι; {Α.} πῶς ἔχομεν;
   {ΕΡΜ.} τί δ᾽ ἄλλο γ᾽ ἢ
ὁ πατὴρ ἄνωθεν ἐς τὸ φρέαρ, ἐμοὶ δοκεῖν,
ὥσπερ τὸν οἶνον τοῦ θέρους καθεῖκέ με.

2 Pollux 7.89

βλαύτῃ, κοθόρνῳ, Θετταλίδι

3 Pollux 10.50

ἀλλὰ τρίμιτός ἐστι πλεκτός.

4 Pollux 7.77

οὐδ᾽ ἀνακνάψας καὶ θειώσας τὰς ἀλλοτρίας ἐπινοίας

---

1 The metre is anapaestic tetrameter catalectic, found often in the parabases of Aristophanes. This fragment may come from a parabasis where Lysippus argues that he will not be revamping

iii . . . L]ysippus won . . .
 . . . in the archonship of Glaucip]us with *Mockeries*
 . . . with *Bacch*]*ae*—this is the only one extant.

Fragments

BACCHAE

A common title in tragedy, Bacchae *is the title also of a comedy by Diocles. There is no way of knowing whether the comedy covered the same ground as Euripides' master-piece. The fragments mention shoes (F 2–3), including the* cothurnus *familiar as part of Dionysus' attire, but all that might imply is that Dionysus might have been a character in the comedy, along with a chorus of his female followers.*

1 (A) Hermon.   (HERMON) What is it?   (A) How are we doing?   (HERMON) Nothing much, except that father's lowered me down into the well, I think, like wine in summer.

2 With a slipper, a high boot, a Thessalian shoe.

3 But it is plaited with triple threads. [of a shoe]

4 Not revamping or retouching someone else's bright ideas.[1]

and retouching the comic ideas of others. "Revamping" is brushing clothes to raise the nap, while "retouching" is cleaning used clothing by fumigating with sulphur. Aristophanes twice uses the metaphor of clothing in connection with the creation of comedy (*Clouds* 554, F 58).

5 Pollux 10.154

αὐτοῖς αὐλοῖς ὁρμᾷ καὶ γλωττοκομείῳ.

6

(a) Athenaeus 344e

καὶ Λάμπωνα δὲ τὸν μάντιν ἐπὶ τοῖς ὁμοίοις κωμῳ-
δοῦσι Καλλίας Πεδήταις καὶ Λύσιππος Βάκχαις.

(b) Hesychius α 461

Λύσιππος ἐν Βάκχαις τὸν αὐτὸν ἀγύρτην κωμῳδεῖ.

7 P. Oxy. 1611

"[...]ον νῦν γ᾽ ὁρᾷ[ς] ἡμᾶς δύ᾽ ὄντας, τέτταρ[α]ς καὶ
τοὺς κριτάς." δηλῶν οὕτως τέτταρας ὄντας, Λύσιπ-
π[ο]ς δ᾽ ἐν Βάκχαις ε´, ὁμοίως δὲ καὶ Κρατῖνος ἐν
Πλούτοις λέγει.

ΘΥΡΣΟΚΟΜΟΣ

ΚΑΤΑΧΗΝΑΙ

5 He/she rushes off with *auloi* and reed case.

6

(a) Callias in his *Men-in-Chains* [F 20] and Lysippus in *Bacchae* make fun of Lampon for similar reasons [as a glutton].

(b) Lysippus in *Bacchae* makes fun of the same person as a mendicant prophet.

7 "And now you see us two in number, but the judges four" [K.-A. VIII 1033], making it clear that there are four, but Lysippus in *Bacchae* says ‹there were› five, and Cratinus in *Wealth-Gods* [F 177] says the same.

THYRSUS-KEEPER

This title is known only from the entry in the Suda *(T 1). Is it an alternative title for* Bacchae?

MOCKERIES

The word katachēnē *is used twice in Aristophanes (*Wasps 575, Ecclesiazusae *631) in the sense of a "snub" or a "sneer" at the rich and powerful. Kaibel suggested on the basis of Hesychius κ 1515 that these might be apotropaic representations (like gargoyles?) on the outside of a building.*

ΑΔΗΛΩΝ ΔΡΑΜΑΤΩΝ

8 Heraclides *On the Greek City* 1.5

εἰ μὴ τεθέασαι τὰς Ἀθήνας, στέλεχος εἶ,
εἰ δὲ τεθέασαι μὴ τεθήρευσαι δ', ὄνος,
εἰ δ' εὐαρεστῶν ἀποτρέχεις, κανθήλιος.

9 Hesychius β 887

κύων δέ τις
ἐβόα δεδεμένος <– ∪> ὥσπερ Βούδιος.

UNASSIGNED FRAGMENTS

8 If you have not seen Athens, you're an idiot. If you have seen her and not been captivated, you're a donkey. If you enjoy her charms and then run off, you're a jackass.

9 A tied-up dog was howling just like Boudius.

Brief fragment: (F 10) "rush-mat."

ΜΑΓΝΗΣ

For the early comic poets, the testimonia outweigh the actual remains of both titles and fragments. This is especially unfortunate as Magnes was the first great name in the history of Greek comedy. Aristophanes (T 8) recalls that Magnes "set up the most trophies of victory," a claim which the eleven victories recorded on the victors' list (T 5) and by the anonymous writer on comedy (T 3) supports. But the ancients seem to have had very little of his work to study or to cite. Only eight fragments remain, two each from Lydians and the comedies about Dionysus, and one apiece from Herb-Woman and Pytakides. Also worrying are the statements by Athenaeus (T 4) about "the works attributed to Magnes" (ad F 1–2, from Dionysus). The scholiast to Knights (T 9) lists a number of titles, which are clearly his deductions from what Aristophanes has said in the text; only Lydians is known independently. Two sources tell us that Lydians was revised—by Magnes or by a later adaptor?

At Knights 518–25 (T 8) Aristophanes is ostensibly complimenting Magnes' comedy, but to both bring him down later and criticise the fickle tastes of the Athenian audience. From what he says we get the picture of a creator of plays with animal choruses, with an emphasis on the

MAGNES

visual and the aural ("flapping wings," "making all sorts of sounds"), but whose comedy in the last part of his career was no match for the vigorous and satirical comedy of Cratinus and others. In this regard, the verb skōptein at Knights 525, in which quality Magnes was lacking, usually means "personal jokes." Is it here that Magnes was seen as especially falling short, especially given the personal and topical comedy that Cratinus and Hermippus were creating in the 430s?

Magnes won a victory at the Dionysia of 472 (T 6), perhaps also in 471 (T 7). Since Aristophanes expects his spectators to remember Magnes' failure as an older poet, he must have been active into the 430s. If his victory in 472 is an early success, then we may place his career from the late 470s to the early 430s; but if he had already won several victories, we may wish to move him back to the late 480s. It has been thought that the two victories recorded by the Suda (T 1) could have been at the Lenaea, but the list of victors at that festival begins with Xenophilus (c. 440), with no room for Magnes.

Recent bibliography: E. Spyropoulos, Aristophane (Thessalonica 1988) 177–216.

THE POETS OF OLD COMEDY

Testimonia

i *Suda* μ 20

Μάγνης, Ἰκαρίου πόλεως Ἀττικῆς ἢ Ἀθηναῖος, κωμικός. ἐπιβάλλει δ᾽ Ἐπιχάρμῳ νέος πρεσβύτῃ. ἐδίδαξε κωμῳδίας θ΄, νίκας δὲ εἷλε β΄. οὗτος ἀρχαίας κωμῳδίας ποιητής.

ii Aristotle *Poetics* 1448a33

Ἐπίχαρμος ὁ ποιητὴς πολλῷ πρότερος ὢν Χιωνίδου καὶ Μάγνητος.

iii Anonymous *On Comedy* (Koster III.9–13, 18–19)

τούτων δέ εἰσιν ἀξιολογώτατοι Ἐπίχαρμος, Μάγνης, Κρατῖνος, Κράτης, Φερεκράτης, Φρύνιχος, Εὔπολις, Ἀριστοφάνης
Μάγνης δὲ Ἀθηναῖος ἀγωνισάμενος Ἀθήνησι νίκας ἔσχεν ια΄. τῶν δὲ δραμάτων αὐτοῦ οὐδὲν σῴζεται· τὰ δὲ ἐπιφερόμενά ἐστιν ἐννέα.

iv

(a) Athenaeus 367f

ὁ τὰ εἰς Μάγνητα ἀναφερόμενα ποιήσας.

MAGNES

Testimonia

i Magnes: from the Attic town of Icaria, or from Athens; comic poet. In his youth he overlapped with Epicharmus in his old age. He produced nine comedies, and won two victories. He was a poet of Old Comedy.

ii The poet Epicharmus, who was much earlier than Chionides and Magnes.

iii The most noteworthy poets [of Old Comedy] are Epicharmus, Magnes, Cratinus, Crates, Pherecrates, Phrynichus, Eupolis, and Aristophanes.

Magnes the Athenian competed at Athens and won eleven victories. None of his plays has survived, but there are nine attributed to him.

iv

(a) The person who wrote the works attributed to Magnes.

THE POETS OF OLD COMEDY

(b) Athenaeus 646e

Μάγνης ⟨ἢ⟩ ὁ ποιήσας τὰς εἰς αὐτὸν ἀναφερομένας
κωμῳδίας.

v *IG* ii2 2325.44

Μάγνη]ς ΔΙ

vi *IG* ii2 2318.7

Ξ]ενοκλείδης ἐχορήγε(ι)
Μάγνης ἐδίδασκεν

vii *IG* ii2 2318.17

[κωμῳδῶν]
ἐχ]ορήγει
[Μάγνης ἐδίδ]ασκεν

viii *Knights* 518–25

ὑμᾶς τε πάλαι διαγιγνώσκων ἐπετείους τὴν φύσιν
  ὄντας
καὶ τοὺς προτέρους τῶν ποιητῶν ἅμα τῷ γήρᾳ
  προδιδόντας·
τοῦτο μὲν εἰδὼς ἄπαθε Μάγνης ἅμα ταῖς πολιαῖς
  κατιούσαις,
ὃς πλεῖστα χορῶν τῶν ἀντιπάλων νίκης ἔστησε
  τροπαῖα·

(b) Magnes mentions this or the man who wrote the comedies attributed to him.

v [from the early part of the list of victors at the Dionysia]

Magne]s 11

vi [the result of the comic competition at the Dionysia of 472]

X]enoclides was the *chorēgus*/Magnes the producer.

vii [the result of the comic competition at the Dionysia of 471]

[of the comic poets]/[. . .] was the *chorēgus*/[Magnes] the producer.[1]

[1] We need a short name (of about six letters) at the beginning of the line for the poet.

viii Because he [Aristophanes] recognised long ago how changeable your nature is, how you betray the poets of the past when they reach old age, and because he was well aware of what happened to Magnes, when he grew old and grey. Magnes had put up the most victory trophies over his

πάσας δ' ὑμῖν φωνὰς ἱεὶς καὶ ψάλλων καὶ
  πτερυγίζων
καὶ λυδίζων καὶ ψηνίζων καὶ βαπτόμενος
  βατραχειοῖς
οὐκ ἐξήρκεσεν, ἀλλὰ τελευτῶν ἐπὶ γήρως, οὐ γὰρ
  ἐφ' ἥβης,
ἐξεβλήθη πρεσβύτης ὤν, ὅτι τοῦ σκώπτειν
  ἀπελείφθη·

ix Σ Knights 522a

ψάλλων· τοὺς Βαρβιτιστὰς ἂν λέγοι· δρᾶμα δέ ἐστι
τοῦ Μάγνητος. ἡ δὲ βάρβιτος εἶδος ὀργάνου μου-
σικοῦ. πτερυγίζων δὲ ὅτι καὶ Ὄρνιθας ἐποίησε
δρᾶμα· ἔγραψε δὲ καὶ Λύδους καὶ Ψῆνας καὶ Βατρά-
χους. ἔστι δὲ χρώματος εἶδος τὸ βατράχειον· ἀπὸ
τούτου καὶ βατραχὶς ἱμάτιον. ἐχρίοντο δὲ τῷ βατρα-
χείῳ τὰ πρόσωπα, πρὶν ἐπινοηθῆναι τὰ προσωπεῖα.
τὸ ψηνίζων δὲ εἶπεν ὡς πρὸς τοὺς Ψῆνας ἀναφέρων.

x Diomedes *Art of Grammar* (Koster XXIV.46–47)

poetae primi comici fuerunt Susarion, Mullus et Magnes.
hi veteris disciplinae iocularia quaedam minus scite ac
venuste pronuntiabant.

xi *The Glossary of Ansileubus* (Koster XXVII.8–13)

sed prior ac vetus comoedia ridicularis extitit; postea civi-
les vel privates adgressa materias in dictis atque gestu uni-

rivals, making every sort of sound for you, strumming the lyre, flapping his wings, playing the Lydian, buzzing like a fly, dyed green like a frog, but it wasn't enough, and in the end, in his old age, never when he was young, he was rejected because he failed in making jokes.

ix "Strumming the lyre": he would be referring to *Lyre-Players*; this is a play by Magnes. The *barbitos* is a type of musical instrument. "Flapping his wings," because he wrote a play called *Birds*. He also wrote *Lydians*, *Fig-Wasps*, and *Frogs*. There is a type of colour called "frog-green," and from this a garment called "froggy." They would smear their faces with frog-green before masks were invented. He says "buzz like a fly" alluding to the *Fig-Wasps*.

x The first comic poets were Susarion, Myllus, and Magnes. They were of the old style and delivered their jokes rather less skilfully and elegantly.

xi But Old Comedy first began as something silly, but later moved on to public and private themes, and seizing upon the shortcomings of everybody in word and deed

versorum delicta corripiens in scaenam proferebat, nec vetabatur poetae pessimum quemque describere vel cuiuslibet peccata moresque reprehendere. auctor eius Susarion traditur; sed in fabulas primi eam contulerunt Magnes †† ita, ut non excederent in singulis versus trecenos.

xii *PAmherst* 13, col. I 3

εἰς Μάγνητα

Fragments

ΒΑΡΒΙΤΙΣΤΑΙ

ΒΑΤΡΑΧΟΙ

would bring them on stage as his subjects. A poet was not forbidden to portray anyone in a very bad light or to find fault with the misdeeds or character of anybody he wanted. The founder of this is said to be Susarion, but Magnes ⟨and . . . ⟩ were the first ⟨to put it⟩ into dramatic form, such that they did not exceed three hundred lines at a time.

xii [a marginal note to a papyrus of Aristophanes = F 593.3]

at Magnes.

Fragments

LYRE-PLAYERS

A barbitos *was a type of lyre, said to have been invented by Terpander (Athenaeus 635d). The title is the scholiast's explanation of "strumming the lyre," and while he may be guessing at some of these titles, the* barbitos *is not an obvious inference from "strumming"* (psallein).

FROGS

Again the title "Frogs" is the scholiast's inference based on Aristophanes' "dyed like a frog." Callias and Aristophanes both wrote plays of this title, and even if Magnes' play was not called "Frogs," we may assume that it had a chorus of (visible) frogs.

ΔΙΟΝΥΣΟΣ

1 Athenaeus 367f

καὶ ταῦτα μέν μοι τῶν κακῶν παροψίδες.

2 Athenaeus 646e

ταγηνίας ἤδη τεθέασαι χλιαροὺς
σίζοντας, ὅταν αὐτοῖσιν ἐπιχέῃς μέλι;

ΛΥΔΟΙ

3 Athenaeus 690c

λούσαντα χρὴ καὶ βακκάριδι κεχριμένον.

4 Pollux 7.188

ὀνειροκρίταισιν, ἀναλύταις

348

DIONYSUS

For both the fragments cited, Athenaeus employs the peri-phrasis "the person who wrote the plays attributed to Magnes" and complicates matters further by referring to a "first Dionysus" (F 1) and a "second Dionysus" (F 2). Dio-nysus is a common character in Old Comedy, but the two fragments give no hint of the plotline, unless Dionysus is the speaker of F 1, complaining of some misfortunes.

1 And these are just the side dishes to my problems.

2 Have you [sing.] ever seen warm pancakes sizzle, when you pour honey over them?

LYDIANS

Foreigners were always good material for both tragedy and comedy. We have titles such as Thracian Women *(Cra-tinus),* Egyptian *(Callias),* Persians *(Pherecrates, as well as Aeschylus' tragedy, whose ending with the wailing Per-sians was enjoyed by Dionysus—Frogs 1028–29),* Babylo-nians *(Aristophanes). The depiction of the Lydians may have been partly aural (one of the "every sort of sound") and partly in dance form.*

3 You must bathe and be anointed with asarabaca.

4 Dream interpreters, breakers of spells.

ΟΡΝΙΘΕΣ

ΠΟΑΣΤΡΙΑ

5 Σ Plato *Theaetetus* 209b

οὐκ ἔστιν οὐδείς, οὐδ᾽ ὁ Μυσῶν ἔσχατος.

ΠΥΤΑΚΙΔΗΣ [ΤΙΤΑΚΙΔΗΣ?]

6 Photius p. 305.9, *Suda* ν 603

εἰπέ μοι· νυνδὴ μὲν ὤμνυς μὴ γεγονέναι, νῦν δὲ
φῄς;

MAGNES

BIRDS

*The scholiast so explains "flapping wings" in Aristophanes'
description of Magnes' comedy, perhaps influenced by
Aristophanes' more famous title.*

LADY GRASS-CUTTER

Ancient writers make it clear that the term poastria *is used
of a woman cutting grass or herbs or generally working in
the fields. Archippus (F 46) conjoins "grass cutters" with
donkey drivers and garden diggers as examples of manual
labourers. Phrynichus wrote a comedy with the plural ti-
tle "Lady Grass-Cutters." We may compare such other
comic titles as* Bread-Women *(Hermippus),* Wool-Carders
(Platon), and Washer-Woman *(Philyllius).*

5 There is nobody, not even the "last of the Mysians."

PYTACIDES OR THE MAN
FROM TITACIDAE (?)

The manuscripts of Photius and the Suda, *who cite F 6,
read either* Pytacides *or* Pitacisci, *neither of which has any
apparent meaning. Earlier editions of the fragments ac-
cepted Bernhardy's correction to* Titacides, *"the man from
Titacidae," a town near Aphidna in Attica, a deme in the
Roman period but not in the fifth century BC.*

6 So tell me, just now you swore that this hadn't hap-
pened, and now you say it did?

THE POETS OF OLD COMEDY

ΨΗΝΕΣ

MAGNES

FIG-FLIES

The title given by the Aristophanic scholiast to explain "buzzing like a fig fly."

UNASSIGNED FRAGMENTS

Brief fragments: (F 7) "little jar," (F 8) "with a dull edge."

ΜΕΤΑΓΕΝΗΣ

We would like to have more than the twenty fragments and
four play titles by Metagenes. His comedy appears to be
very much in the Aristophanic spirit, with plural titles that
suggest an imaginative use of the chorus, jokes against
some of the familiar targets of Old Comedy (F 10, 12, 14), a
parabatic address to the spectators with the metaphor of
comedy as a banquet (F 15), and some instances of engage-
ment with Homer (F 19). He belongs to the last part of the
fifth century. If the betrayal of Naupactus (T 10) refers to

Testimonia

i *Suda* μ 688

Μεταγένης, Ἀθηναῖος, † δύλου παῖς, κωμικός. τῶν δὲ
αὐτοῦ δραμάτων ἐστὶ ταῦτα· Αὖραι <ἢ> Μαμμάκυθος,
Θουριοπέρσαι, Φιλοθύτης, Ὅμηρος ἢ Ἀσκηταί.

ii *IG* ii² 2325.128

Με[ταγέν]ης ΙΙ

354

METAGENES

the capture of that city by the Spartans in the last years of the fifth century (Pausanias 4.26.2), then Homer *(or* Hostage*) belongs to 400 or later. The scandal over Callias' son by Chrysilla (F 14) is also an event of the 400s. On the Lenaean victors' list (T 2), he appears between Poliochus and Theopompus, who belong to the very end of the century.*

Recent bibliography: M. Pellegrino, *in* Tessere *291–339.*

Testimonia

i Metagenes: of Athens, son of . . .]dylus, a comic poet. His plays are: *Breezes* <*or*> *Blockhead, Thurio-Persians, Sacrifice-Lover, Homer* (or *Hostage*) or *Men-in-Training.*

ii [from the list of victors at the Lenaea]
Me[tagen]es 2

ΑΥΡΑΙ

Fragments

1 Σ Aristophanes *Birds* 872

   {A.} τίς ἡ Κολαινὶς Ἄρτεμις;
{B.} ἱερεὺς γὰρ ὢν τετύχηκα τῆς Κολαινίδος.

2 Athenaeus 385b

ἀλλ᾽, ὦγαθέ, δειπνῶμεν ‹× –›, κἄπειτά με πάντ᾽
  ἐπερωτᾶν,
ὅ τι ἂν βούλῃ· νῦν γὰρ πεινῶν δεινῶς πώς εἰμ᾽
  ἐπιλήσμων.

3 Athenaeus 355a

ὥσπερ ἐπειδὰν δειπνῶμέν που, τότε πλεῖστα
  λαλοῦμεν ἅπαντες.

4 Athenaeus 571b

    ὑμῖν ὀρχηστρίδας εἶπον ἑταίρας
ὡραίας πρότερον, νῦν δ᾽ αὖθ᾽ ὑμῖν ἀγορεύω
ἄρτι χνοαζούσας αὐλητρίδας, αἵ τε τάχιστα
ἀνδρῶν φορτηγῶν ὑπὸ γούνατα μισθοῦ ἔλυσαν.

METAGENES

BREEZES

In the Suda *(T 1)* Breezes *and* Blockhead *seem to be listed as separate plays. Of the five fragments, three are cited just from Metagenes'* Breezes *(F 1, 2, 5). F 4, cited by Athenaeus (571b), is attributed to Metagenes'* Breezes *or Aristagoras'* Blockhead, *while F 3, again from Athenaeus (355a), is described as "an iamb from* Blockhead *or* Breezes *by Metagenes". This in fact turns out to be an anapaestic tetrameter catalectic. Dalechamp's supplement "of Aristagoras" would bring the citation into line with Athenaeus' 571b and lessen the possibility of a* Blockhead *by Metagenes. For a chorus of natural phenomena we may compare* Clouds *and* Seasons *by Aristophanes and Cratinus, also Hermippus F 73.*

Fragments

1 (A) Who is Artemis Colaenis?
(B) Well, I happen to be the priest of Colaenis.

2 My dear fellow, let us go to dinner . . . and then ask me anything you wish, because being terribly hungry at the moment I rather forget things.

3 It's just like when we go to dinner, we all start talking the most.

4 I told you [pl.] earlier about the lovely dancing prostitutes, now I am informing you of the *aulos* girls, with the early down of womanhood, who for a fee very quickly sap the strength of stevedores.

357

ΘΟΥΡΙΟΠΕΡΣΑΙ

Testimonium

i Athenaeus 269f

οἶδα δὲ ὅτι καὶ οἱ Θουριοπέρσαι καὶ τὸ τοῦ Νικο-
φῶντος δρᾶμα ἀδίδακτά ἐστι.

Brief fragment: (F 5) "birdcage."

THURIO-PERSIANS

*F 6 is one of the many expressions of Old Comedy of the utopia where food appears "on its own" (*automaton—*ll. 2, 9), in this case in the land of Thurii in Italy. This city was built on the site of Sybaris, whose name was a byword in antiquity for luxury and the good life. Persia enjoyed a similar reputation—cf. the opening scene of* Acharnians—*and Metagenes seems to have combined both ethnic entities in a comedy about the good life in a distant land. We cannot determine whether Persia was meant to suggest a barbarian decadence or a luxury to be envied. That the speaker of F 6 is telling another about the delights of that land suggests that the setting of that scene is not Thurii. F 7 refers to "these men" (the chorus?) dancing in barbarian fashion." Thurii was Athens' sole colonial foundation (in the late 440s); in 412 she abandoned her alliance with Athens to side with the Spartans in the War. For this reason some have dated the play to around 411. Athenaeus (T 1) records that this play was never produced. Was the comedy produced in the West and/or was it just missing from the Athenian records?*

*Recent bibliography: Pellegrino (*Utopie*) 133–40; Revermann 171–72.*

Testimonium

i I know that both *Thurio-Persians* by Metagenes and the play by Nicophon [*Sirens*] were not performed.

Fragments

6 Athenaeus 269f

ὁ μὲν ποταμὸς ὁ Κρᾶθις ἡμῖν καταφέρει
μάζας μεγίστας αὐτόματος μεμαγμένας,
ὁ δ᾽ ἕτερος ὠθεῖ κῦμα ναστῶν καὶ κρεῶν
ἑφθῶν τε βατίδων εἰλυομένων αὐτόσε.
5 τὰ δὲ μικρὰ ταυτὶ ποτάμι᾽ ἐνμεντευθενὶ
ῥεῖ τευθίσιν ὀπταῖς καὶ φάγροις καὶ καράβοις,
ἐντευθενὶ δ᾽ ἀλλᾶσι καὶ περικόμμασι,
τῃδὶ δ᾽ ἀφύαισι, τῇδε δ᾽ αὖ ταγηνίαις.
τεμάχη δ᾽ ἄνωθεν αὐτόματα πεπνιγμένα
10 εἰς τὸ στόμ᾽ ᾄττει, τὰ δὲ παρ᾽ αὐτὼ τὼ πόδε,
ἄμυλοι δὲ περινάουσιν ἡμῖν ἐν κύκλῳ.

7 Photius p. 591.9

τίς τρόπος ἵππων; ὡς δ᾽ ὀρχοῦνται τὸν βαρβαρικὸν
τρόπον οὗτοι.

ΟΜΗΡΟΣ Η ΑΣΚΗΤΑΙ
Η ΣΟΦΙΣΤΑΙ

Fragments

6 The River Crathis carries huge barley loaves, self-kneaded, downstream for us, and the other river [Sybaris] drives a wave of cakes and meats and boiled skates still wriggling along there. The little streams on the far side here teem with roasted squid and sea bream and crawfish, and on this side with sausages and minced meat, over here with minnows, over there with pancakes. Fish slices that barbecue themselves fly from above right into the mouth, others ⟨appear⟩ at our feet, while wheat rolls drift round about us in a circle.

7 What's all this horsing around? These men are dancing in barbarian fashion.

Brief fragments: (F 8) "platter," (F 9) "to beat up" and "I was beaten up."

HOMER (HOSTAGE?) OR MEN-IN-TRAINING OR SOPHISTS

The exact title of this comedy is in doubt. All three citations of the play agree that one title was Homer, *whose name in Greek also means* Hostage; *as F 19 parodies a line from Homer, it has been attributed to this play and taken to indicate that the title was* Homer. *F 10, 12 are cited from* Homer, *F 11 from* Homer *or* Sophists, *while the* Suda *(T 1) knows of a comedy* Homer *or* Men-in-Training. *The matter is complicated somewhat by the fact that Platon wrote a* Sophists *and Aristomenes a* Dionysus in Training. *The reference to the fall of Naupactus c. 400 (Diodorus 14.34.2) argues for a date in the early 390s.*

THE POETS OF OLD COMEDY

Fragments

10 Σ (Arethas) Plato *Apology* 23e

καὶ Λύκων ἐνταῦθά που
<   > προδοὺς Ναύπακτον ἀργύριον λαβὼν
ἀγορᾶς ἄγαλμα ξενικὸν ἐμπορεύεται.

11 Photius ε 662

ἑλοῦσι τοὺς πολέμους

πολέμους cod., πολεμίους Snell.

12 Σ Aristophanes *Birds* 1297

διαβάλλεται δὲ εἴς τε πονηρίαν, ὡς Πλάτων ἐν Νίκαις,
καὶ κλοπῆς δημοσίων, ὡς Μεταγένης ἐν Ὁμήρῳ, καὶ
συκοφαντίᾳ.

ΦΙΛΟΘΥΤΗΣ

Fragments

10 And Lycon, who took a bribe and betrayed Naupactus, the darling of the marketplace, does foreign business there.[1]

> [1] This Lycon is possibly the accuser of Socrates in 399 (Plato *Apology* 23e), but is not the father of Autolycus. *PAA* 611820 needs to be broken down into two or three people.

11 They will win the conflicts.[1]

> [1] Or with Snell's reading: "they will capture the enemy."

12 He [Meidias] is accused of wicked behaviour, so Platon in *Victories* [F 85], and for theft of public funds, so Metagenes in *Homer*, and for being an informer.

SACRIFICE-LOVER

The word philothytēs *means "one who is fond of sacrifices" and is proposed at* Wasps *82 as one of the possible addictions of Philokleon. This may afford a hint of how a generally complimentary term (see Antiphon 2.2.12) might be exploited in comedy. In F 14, "Sacas of Mysia" alludes to the tragic poet Acestor, made fun of from the late 430s to at least* Birds, *while "that bastard of Callias" refers to a scandal of the last decade of the century (Andocides 1.126–29). A date of c. 400 seems appropriate.*

Fragments

13 Pollux 10.115

δίμυξον ἢ τρίμυξον ὡς ἐγὼ δοκῶ.

14 Σ Aristophanes *Wasps* 1221

ὦ πολῖται, δεινὰ πάσχω. τίς πολίτης δ᾽ ἔστὶ
πλὴν ἄρ᾽ εἰ Σάκας ὁ Μυσὸς καὶ τὸ Καλλίου νόθον;

15 Athenaeus 459b

   κατ᾽ ἐπεισόδιον μεταβάλλω τὸν λόγον, ὡς ἂν
καιναῖσι παροψίσι καὶ πολλαῖς εὐωχήσω τὸ
θέατρον.

ΑΔΗΛΩΝ ΔΡΑΜΑΤΩΝ

17 Photius (z) α 3277

κραταιὸν αὐχένισμα τοὐμὸν

18 Erotianus *Collection of Hippocratic Terms* π 62

                                    ῥαφανῖδος,
ἀμύλου, λεκίθων, καρύων, ζωμοῦ, πολφῶν, οἴνου,
κολοκύντης.

364

Fragments

13 In my opinion, a lamp with two or three wicks.

14 Citizens, I am in a terrible situation. What citizen is there now except Sacas of Mysia and that bastard of Callias.[1]

> [1] For Acestor, nicknamed "Sacas," see *PAA* 116685 and *TrGF* I 25. For Callias' illegitimate son, see J. K. Davies, *Athenian Propertied Families* (Oxford 1971) 264–65.

15 I am changing the plot scene by scene, so that I may feast the audience with many original side dishes.[1]

> [1] The metre, anapaestic tetrameter, is frequently used by Aristophanes in his parabatic addresses to the spectators. If F 15 comes from a parabasis, Metagenes would be promising the audience a culinary delight of original "dishes." For the image of drama as a food, see Aeschylus "serving slices from the banquet of Homer" (Athenaeus 347e), the light breakfast served by Crates (*Knights* 538–39), and Aristophanes giving the spectators the "first taste" of his new play (*Clouds* 523).

Brief fragment: (F 16) "to eat unobserved."

UNASSIGNED FRAGMENTS

17 My mighty throat grip.

18 Of radish, wheat roll, porridge, nuts, soup, pasta, wine, squash.

19 Athenaeus 270e

εἷς οἰωνὸς ἄριστος ἀμύνεσθαι περὶ δείπνου.

19 There is only one excellent omen: to fight for one's . . . dinner.[1]

[1] A parody of *Iliad* 12.243: "There is only one excellent omen: to fight for one's country."

Brief fragment: (F 20) "slave woman."

ΜΥΛΛΟΣ

Testimonia

i *Suda* ε 2766

Ἐπίχαρμος . . . ἦν δὲ πρὸ τῶν Περσικῶν ἔτη ἕξ, διδάσκων ἐν Συρακούσαις· ἐν δὲ Ἀθήναις Εὐέτης καὶ Εὐξενίδης καὶ Μύλλος ἐπεδείκνυντο.

ii Diomedes *Art of Grammar* (Koster XXIV.46–48)

poetae primi comici fuerunt Susarion, Mullus et Magnes. hi veteris disciplinae iocularia quaedam minus scite ac venuste pronuntiabant.

iii

(a) Hesychius μ 1858

μύλλον· καμπύλον, σκολιόν, κυλλόν, στρεβλόν . . . ἔστι δὲ καὶ κωμῳδιῶν ποιητὴς οὕτως καλούμενος

MYLLUS

A shadowy figure from the very beginning of Old Comedy, Myllus has no titles or fragments extant.

Testimonia

i Epicharmus: he was active six years before the Persian Wars [486/5] producing plays in Syracuse. At Athens Euetes and Euxenides and Myllus were putting on plays.

ii The first comic poets were Susarion, Myllus, and Magnes. They were of the old style and delivered their jokes rather less skilfully and elegantly.

iii

(a) *"Myllon"*: bent, crooked, hooked, twisted . . . and there is a comic poet so called.

THE POETS OF OLD COMEDY

(b) Zenobius *Common Proverbs* 5.14

Μύλλος πάντα ἀκούων· αὕτη τέτακται ἐπὶ τῶν κωφό-
τητα προσποιουμένων καὶ πάντα ἀκουόντων. μέμνη-
ται αὐτῆς Κρατῖνος ἐν Κλεοβουλίναις. ἐστι δὲ καὶ
κωμῳδιῶν ποιητὴς ὁ Μύλλος.

iv

(a) Hesychius λ 1405

Λύλιος ἢ Μύλλος· οὗτος ἐπὶ μωρίᾳ ἐκωμῳδεῖτο.

(b) Photius p. 236.10

Λυλλος· ποιητὴς ἐπὶ μωρίᾳ κωμῳδούμενος.

v

(a) Arcadius p. 53.14 Barker

Μύλλος ποιητὴς κωμικός.

(b) Eustathius *On the Odyssey* p. 1885.21

Μύλλος, ὅπερ ἐστὶ κύριον ὑποκριτοῦ τοῦ παλαιοῦ, ὃς
μιλτωτοῖς, φασί, προσωπείοις ἐχρήσατο.

(b) "Myllus hears all": this is said of those who feign deafness and hear everything. Cratinus refers to it in *Cleoboulinas* [F 96]. There is also Myllus, the comic poet.

iv

(a) Lylius or Myllus: this man was made fun of for stupidity.

(b) Lyllus: a poet made fun of for stupidity.

v

(a) Myllus, a comic poet.

(b) Myllus, which is the proper name of the old actor, who, they say, used masks painted with red ochre [*miltos*].

ΜΥΡΤΙΛΟΣ

Testimonia

i *Suda* μ 1460

Μυρτίλος, Ἀθηναῖος, κωμικός, υἱὸς μὲν Λύσιδος, ἀδελφὸς δὲ τοῦ κωμικοῦ Ἑρμίππου. δράματα αὐτοῦ Τιτανόπανες, Ἔρωτες.

ii Athenaeus 566e

καὶ ὁ Κύνουλκος "ταυτὶ καὶ τολμᾷς σὺ λέγειν, οὐ ῥοδοδάκτυλος οὖσα;' κατὰ τὸν Κρατῖνον, ἀλλὰ βολίτινον ἔχων θάτερον σκέλος, ἐκείνου τοῦ ὁμωνύμου σοι ποιητοῦ τὴν κνήμην φορῶν, ὃς ἐν τοῖς καπηλείοις καὶ τοῖς πανδοκείοις αἰεὶ διαιτᾷ."

iii *IG* ii² 2325.125

Μύρτιλος I

MYRTILUS

A minor figure in the history of Old Comedy, Myrtilus was the brother of Hermippus and victor at the Lenaea in 428 or 427 (T 3). The Suda *(T 1) gives two titles, but only the second,* Titan-Pans, *was known in antiquity.*

Testimonia

i Myrtilus: of Athens, comic poet, son of Lysis and brother of the comic poet, Hermippus. His plays are *Titan-Pans*, *Love-Gods*.

ii [to a banqueter named Myrtilus] Cynulcus ⟨said⟩, "In the words of Cratinus [F 351], 'you dare say this,' although you 'are not rosy-fingered,' but with one leg made of cow dung [*Frogs* 295], and with the shin of that poet with the same name as yours, who spends all his time in the pubs and taverns."

iii [from the list of victors at the Lenaea, in the early 420s]

Myrtilus 1.

373

THE POETS OF OLD COMEDY

Fragments

ΕΡΩΤΕΣ

ΤΙΤΑΝΟΠΑΝΕΣ

1 *Commentaria in Aristotelem Graeca* XX p. 186.9 (Heylbut)

σύνηθες ἐν κωμῳδίᾳ παραπετάσματα δέρρεις ποιεῖν
οὐ πορφυρίδας. Μύρτιλος ἐν Τιτανόπασι.

2 Σ Aristophanes *Birds* 1490

οἱ ἥρωες δὲ δυσόργητοι καὶ χαλεποὶ τοῖς ἐμπελάζουσι
γίνονται . . . διό μοι δοκοῦσι καὶ οἱ τὰ ἡρῷα παριόντες
σιγὴν ἔχειν, ὡς Μύρτιλος ἐν Τιτανόπασί φησιν.

374

MYRTILUS

Fragments

LOVE-GODS

Although Eros in the singular is the child of Aphrodite and the god of love, vases depicting amorous encounters show scenes with several winged love gods. Hence a chorus of such deities would not be greatly surprising. We know the play only from the mention in the Suda *(T 1), which Kaibel considered a gloss explaining a love theme in* Titan-Pans.

TITAN-PANS

A splendid calyx crater in the British Museum (ARV² 601.23, c. 460) shows dancers dressed as Pans performing before an aulos *player, and there is a possibility that such a chorus might have been substituted on occasion for a satyr chorus. But what were Titan-Pans? Hesychius (τ 971) says that "Titan" is a slang word for "paederast," and elsewhere (π 339) describes Pans as "those very keen on sex," but what sort of chorus are we to imagine and how costumed? Perhaps they were a hybrid race, the result of unions between Pan(s) and female Titans. F 2 might imply that the* skēnē *represented their shrine.*

1 It was customary in comedy to use leather hangings, not purple, so Myrtilus in *Titan-Pans*.

2 Heroes can get angry and upset with people who get too close . . . that is why I think that people who pass by the shrines of heroes keep silence, as Myrtilus says in *Titan-Pans*.

ΑΔΗΛΩΝ ΔΡΑΜΑΤΩΝ

4 Theodosius *On the Declension of Barytone Nouns in –ōn*, p. 21.25 Hilgard.

Φέρωνος ἆρά που 'στιν ἡ ξυναυλία;

5 Phrynichus *Selection* 402

ὡς ὁ μὲν κλέπτης, ὁ δ' ἅρπαξ,
ὁ δ' ἀνάπηρος πορνοβοσκὸς
καταφαγᾶς.

Brief fragment: (F 3) "a tongue blister."

UNASSIGNED FRAGMENTS

4 Is Pheron's *aulos* company anywhere about?

5 One man is a thief, another is a bandit, another is a maimed glutton who keeps a brothel.

ΝΙΚΟΧΑΡΗΣ

Nicochares belongs to the last phase of Old Comedy. The one secure date is the production of his Men of Laconia *in 388, competing against Aristophanes'* Wealth. *The one kōmōidoumenos in the fragments, Philonides of Melite (F 4), is made fun of by Aristophanes in that same comedy of 388. If Nicochares' name is to be restored in T 4, then he won a victory at the Lenaea at the same time as other comic poets of the early fourth century. The titles suggest that he wrote mainly mythological burlesques, and while we have no direct parody of tragedy, some of the titles suggest an engagement with the dramatic versions of myth from the*

Testimonia

i *Suda* ν 407

Νικοχάρης, Φιλωνίδου τοῦ κωμικοῦ, Ἀθηναῖος, κωμικός, σύγχρονος Ἀριστοφάνους. τῶν δραμάτων αὐτοῦ Ἀμυμώνη ⟨ἢ⟩ Πέλοψ, Γαλάτεια, Ἡρακλῆς γαμῶν, Ἡρακλῆς χορηγός, Κρῆτες, Λάκωνες, Λήμνιαι, Κένταυροι, Χειρογάστορες.

NICOCHARES

fifth century, Lemnian Women, Agamemnon. *The last title cited by the* Suda, Hand-Bellies, *has been confused with the attested comedy of that title by Nicophon.*

Perhaps the most striking thing about Nicochares is the indirect connection with Aristophanes. The Suda *(T 1) describes him as "the son of Philonides the comic poet," who must be the man whom Aristophanes used on a number of occasions to produce his comedies. T 2 assigns a "Nicochares the comic poet" to the deme of Cydathenaeum, the deme known for Aristophanes and strongly indicated for Philonides (q.v.).*

Testimonia

i Nicochares: the son of Philonides the comic poet, of Athens, a comic poet, a contemporary of Aristophanes. His plays are: *Amymone <or> Pelops, Galateia, The Marriage of Heracles, Heracles the Producer, Cretans, Men of Laconia, Lemnian Women, Centaurs, Hand-Bellies.*

379

ii Stephanus of Byzantium p. 390.1

Κυδαθήναιον, δῆμος τῆς Πανδιονίδος φυλῆς. ὁ δημό-
της Κυδαθηναιεύς. ἐντεῦθεν ἦν Νικοχάρης ὁ κωμικός.

iii *Inscript. Agora* I 7168

Ὀνήσιππος Αἰτίο Κηφισιεὺς βασιλεὺς ἀνέθηκε[ν.
ο[ἷδ]ε Ὀνησίππο βασιλεύοντος χορηγοῦντες ἐνίκων·

κωμῳδῶν	τραγῳδῶν
Σωσικράτης ἐχορήγε	Στρατόνικος ἐχορήγε
χαλκοπώλης	Στράτωνος
Νικοχάρης ἐδίδασκε	Μεγακλείδης ἐδίδασκε

iv *IG* ii² 2325.134

Νι[κοχάρης

v Aristotle *Poetics* 1448a11

οἷον Ὅμηρος μὲν βελτίους, Κλεοφῶν δὲ ὁμοίους,
Ἡγήμων δὲ ὁ Θάσιος ⟨ὁ⟩ τὰς παρῳδίας ποιήσας
πρῶτος καὶ Νικοχάρης ὁ τὴν Δειλιάδα χείρους·

ii Cydathenaeum: deme of the tribe of Pandion. The demotic is Cydathenaean. This is where Nicochares the comic poet was from.

iii [inscription from the end of the fifth century]
Onesippus the son of Aetias of Cephisia, archon basileus, put this up:
These are the victorious *chorēgi* during Onesippus' term of office

comedy

Sosicrates the bronze seller was producer
Nicochares presented the play.

tragedy

Stratonicus son of Straton was producer
Megaclides presented the play.

iv [from the list of victors at the Lenaea]
Ni[cochares.

v Homer ⟨represented⟩ superior people, Cleophon as similar to real life, while Hegemon of Thasus, the first to write *paroidia* and Nicochares, the ⟨author of⟩ the *Deiliad*, people as worse than they are.[1]

---

[1] Nicochares is not a common name, and it is an attractive identification to see the comic poet meant here. The title of his poem could be *Deiliad* (A Coward's Tale) or *Deliad* (A Tale of Delos), but in light of the association with the parodist Hegemon, *Deiliad* (or *Deliad*) is probably not a lost comedy, but another instance of a *parōidia*, written in the epic metre and style.

381

ΑΓΑΜΕΜΝΩΝ

Fragment

1 Photius (S^z) α 3479

οἶδα δ' ὡς
ἀψευδόμαντις ἥδε καὶ τελεσφόρος

γνώσῃ δὲ τέχνην τὴν ἐμὴν ἐτητύμως
ἀψευδόμαντιν οὖσαν

ΑΜΥΜΩΝΗ

AGAMEMNON

*Hermippus also wrote a play with this title. Nicochares'
comedy is not mentioned in the* Suda *and is cited only by
Photius. Changing the citation to "in Amymone" has been
suggested, but F 1 refers to a woman who is "no false
prophet," very likely to be Cassandra—cf. her use of the
words "false prophet" and "true prophet" at* Agamemnon
*1195, 1241. Thus this comedy appears to have covered
humorously the same ground as Aeschylus' great play.*

Fragment

1 I know that this woman is no false prophet, and one who
brings fulfilment.

You will truly come to know my skill, that I [fem.] am no
false prophet.

AMYMONE ⟨OR⟩ PELOPS

Meineke's insertion of "or" into the Suda's *list of plays does
preserve the mostly alphabetical listing of the plays. But
the two titles suggest two very different stories. Aeschylus'
satyr play,* Amymone, *told the story of one of the daughters
of Danaus, who was threatened by a satyr, rescued by Po-
seidon, to whom she bore a son Nauplius. Pelops, on the
other hand, is most famous for the chariot race by which he
won the daughter of Oenomaus in marriage. The one frag-
ment that we have is cited from "Amymone" and mentions
Pelops' eventual father-in-law by name.*

Fragment

2 Athenaeus 426e

Οἰνόμαος οὗτος χαῖρε· πέντε καὶ δύο,
κἀγώ τε καὶ σὺ συμπόται γενοίμεθα.

ΓΑΛΑΤΕΙΑ

Fragments

3 Pollux 10.93

σοφαῖσι παλάμαις τεκτόνων εἰργασμένον
⟨καὶ⟩ πόλλ᾽ ἐν αὐτῷ λέπτ᾽ ἔχον καδίσκια
κυμινοδόκον

4 Σ Aristophanes *Wealth* 179b

τί δῆτ᾽; ἀπαιδευτότερος εἶ Φιλωνίδου
τοῦ Μελιτέως;

---

[1] Philonides (*PAA* 957480), son of Onetor, hence his nickname Onos (ass), was a large, awkward, not very bright, but rich Athenian, said to be the lover of the hetaera Nais. See *Wealth* 179, 303; Platon F 65; Nicochares F 4; Theopompus F 5; and the comedy *Philonides* by the Middle Comic poet Aristophon.

NICOCHARES

Fragment

2 Hey, Oenomaus, hello. Let's you and I become drinking buddies, five-and-two.[1]

[1] The joke turns on the fact that the first two syllables of Oenomaus' name form the Greek word for "wine." "Five-and-two" refers to the standard mixture of five parts water to two parts wine.

GALATEA

The sea nymph Galatea is one of the daughters of Nereus in Homer and Hesiod. Douris of Samos (FGrHist 76 F 58) tells the story of how the poet, Philoxenus of Cythera, found a shrine on the slopes of Mount Etna, allegedly constructed by the Cyclops Polyphemus for the nymph Galatea. Unable to ascertain the origin, he made up the story that Polyphemus was in love with Galatea. Philoxenus' dithyramb called "Cyclops or Galatea" was parodied by Aristophanes at Wealth *288–321 (388), and if Philoxenus did create the story of Polyphemus and Galatea, then Nicochares' play belongs after the production of that dithyramb, probably in the 380s.*

Fragments

3 A spice box, wrought by the skilled hands of craftsmen, containing many small bottles inside it.

4 What is this? Are you even stupider than Philonides of Melite?[1]

5 Photius (b, S^z) α 1552

τὸν ἀναλφάβητον, τὸν ἄπονον

ΗΡΑΚΛΗΣ ΓΑΜΩΝ

ΗΡΑΚΛΗΣ ΧΟΡΗΓΟΣ

Fragments

8 Pollux 7.45

φέρε νῦν ταχέως χιτῶνα τόνδ' ἐπενδύτην.

9 Athenaeus 619a

καὶ τῶν πτισσουσῶν ἄλλη τις, ὡς . . . Νικοχάρης ἐν
Ἡρακλεῖ Χορηγῷ.

5 An illiterate fellow, and lazy.

Brief fragment: (F 6) "daughters of Nereus."

THE MARRIAGE OF HERACLES

The comedy is listed in the Suda *(T 1) as* Heracles Marrying *(as the groom), while Pollux (F 7) cites the play as* Heracles being Married *(as the bride). On that basis some have seen a reference to Heracles' service to Omphale as sort of "marriage," in which the hero takes the passive role. A safer course is to regard this comedy and that of the same name by Archippus as dramatising Heracles' marriage to Hebe on Olympus—cf. Epicharmus' comedy,* The Marriage of Hebe.

Brief fragment: (F 7) "fuller's earth."

HERACLES THE PRODUCER

Heracles was a favourite of satyr play and Old Comedy. Like Dionysus, the humour would focus on Heracles in an unfamiliar and incongruous situation. At Frogs 105–7 Dionysus and Heracles agree to leave things culinary to Heracles and things dramatic to Dionysus. Nicochares appears to have taken Heracles across that line.

Fragments

8 Quickly now, ⟨put on⟩ this tunic as an overgarment.

9 There was another ⟨song⟩, that of women winnowing grain, so . . . Nicochares in *Heracles the Producer.*

ΚΕΝΤΑΥΡΟΣ

ΚΡΗΤΕΣ

Fragment

12 Pollux 10.141

τοῖς τρυπάνοις ἀντίπαλον † ὅπερ ἀρχίλιον †

ΛΑΚΩΝΕΣ

CENTAUR

Aristophanes wrote a comedy with the twin titles, Plays or
Centaur, *which may have been produced at the Lenaea of
426 with Euripides as a character. The connection between
the two titles may have been a dramatic parody of a play
about a centaur (Chiron or Nessus). Cratinus' comedy,*
Chirons, *will have had a chorus of centaurs, and whatever
Old Comedy lies behind the Chiron vase (V 9) had a scene
in which (a drunken?) Chiron navigates stairs with dif-
ficulty. Is this a scene from Nicochares'* Centaur?

Brief fragments: (F 10) "auction," (F 11) "thrashed."

CRETANS

*Apollophanes wrote a comedy with this title, but the most
likely parallel would be the tragedy of that name by Euripi-
des, from the earlier part of his career. Enough remains to
show that Euripides treated the story of Minos, Pasiphae,
and the Bull, a tragedy with obvious potential for comedy.*

Fragment

12 An awl, a match for a thousand drills.[1]

[1] The text is uncertain. Was Daedalus a character in the play?

MEN OF LACONIA

*Comedies with this title are recorded for Eupolis (probably
incorrectly) and for Platon. It was produced in 388 as one
of the rival plays to Aristophanes'* Wealth.

ΛΗΜΝΙΑΙ

Fragments

14 Athenaeus 328e

τριχίας δὲ καὶ τὰς πρημνάδας {τὰς θυννίδας}
ἐπὶ δεῖπνον ἠκούσας ὑπερπληθεῖς

15 *Etymologicum Genuinum*

ἐπλέομεν, ὦ κόρη, 'πὶ κῶς.

390

NICOCHARES

Testimonium

i ⟨*Wealth*⟩ was produced in the archonship of Antipater [389/8], the other entrants being Nicochares with *Men of Laconia*, Aristomenes with *Admetus*, Nicophon with *Adonis*, and Alcaeus with *Pasiphae*.

Brief fragment: (F 13) "the Manes" [target in cottabus*].*

LEMNIAN WOMEN

"Lemnian women" should refer to the women of Lemnos who murdered their husbands and then enjoyed a liaison with Jason and the Argonauts on their voyage to Colchis. It was a popular subject for drama. Aeschylus may have written a play with this title, while two plays are attributed to Sophocles. Aristophanes wrote a comedy of this name, usually regarded as a parody of Euripides' Hypsipyle; *the theme lies also beneath the surface of his* Lysistrata. *Strattis wrote a* Lemnomeda, *which seems to have combined the stories of Hypsipyle and Andromeda. The reference to "sailing to Cos" (F 15) makes it likely that we do have here the story of Jason and Hypsipyle.*

Fragments

14 Sardines and young tunny fish coming to dinner in great numbers.

15 My girl, we were sailing to Cos.

THE POETS OF OLD COMEDY

16 Athenaeus 426ef

οἱ δ' ἐπιτεταμένως χρώμενοι τῷ ποτῷ δύο οἴνου ἔπινον
πρὸς πέντε ὕδατος. Νικοχάρης γοῦν ἐν Ἀμυμώνῃ
πρὸς τοὔνομα παίζων ἔφη . . . τὰ παραπλήσια εἴρηκε
καὶ ἐν Λημνίαις.

ΧΕΙΡΟΓΑΣΤΟΡΕΣ

ΑΔΗΛΩΝ ΔΡΑΜΑΤΩΝ

18 Athenaeus 34e

εἰς αὔριον ⟨δ'⟩ ἀντὶ ῥαφάνων ἑψήσομεν
βαλάνιον, ἵνα νῷν ἐξάγῃ τὴν κραιπάλην.

19 Photius (b, z) α 443

εἰ πεύσομαι ⟨σε κἂν⟩ τὸν ἀηδόνιον ὕπνον
τῆς νυκτὸς ἀποδαρθόντα, σαυτὸν αἰτιῶ.

20 Photius (b, Sᶻ) α 1643

ῥηγνὺς δὲ πολλὰς κυμάτων ἀναρρόας.

21 Photius (Sᶻ) α 3411

                              ἀλλ' εἰλήμμεθα
λαβὴν ἄφυκτον, ἀδιάγλυπτον.

392

16 Those who engaged in hard drinking would consume two parts of wine to five parts of water. At least Nicochares says so in jest in *Amymone* [F 2] . . . and much the same sort of thing in *Lemnian Women*.

Brief fragment: (F 17) "pots with three legs."

HAND-BELLIES

The Suda *(or his source) has very probably misassigned this comedy to Nicochares. A comedy with a very similar title (with seven secure fragments) is known for Nicophon.*

UNASSIGNED FRAGMENTS

18 Tomorrow instead of cabbages we shall boil up an acorn broth, to get rid of both our hangovers.

19 If I find out that during the night you took even a nightingale's nap, blame yourself . . .

20 Breaking many back-swells of waves.

21 But we are caught in an unbreakable hold, inescapable.

22 Athenaeus 657a

κυοῦσαν δέλφακα

23 Photius α 898

τὴν ἀλάστορα Σφίγγα

NICOCHARES

22 A pregnant young sow.

23 The avenging Sphinx.

Brief fragments: (F 24) "to say 'ah,'" (F 25) "to munber"
["number" mispronounced], (F 26) "without pity," (F 27)
"bran seller," (F 28) "childish."

ΝΙΚΟΦΩΝ

Occasionally confused with Nicochares, a comic poet of the same time and a similar style, Nicophon can be firmly dated to the late fifth and early fourth centuries. On the list of victors at the Dionysia (T 3), he comes before Cephisodorus, for whom a victory in 402 is attested, and his Adonis (see below) competed against Aristophanes' Wealth in 388. The Suda (T 1) gives five titles, which do not include Adonis. Thus six plays over a period of at least fifteen years suggest a poet of the second rank. Four titles indicate that burlesques of myth were his principal sort of comedy.

Testimonia

i *Suda* ν 406

Νικόφων Θήρωνος, Ἀθηναῖος, κωμικός, σύγχρονος Ἀριστοφάνους τοῦ κωμικοῦ. τῶν δραμάτων αὐτοῦ καὶ ταῦτα· Ἐξ Ἅιδου ἀνιών, Ἀφροδίτης γοναί, Πανδώρα, Ἐγχειρογάστορες, Σειρῆνες.

ii Herodian *Singular Vocabulary* II p. 915.3

ἀλλ' οὐδὲν εἰς ων λῆγον περισπώμενον ὑπὲρ δύο συλλαβὰς φύσει μακρᾷ παραλήγεται. Ἀντιφῶν, Ξενοφῶν, Εὐρυφῶν Ὁμήρου υἱός, Νικοφῶν ὁ κωμικός.

NICOPHON

There are no kōmōidoumenoi *among the thirty fragments, nor anything that implies a political theme. Four of the comedies (Adonis, Birth of Aphrodite, Pandora, Sirens) have very alluring and attractive women as main characters or chorus, and Nicophon's comedy may have turned on the potential in beauty for comic rivalry and disaster. The Suda gives his father's name as Theron, a rare name at Athens, with no other instance known for the late fifth century.*

Recent bibliography: M. Pellegrino, AFLB 49 (2006) 43–97.

Testimonia

i Nicophon: son of Theron, of Athens, comic poet, a contemporary of the comic poet Aristophanes. His plays include: *Back from Hades, Birth of Aphrodite, Pandora, Hands-to-Mouth, Sirens.*

ii No word ending in *–ōn* with a circumflex on the last syllable and containing more than two syllables has a penultimate syllable which is long: Antiphon, Xenophon, Euryphon the son of Homer, Nicophon the comic poet.

iii *IG* ii² 2325.67

Νικοφῶ[ν

iv *IG* ii² 2325.131

Νικοφ[ῶν

ΑΔΩΝΙΣ

Testimonium

i Hypothesis III *Wealth*

ἐδιδάχθη ἐπὶ ἄρχοντος Ἀντιπάτρου, ἀνταγωνιζομένου αὐτῷ Νικοχάρους μὲν Λάκωσιν, Ἀριστομένους δὲ Ἀδμήτῳ, Νικοφῶντος δὲ Ἀδώνιδι, Ἀλκαίου δὲ Πασιφάῃ.

ΑΦΡΟΔΙΤΗΣ ΓΟΝΑΙ

One of the several comedies from the early fourth century featuring the birth of gods or heroes, for which see Nesselrath in Dobrov (BA) 1–27. A less probable explanation of the title is "offspring of Aphrodite." The shorter Homeric Hymn to Aphrodite (Hymn 6) gives a possible comic

iii [from the list of victors at the Dionysia, before 402]

Nicopho[n].

iv [from the list of victors at the Lenaea]

Nicoph[on].

ADONIS

This comedy is known only from the hypothesis to Wealth.
*If these plays are being cited in the order of finish, rather
than the order of production, then* Adonis *finished fourth
in 388. Platon also wrote a comedy called* Adonis. *A major
festival for women, called the Adonia (see* Lysistrata 393,
Pherecrates F 181, *and Menander* Samian Woman 39), *was
held in the summer to mourn the death of Adonis, the
young and beloved companion of Aphrodite or the Great
Mother.*

Testimonium

i [*Wealth*] was produced in the archonship of Antipater
[389/8], the other entrants being Nicochares with *Men of
Laconia*, Aristomenes with *Admetus*, Nicophon with
Adonis, and Alcaeus with *Pasiphae*.

BIRTH OF APHRODITE

*plotline, the birth and arrival of Aphrodite among the
(male) gods at Olympus, each of them wishing to have her
to wife. A good comedy could be made from the eventual
successful suit by Hephaestus, especially if Aphrodite were
less than willing.*

Fragments

1 Σ Aristophanes *Birds* 82

ἅπερ ἐσθίει ταυτὶ τὰ πονήρ᾽ ὀρνίθια,
σέρφους ἴσως, σκώληκας, ἀκρίδας, πάρνοπας.

2 Σ Aristophanes *Birds* 1283

οὐκ ἐς κόρακας τὼ χεῖρ᾽ ἀποίσεις ἐκποδὼν
ἀπὸ τοῦ σκυταλίου < > καὶ τῆς διφθέρας;

3 *Suda* α 3750

ἆρ᾽ ἀράχνιόν τι φαίνετ᾽ ἐμπεφυκέναι;

5 P. Oxy. 3710

$$\text{ἐὰν τρέχῃς}$$
α[   ]ας βλέψεις πάνυ
π[

ΕΓΧΕΙΡΟΓΑΣΤΟΡΕΣ

Fragments

6 Athenaeus 645bc

ἐγὼ μὲν ἄρτους, μᾶζαν, ἀθάρην, ἄλφιτα,
κόλλικας, ὀβελίαν, μελιτοῦτταν, ἐπιχύτους,
πτισάνην, πλακοῦντας, δενδαλίδας, ταγηνίας.

NICOPHON

Fragments

1 The sort of things these nasty little birds eat: gnats, I suppose, worms, grasshoppers, locusts.

2 Why don't you [sing.] take your hands off the ["my"?] staff and jacket and go to hell?

3 Does a spider's web seem to be rooted in there?

5 . . . if you [sing.] run . . . you will see very . . .

Brief fragment: (F 4) "baited trap."

HANDS-TO-MOUTH

For the title, the tradition gives both cheirogastores *and* encheirogastores. *The ancient lexicographers usually explain the word as meaning "those who feed themselves by manual labour," while Eustathius* (On the Iliad *p. 286.21) says that it is used to describe the Cyclopes, who built the walls of cities in the Argolid in return for food. The scholiast to Aelius Aristeides (p. 408.25 Dindorf) distinguishes three sorts of Cyclopes, those in Sicily whom Odysseus encountered, these "hands-to-mouth," and the "heavenly ones." A crew of hungry Cyclopes, willing to work for food, could have made a good comic chorus.*

Fragments

6 I ‹have, provide› loaves of bread, barley cake, porridge, barley groats, rolls, bread on a spit, honey cake, cupcakes, barley gruel, flat-cakes, barley cakes, pancakes.

7 Σ Aristophanes *Birds* 1551

† γεννα ὁ αὐτὸς † ὀλίγον ἀνάγαγε
ἀπὸ τῆς διφροφόρου· χρηστὸς εἶ καὶ κόσμιος.

8 Pollux 4.55

ἀλλ᾽ ἴθι προσαύλησον σὺ νῷν πτισμόν τινα.

9 Athenaeus 389a

τοὺς ἑψητοὺς καὶ τοὺς πέρδικας ἐκείνους

10 Athenaeus 126e

μεμβραδοπώλαις, ἀνθρακοπώλαις,
ἰσχαδοπώλαις, διφθεροπώλαις,
ἀλφιτοπώλαις, μυστριοπώλαις,
βιβλιοπώλαις, κοσκινοπώλαις,
5   ἐγκριδοπώλαις, σπερματοπώλαις

11 The Antiatticist p. 89.28

δευτέριον οἶνον

ΕΞ ΑΙΔΟΥ ΑΝΙΩΝ

7 You there, please move a little bit away from the footstool carrier—there's a good and decent fellow.[1]

[1] The "footstool carrier" refers to an attendant in the procession at the Panathenaea, who might carry also a parasol for the comfort of the priestess in the parade. Such a scene may be found on the East Frieze of the Parthenon.

8 Now go and play for the two of us a winnowing song.

9 The boiled sprats and those partridges.

10 Sardine sellers, charcoal sellers, fig sellers, leather sellers, barley-groat sellers, spoon sellers, booksellers, sieve sellers, cake sellers, seed sellers.

11 Second-rate vintage.

Brief fragment: (F 12) "raisins."

BACK FROM HADES

We know this comedy only from the list in the Suda *(T 1). Journeys to and from the world of the dead are a regular part of Greek drama. For tragedy we have the ghosts of Darius (Aeschylus'* Persians*) and Polydorus (Euripides'* Hecuba*), in comedy the return of the four in Eupolis'* Demes *and the ghost of Solon in Cratinus'* Chirons*), in Aeschylus' satyr play* Sisyphus the Runaway*. This last play was very much about a man "back from Hades."*

THE POETS OF OLD COMEDY

ΠΑΝΔΩΡΑ

Fragments

13 Pollux 7.32

ὁ δ' ἐξυφαίνεθ' ἱστός, ὁ δὲ διάζεται.

14 Athenaeus 323b

κέστραι τε καὶ λάβρακες

15 *Suda* κ 2546

κοιμίσαι τὸν λύχνον

16 The Antiatticist p. 89.14

δεύτερον αὐτόν

17 The Antiatticist p. 115.24

φίλημα δοῦναι

404

PANDORA

The myth of Pandora is as old as Hesiod (Theogony 561–616, Works & Days 59–105), *and was popular with the dramatists and with vase painters. A representation of the myth of Pandora was said also to have been sculpted on the statue of Athena in the Parthenon. Sophocles wrote a satyr play called* Pandora or the Hammerers, *and on one vase, satyrs are shown hammering at the earth to release a female figure. Her name "all gifts" can be applied to the earth as mother.*

Fragments

13 The beam of the loom begins to weave, and the . . . gets going.

14 Grey mullets and sea bass.

15 To put the lamp to sleep.

16 Himself the second.

17 To give a kiss.

Brief fragments: (F 18) "youngsters," (F 19) "to drink freely."

THE POETS OF OLD COMEDY

ΣΕΙΡΗΝΕΣ

Testimonium

i Athenaeus 270a

οἶδα δὲ καὶ οἱ Θουριοπέρσαι καὶ τὸ τοῦ Νικοφῶντος δρᾶμα ἀδίδακτά ἐστι, διόπερ καὶ τελευταίων αὐτῶν ἐμνήσθην.

Fragments

20 Athenaeus 80b

ἐὰν δέ γ᾽ ἡμῶν σῦκά τις μεσημβρίας
τραγὼν καθεύδῃ χλωρά, πυρετὸς εὐθέως
ἥκει τρέχων, οὐκ ἄξιος τριωβόλου·
κᾆθ᾽ οὗτος ἐπιπεσὼν ἐμεῖν ποιεῖ χολήν.

21 Athenaeus 269e

νειφέτω μὲν ἀλφίτοις,
ψακαζέτω δ᾽ ἄρτοισιν, ὑέτω δ᾽ ἔτνει,
ζωμὸς διὰ τῶν ὁδῶν κυλινδείτω κρέα,
πλακοῦς ἑαυτὸν ἐσθίειν κελευέτω.

NICOPHON

SIRENS

According to Athenaeus, this play, like the Thourio-Persians *of Metagenes, was never produced, although he is able to quote three times from it and include F 21 as part of his citations on the good life in comedy. Theopompus also wrote a comedy with this title. Nicophon may have created a mythological burlesque along the lines of Cratinus'* Odysseus and Company *(or Euripides'* Cyclops*), dramatising the encounter with the Sirens at* Odyssey *12.37–58, 153–200). But could Nicophon have increased the traditional three Sirens to make up a comic chorus of twenty-four? F 21 suggests that the temptation of the Sirens is not so much their enchanting song, but the offer of an ideal existence.*

*Recent bibliography: Pellegrino (*Utopie*) 127–32.*

Testimonium

i I am aware that both *Thurio-Persians* and the play by Nicophon [*Sirens*] were not performed, which is why I mentioned them last.

Fragments

20 If one of us munches green figs at midday and then goes to sleep, a good-for-nothing fever immediately comes running, attacks him, and makes him vomit up bile.

21 Let it snow with barley groats, hail with loaves of bread, pelt down with soup, let gravy roll pieces of meat throughout the streets, let a flat-cake demand to be eaten.

22 Athenaeus 368b

ἀλλᾶς μαχέσθω περὶ ἕδρας παροψίδι.

ΑΔΗΛΩΝ ΔΡΑΜΑΤΩΝ

23 Pollux 3.18

νυνὶ δὲ Κρόνου καὶ Τιθωνοῦ παππεπίπαππος
νενόμισται.

408

22 Let a sausage vie with a side dish for precedence.

UNASSIGNED FRAGMENTS

23 Now he is considered the great-great-grandfather of Cronus and Tithonus.[1]

[1] One MS of Pollux names the comic poet as Philonides [F 17] and not Nicophon.

Brief fragments: (F 24) "silence," (F 25) "saucers," (F 26) "dancing the cordax," *(F 27) "on bell duty," (F 28) "silent," (F 29) "the uvula," (F 30) "friend" [vocative used of more than one person].*

ΦΕΡΕΚΡΑΤΗΣ

The loss of Pherecrates' comedies is a considerable one, as a more representative triad for Old Comedy could well be Cratinus, Pherecrates, and Aristophanes. A victory in 437 (T 2) is recorded; he thus belongs to that group of successful comic poets who immediately precede Aristophanes and Eupolis. Dates are difficult to determine for his lost comedies, since there are so few topical allusions. He seems remarkably absent from the records of the 420s, but his Wild-Men *is firmly dated by Athenaeus (T 1 to that comedy) to the Lenaea of 420. I suspect that once comedy returned to five productions after the Peace of 421, Pherecrates, like other poets, got more of a look-in. Certain other comedies (Kitchen, Chiron) have been plausibly dated to the 410s or even later. A career of c. 440–410 would seem reasonable.*

Pherecrates is credited with seventeen (T 1) or eighteen (T 4) comedies. We have nineteen titles, and if Metics *is actually by Platon and the two Heracles plays (Heracles the Mortal, False Heracles) are the same comedy, that nineteen is nicely reduced to seventeen. The authenticity of three comedies in particular has been disputed, especially by Athenaeus, (Miners, Persians, Chiron), unfortunately so, since they are three of the plays best represented among the remains of Pherecrates. Athenaeus knows of a tradition*

410

PHERECRATES

that attributed Miners and Chiron to "Nicomachus the rhythmist," and also assigns Good Men to "Pherecrates or Strattis." Disputed authorship is nothing unusual for Old Comedy, but it does seem as if Pherecrates' plays were especially susceptible to suspicions about who wrote them. We might consider a number of possibilities: production by someone other than Pherecrates (but the ancients seem to have been able to ferret out the real author), or perhaps revision by a later poet, either of an unfinished play or one actually produced before. Pollux (2.33) does use the verb "revised" of the plays of Pherecrates.

The ancient critics found in the comedy of Crates and Pherecrates something different from the abusive and topical comedy of Aristophanes and Eupolis that came to be seen as stereotypical of Old Comedy. The anonymous writer on comedy (T 2) makes him an actor and follower of Crates in avoiding personal humour and in writing comedy with strong plotlines. The first claim is certainly borne out by the fragments that we have. Of the nearly three hundred fragments, perhaps ten contain any personal jokes, and none is of the politically charged sort that permeates Aristophanes' comedy. We do not have enough of the comedies to justify the second judgement. Chiron, the one comedy for which we have any hints about scenes and characters, is confusing in the extreme.

THE POETS OF OLD COMEDY

While one or two plays (Chiron *and* Ant-Men *) seem to be burlesques of myth, the sort which Cratinus and Hermippus were fond of writing in the 430s, Pherecrates' plays have more largely to do with domestic themes and female characters, perhaps anticipating the comedy of Menander and the other poets of New Comedy. There are hints of the theme of women in control in* Tyranny, *and as many as five plays may have featured a hetaera as a principal character* (Corianno, Kitchen *or* Pannychis, Forgetful Man *or* Thalassa, Petale, Tyranny). *There is also the presentation of Music as a high-class hetaera in* Chiron *(F 155). Other lost comedies suggest social themes:* Good

Testimonia

i *Suda* φ 212

Φερεκράτης, Ἀθηναῖος, κωμικός· {ὃς Ἀλεξάνδρῳ συν-εστράτευσεν.} ἐδίδαξε δράματα ιζ΄.

ii Anonymous *On Comedy* (Koster III.9–13, 29–31)

τούτων δέ εἰσιν ἀξιολογώτατοι Ἐπίχαρμος, Μάγνης, Κρατῖνος, Κράτης, Φερεκράτης, Φρύνιχος, Εὔπολις, Ἀριστοφάνης

Φερεκράτης Ἀθηναῖος. νικᾷ ἐπὶ Θεοδώρου· γενόμενος δὲ ὑποκριτὴς ἐζήλωσε Κράτητα, καὶ αὖ τοῦ μὲν λοιδορεῖν ἀπέστη, πράγματα δὲ εἰσηγούμενος καινὰ ηὐδοκίμει, γενόμενος εὑρετικὸς μύθων.

θεάτρου cod., Θεοδώρου Dobree.

412

Men, Wild-Men, Slave-Trainer, *and* Accessories. Persians *and* Miners *appear to have contained the popular utopian sentiments of the life free from toil, where things happen "on their own." Perhaps most intriguing is* Tiddlers, *almost certainly earlier than* Frogs, *but set in the Underworld with Aeschylus as a speaking character.*

Recent bibliography: Conti Bizzarro, MCr 25–28 (1990–1993) 79–121, MCr 23–24 (1988–1989) 259–92; *Dobrov and Urios Aparisi, in Dobrov* (BA) 139–75; *Henderson, in* Rivals 135–50; *R. Quaglia,* Acme 56 (2003) 255–70, AFLB 46 (2003) 253–95, 48 (2005) 99–170.

Testimonia

i Pherecrates: of Athens, comic poet {who served in Alexander's army}. He produced seventeen plays.

ii The most noteworthy of these ⟨poets⟩ are Epicharmus, Magnes, Cratinus, Crates, Pherecrates, Phrynichus, Eupolis, Aristophanes

Pherecrates: of Athens. He won a victory in the archonship of Theodorus [438/7]. He had been an actor and emulated Crates, and also refrained from personal jokes. His success lay in introducing new themes and in inventing plots.

iii *Canons of the Comic Poets*

κωμῳδοποιοὶ ἀρχαίας ζ· Επιχαρμος, Κρατῖνος, Εὔ-
πολις, Ἀριστοφάνης, Φερεκράτης, Κράτης, Πλάτων.

iv *The Names and Plays of the Poets of Old Comedy*
  (Koster VIII.3)

Φερεκράτους δράματα ιη΄.

v *Suda* π 1708

Πλάτων, Ἀθηναῖος, κωμικός, γεγονὼς τοῖς χρόνοις
κατὰ Ἀριστοφάνην καὶ Φρύνιχον, Εὔπολιν· Φερε-
κράτην.

vi *IG* ii² 2325.56

  Φερ[εκράτης

vii *IG* ii² 2325.122

  Φερεκράτης II

viii

(a) Tzetzes *Distinctions among Poets* (Koster XXIa.82–
  84)

τῆς δευτέρας ἦν ὁ ψόγος κεκρυμμένος,
ἧς ἦν Κρατῖνος, Εὔπολις, Φερεκράτης,
Ἀριστοφάνης, Ἕρμιππός τε καὶ Πλάτων

iii There were seven poets of Old Comedy: Epicharmus, Cratinus, Eupolis, Aristophanes, Pherecrates, Crates, Platon.

iv The plays of Pherecrates: 18.

v Platon: of Athens, comic poet, a contemporary of Aristophanes and Phrynichus [T 4], Eupolis [T 8], and Pherecrates.

vi [list of victors at the Dionysia—from the mid-430s]

    Pher[ecrates

vii [list of victors at the Lenaea—from the late 430s]

    Pherecrates 2

viii

(a) Indirect insult was characteristic of second ‹comedy›, of which there were Cratinus, Eupolis, Pherecrates, Aristophanes, Hermippus, and Platon.

THE POETS OF OLD COMEDY

(b) Tzetzes *Proem* (Koster XIa I.78)

οὕτως ἡ πρώτη κωμῳδία τὸ σκῶμμα εἶχεν ἀπαρα-
κάλυπτον· ἐξήρκεσε δὲ τὸ ἀπαρακαλύπτως οὑτωσὶ
κωμῳδεῖν μέχρις Εὐπόλιδος . . . ἀλλὰ ψήφισμα θέν-
τος Ἀλκιβιάδου κωμῳδεῖν ἐσχηματισμένως καὶ μὴ
προδήλως αὐτός τε ὁ Εὔπολις Κρατῖνός τε καὶ Φερε-
κράτης καὶ Πλάτων, οὐχ ὁ φιλόσοφος, Ἀριστοφάνης
τε σὺν ἑτέροις τὰ συμβολικὰ μετεχειρίσαντο σκώμ-
ματα, καὶ ἡ δευτέρα κωμῳδία τῇ Ἀττικῇ ἀνεσκίρ-
τησεν.

(c) Tzetzes *Prolegomena to Lycophron* (Koster XXIIb.39)

κωμῳδοὶ πραττόμενοί εἰσιν οὗτοι οἷοι Ἀριστοφάνης,
Κρατῖνος, Πλάτων, Εὔπολις, Φερεκράτης καὶ ἕτεροι.

(d) Tzetzes *Prolegomena to Hesiod*

τῶν ποιητῶν οἱ μὲν εἰσι λυρικοί, οἱ δὲ μονῳδοί, οἱ δὲ
κωμικοί, καὶ ἕτεροι τραγικοί . . . κωμικῶν δὲ ὁ γέλως
μετὰ χορευτῶν καὶ προσώπων, οἷος Ἀριστοφάνης,
Εὔπολις, Φερεκράτης.

ix

(a) Phrynichus F 8

ὁ Φερεκράτης ἀττικώτατος ὤν

416

(b) First comedy had personal jokes that were open and direct, and this direct humour was accepted until the time of Eupolis . . . but when Alcibiades passed a law to make fun of people indirectly and not openly, Eupolis himself and Cratinus and Pherecrates and Platon (not the philosopher) Aristophanes with the rest fashioned their jokes allusively and so second comedy was at its height.

(c) The comic poets that are studied are those such as Aristophanes, Cratinus, Platon, Eupolis, Pherecrates, and others.

(d) There are lyric poets, writers of monody, comic poets, and tragedians . . . ‹characteristic› of comic poets is laughter along with dancers and masks, for example Aristophanes, Eupolis, Pherecrates.

ix

(a) Pherecrates, very much in the Attic style.

(b) Athenaeus 268e

ὁ ἀττικώτατος Φερεκράτης

x Hephaestion *Handbook* 10.2

ἐφθημιμερὲς δὲ τὸ καλούμενον Φερεκράτειον

ΑΓΑΘΟΙ

Fragments

1 Athenaeus 415c

{Α.} ἐγὼ κατεσθίω μόλις τῆς ἡμέρας
πένθ᾽ ἡμιμέδιμν᾽, ἐὰν βιάζωμαι. {Β.} μόλις;
ὡς ὀλιγόσιτος ἦσθ᾽ ἄρ᾽, ὃς κατεσθίεις
τῆς ἡμέρας μακρᾶς τριήρους σιτία.

2 Athenaeus 685b

λουσάμενοι δὲ πρὸ λαμπρᾶς ἡμέρας
   ἐν τοῖς στεφανώμασιν, οἱ δ᾽ ἐν τῷ μύρῳ
λαλεῖτε περὶ σισυμβρίων κοσμοσανδάλων τε.

418

(b) That most Attic ⟨of poets⟩, Pherecrates.

x The hephthemimer ["seven-footed"] called "the Phere-cratean" [citing **F 84**].

GOOD MEN

The comedy is cited five times, three times by Athenaeus as the work of "Pherecrates or Strattis," and twice by Pollux as the work of Pherecrates. The Suda *(Strattis T 1) cites a title "Good Men or The Money Vanishes," which may give us a clue to the plot: good men becoming rich (in the manner of Aristophanes' Wealth—see l. 495) and then quickly going through their newly acquired wealth. The title might suggest the chorus—but what would be distinctive or comic about a group of virtuous men—or the principal characters? The fragments do suggest people enjoying a luxurious way of life.*

Fragments

1 (A) If I am forced to, I can eat five half-bushels a day, just.
(B) "Just." You really are a light eater, if you eat in one day the food ration for a warship.

2 Bathed before the light of day, you people are already gossiping, some in the wreath stalls, others in the perfume market, about bergamot mint and larkspur.

419

3 Pollux 10.47

δίφροι διωχεῖς

ΑΓΡΙΟΙ

3 Chariots built for two.

Brief fragment: (F 4) "of fig buyers."

WILD MEN

This comedy is one of several dramas of the 410s on the theme of leaving civilisation for a better life elsewhere. The best-known is Birds *(D-414), where two Athenians abandon the litigious atmosphere of Athens for a life of freedom among the birds, only to recreate Athens in the sky. The same festival saw Phrynichus' comedy,* The Hermit, *where the title character (Monotropos) "leads the life of Timon," the infamous misanthrope of Athens. The testimony of Plato and Athenaeus (T 1–2) shows that the chorus was made up of "wild men" and that two "misanthropes" (precursors, very likely, of Peithetaerus and Euelpides in* Birds*) have come to the country of the wild men, who have no features of civilisation. T 3 suggests that the wild men do live in a community and are not the solitary and lawless individuals of* Odyssey *9.*

F 5 suggests a confrontation between the visitors and the wise men (also F 12, although how a naval encounter would be worked in is unclear). F 8–10, 13–14 reveal that the simpler life was also a theme, but a larger question remains, whether the newcomers repented of their desire for a less complicated life, when confronted by the reality of the "wild men," or whether, as in Birds, *they were able to co-opt the inhabitants to their own advantage.*

Recent bibliography: P. Ceccarelli, in Rivals *455–58; I. Ruffell, in* Rivals *493–95.*

THE POETS OF OLD COMEDY

Testimonia

i Athenaeus 217c

ἐδιδάχθησαν δὲ οἱ Ἄγριοι ἐπ᾿ Ἀριστίωνος ἄρχοντος

ii Plato *Protagoras* 327cd

οἵου καὶ νῦν, ὅστις σοι ἀδικώτατος φαίνεται ἄνθρωπος τῶν ἐν νόμοις καὶ ἀνθρώποις τεθραμμένων, δίκαιον αὐτὸν εἶναι καὶ δημιουργὸν τούτου τοῦ πράγματος, εἰ δέοι αὐτὸν κρίνεσθαι πρὸς ἀνθρώπους οἷς μήτε παιδεία ἐστὶν μήτε δικαστήρια μήτε νόμοι μηδὲ ἀνάγκη μηδεμία διὰ παντὸς ἀναγκάζουσα ἀρετῆς ἐπιμελεῖσθαι, ἀλλ᾿ εἶεν ἄγριοί τινες οἷοίπερ οὓς πέρυσιν Φερεκράτης ὁ ποιητὴς ἐδίδαξεν ἐπὶ Ληναίῳ. ἦ σφόδρα ἐν τοῖς τοιούτοις ἀνθρώποις γενόμενος, ὥσπερ οἱ ἐν ἐκείνῳ τῷ χορῷ μισάνθρωποι, ἀγαπήσαις ἂν εἰ ἐντύχοις Εὐρυβάτῳ καὶ Φρυνώνδᾳ, καὶ ἀνολοφύραι᾿ ἂν ποθῶν τὴν τῶν ἐνθάδε ἀνθρώπων πονηρίαν.

iii Themistius 26 p. 323c

ἐπαινεῖν μὲν τὸν Προμηθέα . . . ὅτι οὐκ ἐποίησε τοὺς ἀνθρώπους μονήρεις καὶ μονοτρόπους ὥσπερ τοὺς λύκους ἢ τὰς παρδάλεις, αὐτοὺς δὲ ἰλιγγιᾶν πρὸς τὸ πλῆθος, καθάπερ τοὺς Ἀγρίους οὓς ἐδίδαξε Φερεκράτης.

Testimonia

i But *Wild Men* was produced in the archonship of Aristion [421/0].

ii So consider even now that the person, who seems to be the most wicked of those reared in human company and among laws, is himself a just person and a model of such behaviour, if we should compare him to people who have no system of education, no courts or laws, and no necessity that forces them to care about virtue at all, and if they were wild men, such as those that the poet Pherecrates produced at the Lenaea last year. Indeed if you were to find yourself among such folk, like the misanthropists among that chorus, you would be delighted to encounter Eurybatus or Phrynondas, and you would be very sorry and actually miss the wickedness of men here.

iii To praise Prometheus . . . because he did not make men solitary individuals like wolves or leopards, but made them coalesce into a group, like the wild men that Pherecrates put on stage.

Fragments

5 Pollux 10.150

{A.} ἦ μὴν σὺ σαυτὸν μακαριεῖς < > ὅταν
οὗτοί σε κατορύττωσιν. {B.} οὐ δῆτ᾽, ἀλλ᾽ ἐγὼ
τούτους πρότερον, οὗτοι δὲ μακαριοῦσί με.
καίτοι πόθεν ληνοὺς τοσαύτας λήψομαι;

6 Σ Aristophanes *Birds* 858

{A.} φέρ᾽ ἴδω, κιθαρῳδὸς τίς κάκιστος ἐγένετο;
{B.} <ὁ> Πεισίου Μέλης. {A.} μετὰ <τὸν> Μέλητα
   <δ᾽> ἦν;
{B.} ἔχ᾽ ἀτρέμ᾽, ἐγῷδα, Χαῖρις.

7 Athenaeus 171c

                    μὴ θαυμάσῃς·
τῶν γὰρ προτενθῶν ἐσμεν· ἀλλ᾽ οὐκ οἶσθα σύ

8 *Suda* α 3194

πρὶν ἀνακυκῆσαι τὰς ἀπίους ἁρπάζετε.

9 Photius (z) α 2610

{A.} οὐδ᾽ ἀποπροσωπίζεσθε κυάμοις; {B.} πώμαλα.

.

Fragments

5 (A) I suppose you will consider yourself a lucky man, when these people lay you beneath the ground.

(B) Not at all, I <shall bury> them first, and they will think me lucky. But where will I get so many coffins?

6 (A) Well then who was the worst lyre singer of all?

(B) Meles, the son of Peisias. (A) And after Meles, who?

(B) Hold on, I know, Chairis.[1]

1 K.-A. give all of l. 2 to B, and l. 3 to A.

7 Don't you [sing.] be surprised, for we belong to the Fore-tasters. But you don't know . . .

8 You [pl.] snatch the pears before stirring up.

9 (A) And you people don't wash and wipe your faces with beans? (B) Not at all.

10 Athenaeus 263b

οὐ γὰρ ἦν τότ᾽ οὔτε Μάνης οὔτε Σηκὶς οὐδενὶ
δοῦλος, ἀλλ᾽ αὐτὰς ἔδει μοχθεῖν ἅπαντ᾽ ἐν τῇ οἰκίᾳ.
εἶτα πρὸς τούτοισιν ἤλουν ὄρθριαι τὰ σιτία,
ὥστε τὴν κώμην ὑπηχεῖν θιγγανουσῶν τὰς μύλας.

11 Σ Aristophanes *Birds* 1294

οἶμαι δ᾽ αὐτὸν κινδυνεύειν εἰς τὴν Αἴγυπτον ⟨   ⟩
† οἴκους λέξεις, ἵνα μὴ συνέχῃ τοῖσι Λυκούργου
    πατριώταις.

12 Σ Aristophanes *Knights* 762a

ὁ δὲ δὴ δελφίς ἐστι μολιβδοῦς, δελφινοφόρος τε
    κεραία,
ὃς διακόψει τοὔδαφος αὐτῶν ἐμπίπτων καὶ
    καταδύων.

13 Photius α 879

καὶ τὰς βαλάνους καὶ τὰς ἀκύλους καὶ τὰς ἀχράδας
    περιόντας.

10 At that time there was no slave for anyone, no Manes nor Sekis, but the women had to do all the chores in the home themselves. Then in addition they would grind the grain early in the morning, and the village echoed as they worked the mills.

11 I think that he is in danger . . . to Egypt. . . . so that he may contend with the forebears of Lycurgus.[1]

1 Line 2 may be spoken by someone else in response to the first line. Lycurgus (*PAA* 611320) was an Athenian, probably grandfather of the 4th- c. orator, and had some connection with Egypt— see *Birds* 1294, Cratinus F 32.

12 Now this dolphin is made of lead, and the yardarm is a dolphin bearer, and it will fall and break through their hull and sink.

13 Going around <after> oak acorns and holm acorns and wild pears.

14 Athenaeus 316e

ἐνθρύσκοισι καὶ βρακάνοις
καὶ στραβήλοις ζῆν· ὁπόταν δ᾽
   ἤδη πεινῶσι σφόδρα,
ὡσπερεὶ τοὺς πουλύποδας
5 < > νύκτωρ περιτρώ-
   γειν αὐτῶν τοὺς δακτύλους.

15 Σ Aristophanes Wasps 1502c

καὶ Καρκίνος μέν τις ἦν ὁ Θωρυκίου υἱός. ἦσαν δὲ
αὐτῷ τρεῖς τινες μικροὶ κομῆται τότε καὶ νῦν εἰσὶν
μικροὶ καὶ κομῆται. φίλορχοι τότε παῖδες ἦσαν ὄντες
νῦν φιλαρχικώτεροι. μὰ τὸν Δία οὐ τρεῖς τε ἐκεῖνοί
εἰσιν οἱ τέσσαρες.

   φίλαρχοι . . . φιλαρχικώτεροι codd., φίλορχοι . . .
φιλορχικώτεροι Meineke.

16 *Bodleian Proverbs* 57

Ἀντρώνειος ὄνος

17 Pollux 7.192

βύρσης γλευκαγωγοῦ

18 Σ Lucian *Anacharsis* 32

γέρροις ἀποσταυροῦνται

14 To live on chervil and wild herbs and wild olives, when they get really hungry, like octopus . . . to chew at their fingers at night.

15 [The scholiast appears to be citing the actual words of Pherecrates, but the actual reading is in some dispute and attempts to create trimeters or tetrameters have not been persuasive. The text that I have printed reflects a likely pun operating on *philarchoi* (fond of power) and *philorchoi* (fond of dancing), since Carcinus (*PAA* 564125) served as a general at Corcyra and he and his sons appear as dancers at the end of *Wasps*.]

There was a man named Carcinus, the son of Thorycion. He had three sons, small with long hair then, and small and long-haired now. When they were children, they loved to dance, but now they are even fonder of power. No by Zeus, these aren't three—there are four of them.

16 An ass from Antron.

17 A leather bottle for carrying new wine.

18 They are being fenced off with wicker stakes.

Brief fragments: (F 19) "with wool on both sides," (F 20) "being too subtle."

ΑΝΘΡΩΦΗΡΑΚΛΗΣ

Fragment

21 Photius (b) α 2064

ὦ Ζεῦ, καλῶς γ᾽ ἀνταποδίδως μοι τὴν χάριν

ΑΥΤΟΜΟΛΟΙ

PHERECRATES

HERACLES THE MORTAL

Only one fragment is attested for this comedy, whose title reminds one of Strattis' Orestes the Mortal. *There are several other examples of titles composed of two names, but the force of the two parts does not always seem to be consistent, e.g.,* Dionysalexander *(Dionysus as Alexander), but* Anthropheracles *should mean "Heracles as mortal." See also* False Heracles.

Fragment

21 Zeus, this is a fine way to show your thanks to me.

DESERTERS

Given the parallels with Knights *465–67 and* Peace *475–77, the mention of the Argives in F 22 suggests a date in the 420s when Argos was playing Athens and Sparta off against each other. In 421/0 Argos would enter into a four-way accord with Athens. This is the only hint of a political theme for* Deserters, *and the mention of the gods (F 24, 28) and of a journey into the sky might imply a theme like that of* Peace, *and perhaps a source for the first book of Lucian's "True" Story (?). Are the "deserters" men from Athens (or Greece) who have said "no" to the war—compare titles such as Cratinus'* Run-Aways *or Eupolis'* Draft-Dodgers*? F 24 and 28 suggest that gods appeared as characters—is it perhaps the gods who have deserted humanity? The anapaestic tetrameters of F 28 have suggested an agon to some, perhaps an exposition to the chorus like that of Peithetaerus in* Birds.

Fragments

22 Σ Aristophanes *Peace* 477b

οὗτοι γὰρ ἡμῖν οἱ κακῶς ἀπολούμενοι
ἐπαμφοτερίζουσ᾽ ἐμποδὼν καθήμενοι.

23 Photius (z) ε 743

μετέωρον αἴρουσ᾽ αἱ πτέρυγες τὴν ναῦν ‹ ›
ἕως ἂν ἐμπέσωσιν ἐς τὸν οὐρανόν.

24 Harpocration p. 168.11

ὁπόταν σχολάζῃς, νεῖψον, ἵνα τὰ λήια
συγκαρκινωθῇ.

25 Photius p. 541.5

ὑμεῖς γὰρ ἀεὶ στραγγαλίδας ἐσφίγγετε.

26 Athenaeus 119d

ἡ γυνὴ δ᾽ ἡμῶν ἑκάστῳ λέκιθον ἕψουσ᾽ ἢ φακῆν
ἀναμένει καὶ σμικρὸν ὀπτῶσ᾽ ὀρφανὸν ταρίχιον.

27 Photius (b) α 1638

ἀνὴρ ἀναρριπίζεται.

Fragments

22 These damned people [the Argives] are just sitting in our way and playing both sides against the middle.

23 Their wings lift the ship up into the air . . . until they plunge into the sky.

24 ‹to Zeus?› Whenever you have the time, let it snow, so that the crops may get their roots firmly planted.

25 For you [pl.] always tied knots really tight.

26 Each of our wives is waiting, boiling up some pulse or lentil soup and roasting a lonely little salt fish.

27 The man is getting heated up again.

28 Clement of Alexandria *Miscellanies* 7.30.3

ὅ τι τοῖσι θεοῖς θύετε, πρώτιστ᾽ ἀποκρίνετε <   >
τὸ νομιζόμενον † ὑμῶν αἰσχύνῃ· τῷ κατ᾽ εἰπεῖν †
εὖ τὼ μηρὼ περιλέψαντες {κομιδῇ} μέχρι βουβώνων
    <   >
καὶ τὴν ὀσφὺν κομιδῇ ψιλήν, λοιπὸν τὸν σφόνδυλον
    αὐτὸν
5 † ὥσπερ ῥινήσαντες νέμεθ᾽ ὥσπερ καὶ τοῖς κυσὶν
    ἡμῖν
    εἶτ᾽ ἀλλήλους αἰσχυνόμενοι θυλήμασι κρύπτετε
    πολλοῖς.

1 ὅτι cod., ὅτε Sylburg

29 Photius (b, z) α 705

νὴ τὴν Δήμητρ᾽, ἀνιαρὸν <γ᾽> ἦν τὸ κακῶς ᾄδοντος
    ἀκούειν·
βουλοίμην γὰρ κἂν ἀκαλήφαις τὸν ἴσον χρόνον
    ἐστεφανῶσθαι.

30 Athenaeus 648c

ὥσπερ τῶν αἰγιδίων ὄζειν ἐκ τοῦ στόματος
    μελικήρας.

31 Photius (z) α 3109

ἀτραπίζοντες τὰς ἁρμονίας διὰ πασῶν.

28 What [when?] you [pl.] sacrifice to the gods, sepa-
rate off the customary part ‹for the priests?›—it is a
shame on you to mention this (?)—cutting off the thigh
meat right up to the groin . . . the bone completely bare,
and the rest of the spine . . . you apportion to us, as if we
were dogs, but being ashamed of one another you hide it
with many offerings.

29 By Demeter, it is tiresome to listen to someone singing
badly. I would prefer to spend the same amount of time
wearing a garland of nettles.

30 Just like smelling honeycombs on the breath of goats.

31 Following the harmonies through all.

32 Athenaeus 385e

τοὐψάριον τουτὶ παρέθηκέ τις ἡμῖν.

33 Athenaeus 396c

οὐ γαλαθηνὸν ἄρ' ὗν θύειν μέλλεις.

34 Photius α 238

πίνειν ἀεὶ καὶ μεθύειν πρὶν ἀγορὰν πεπληθέναι.

35 Pollux 2.33

ἐν χρῷ κουριῶντας

ΓΡΑΕΣ

Fragments

37 Athenaeus 246f

{A.} σὺ δ' οὐδὲ θᾶττον, Σμικυθίων, ἐπισιτιεῖ;
{B.} τίς δ' οὗτος ὑμῖν ἐστι; {A.} τοῦτον πανταχοῦ
ἄγω λαρυγγικόν τιν' ἐπὶ μισθῷ ξένον.

32 Someone has put this hors d'oeuvre before us.

33 You are not going to sacrifice a suckling pig then?

34 Always to be drinking and to get drunk before the marketplace is full.

35 Their hair trimmed.

Brief fragment: (F 36) "entirely."

OLD WOMEN

The title implies a chorus of old women, and at Lysistrata *177 the older women are entrusted with seizing the Acropolis (from which a pigeon could well have been sent with news—F 38). F 39 does sound as if a treaty or some formal negotiation was part of the action. However, old women in Aristophanes are usually figures of fun, and a chorus of decrepit hags would have been good comic material. In both* Assemblywomen *and* Wealth, *old women are involved romantically with younger males.*

Fragments

37 (A) Smicythion, won't you go quickly and locate some food?

(B) What's this fellow to you people?

(A) I take this fellow everywhere, a guest glutton on retainer.

38 Athenaeus 395ab

ἀπόπεμψον ἀγγέλλοντα τὸν περιστερόν.

39 Photius (b, z) a 466

Ἀθηναίαις αὐταῖς τε καὶ ταῖς ξυμμάχοις.

40 Bachmann's *Lexicon* p. 9.24

εὐθὺς γὰρ ὡς ἐβαδίζομεν ἐξ Ἄγρας

ΔΟΥΛΟΔΙΔΑΣΚΑΛΟΣ

38 Send off the pigeon with the news.

39 For the Athenian women themselves and the allied women.

40 Straightaway as we were walking out of Agra.[1]

[1] A village southeast of Athens in the Ilissus valley, where the Lesser Mysteries of Demeter were celebrated in the month of Anthesterion.

Brief fragments: (F 41) "belt," (F 42) "felt shoe."

SLAVE-TRAINER

The comedy seems to have turned on how slaves need to be taught to be proper slaves. Teaching scenes are always good value in Old Comedy: Strepsiades and Socrates at Clouds *627–888, "bringing up father" at* Wasps *1122–1264, Dionysus undergoing basic training in Eupolis'* Officers, *the sophist teaching the countryman how to dance in Eupolis'* Goats. *The humour could also have been intensified if one of those being trained was not a slave in the first place. F 44–45, 50–51, 53 could all come from scenes where the slaves are being instructed or where the results of the training are displayed for comic effect. F 46 has a Callaeschrus sitting at the Theseum, a precinct near the agora where slaves and others in distress could take refuge. F 43 appears to narrate a dream—cf. those of the slaves in the prologue of* Wasps—*and may have come from the opening scene.*

Testimonia

i Athenaeus 262b

τεθαύμηκα τὸ τῶν δούλων γένος ὥς ἐστιν ἐγκρατὲς
τοσαύταις ἐγκαλινδούμενον λιχνείαις. ταύτας γὰρ
ὑπερορῶσιν οὐ μόνον διὰ φόβον ἀλλὰ καὶ κατὰ
διδασκλαίαν, οὐ τὴν ἐν Δουλοδιδασκάλῳ Φερεκρά-
τους, ἀλλὰ ἐθισθέντες.

ii Pollux 3.80

εὔδουλος δὲ ὁ τοῖς δούλοις εὖ χρώμενος, παρὰ Φερε-
κράτει, καὶ τὸ δρᾶμα Δουλοδιδάσκαλος.

iii Σ Euripides *Hecuba* 467

οὐ μόνον γὰρ παρθένοι ὕφαινον, ὥς φησιν Ἀπολλό-
δωρος ἐν τῷ περὶ θεῶν † αὐλῆς †, ἀλλὰ καὶ τέλειαι
γυναῖκες, ὡς Φερεκράτης ἐν Δουλοδιδασκάλῳ.

Fragments

43 Athenaeus 306a

{Α.} κίθαρος γεγενῆσθαι κἀγοράζειν κίθαρος ὤν.
{Β.} ἀγαθόν γ᾽ ὁ κίθαρος καὶ πρὸς Ἀπόλλωνος
πάνυ.
{Α.} ἐκεῖνο θράττει μ᾽, ὅτι λέγουσιν, ὦ ᾽γαθή,
ἔνεστιν ἐν κιθάρῳ τι κακόν.

440

Testimonia

i I have wondered about the race of slaves, how they are able to restrain themselves even though they are surrounded by so many items of luxury. They ignore them not only through fear but also through instruction, not the sort as in Pherecrates' *Slave-Trainer*, but through habit.

ii "Good to his slaves": that is, one who treats his slaves well, as in Pherecrates [F 244], and there is also a play *Slave-Trainer*.

iii Not only girls wove, as Apollodorus says in his *On the Courtyard (?) of the Gods*, but also grown women as Pherecrates says in his *Servant-Trainer*.

Fragments

43 (A) ‹I dreamed that I› turned into a flatfish [*kitharos*] and was going shopping.

(B) A flatfish is a good omen and has much to do with Apollo.

(A) But what bothers me, my good woman, is that they say "There's trouble with a *kitharos*."[1]

---

[1] The joke operates on a pun on *kitharos* (flatfish) and *kithara* (lyre), the latter providing the connection with Apollo. The proverb was "there's trouble even with the lyre" ("trouble lurks even when you're happy").

44 Athenaeus 699f

ἄνυσόν ποτ᾽ ἐξελθών, σκότος γὰρ γίγνεται,
καὶ τὸν λυχνοῦχον ἔκφερ᾽ ἐνθεὶς τὸν λύχνον.

45 Athenaeus 480b

νυνὶ δ᾽ ἀπονίζε τὴν κύλικα δώσων πιεῖν,
ἔγχει δ᾽ ἐπιθεὶς τὸν ἠθμόν.

46 Etymologicum Genuinum AB

Κάλλαισχρον ἐν τῷ Θησέῳ καθήμενον

47 Bachmann's *Lexicon* p. 128.7

οὐκ ἀπολιβάξεις καὶ τριγώνους καὶ λύρας;

48 Bachmann's *Lexicon* p. 154.20

ἀντ᾽ ἀστραγάλων κονδύλοισι παίζεται.

49 Athenaeus 396c

γαλαθήν᾽ ἔκλεπτον, οὐ τέλεα.

50 Athenaeus 96b

{A.} † ὡς παρασκευάζεται δεῖπνον πῶς ἂν εἴπαθ᾽
ἡμῖν.†
{B.} καὶ δῆθ᾽ ὑπάρχει τέμαχος ἐγ-
χέλειον ὑμῖν, τευθίς, ἄρ-

442

44 Hurry up [masc.] and come outside, for it's getting dark; put a lamp in the lamp stand and bring it out here.

45 Now to give someone a drink, wash out the cup, put the strainer in place, and pour.

46 Callaeschrus sitting in the Theseum.[1]

[1] The Theseum, often misidentified as the prominent temple of Hephaestus beside the agora, was the precinct where the bones of Theseus were laid. Callaeschrus could be the father of Critias the oligarch (*PAA* 552225), or the member of the Four Hundred in 411 (552220), or the man whom Lysias defended in his *On Behalf of Callaeschrus* (552195).

47 Won't you get rid of lutes and lyres?

48 He plays knuckle-bones with real knuckles.

49 I was [they were?] stealing suckling pigs, not full-grown ⟨hogs⟩.

50 (A) Tell us how dinner is coming along.
(B) To be sure, you [pl.] have sliced eel, squid, lamb

νειον κρέας, φύσκης τόμος,
5   ποὺς ἐφθός, ἧπαρ, πλευρόν, ὀρ-
νίθεια πλήθει πολλά, τυ-
ρὸς ἐν μέλιτι, μερὶς κρεῶν.

51 Photius (b, z) α 1965

ταχὺ τῶν ἐρίων καὶ τῶν ἀνθῶν τῶν παντοδαπῶν
κατάγωμεν.

52 Photius (b, z) α 1733

κἀναψηφίσασθ᾽ ἀποδοῦναι πάλιν τὰ χρυσία.

53 Photius (b) α 1508

ῥαίνειν, ἀνακορεῖν ἀγοράς

ΕΠΙΛΗΣΜΩΝ Η ΘΑΛΑΤΤΑ

Fragments

56 Σ Aristophanes *Wasps* 1034a

κἂν μὲν σιωπῶ, † φέρεται † πνίγεται,
καί φησι "τί σιωπᾷς;" ἐὰν δέ <γ᾽> ἀποκριθῶ,
"οἴμοι τάλας", φησίν, "χαράδρα κατελήλυθεν."

444

chop, a slice of sausage, a boiled pig's foot, liver, ribs, all sorts of birds, cheese in honey, a portion of meat.

51 Let us draw down some of the wool and the various colours.

52 To rescind the decision to give back the gold.

53 To wash down, to sweep out marketplaces.

Brief fragments: (F 54) "spurs," (F 55) "to beat with a club."

FORGETFUL MAN OR THALATTA

On six occasions a comedy by Pherecrates is cited with the title "Forgetful Man (or Men)," on one occasion Athenaeus (citing F 57) attributes a "Forgetful Man or Thalatta," and Erotianus (citing F 58) mentions only a "Thalatta." Athenaeus (567c) cites a "Thalatta" by Diocles with the comment that Thalatta was the name of a prostitute. The fragments do not allow us to determine much about the comedy, apart from the references to food and entertainment.

Fragments

56 And if I keep silent, he . . . and fumes and says, "Why are you silent?". But if I answer, then he says, "Oh no, woe is me, a torrent has descended."

57 Athenaeus 365a

συσκευασάμενος δεῖπνον εἰς τὸ σπυρίδιον,
ἐβάδιζεν ὡς †πρὸς ωφελην†.

58 Eustathius *On the Iliad* p. 707.36

τὸν ἱδρῶτα καὶ τὴν ἄρδαν ἀπ᾽ ἐμοῦ σπόγγισον.

59 Photius ε 910

ἐνεχυριμαῖός ἐστί τις παρά σοι χίτων

60 Σ Aristophanes *Wasps* 968d

ὅστις παρέθηκε κρανί᾽ ἢ ⟨τραχήλια⟩.

61 Athenaeus 111b

†ὦλεν ὀβελίαν σποδεῖν, ἄρτου δὲ μὴ προτιμᾶν.

62 Athenaeus 308f

τοῖς σοῖσι συνὼν κορακινιδίοις
καὶ μαινιδίοις.

ΙΠΝΟΣ Η ΠΑΝΝΥΧΙΣ

57 He packed his dinner into the picnic basket and started off to . . . (?)[1]

  [1] Athenaeus' text gives ωφελην, which might be a garbled form of the documented name "Ophelion," or perhaps of "Ophelime" ("beneficial," an appropriate name for a prostitute).

58 Sponge the sweat and dirt off me.

59 There is a tunic at your house as a security.

60 Who served fish heads or ‹scraps›.

61 . . . to devour an obol loaf, but pay no attention to bread.

62 Getting together with tiny crow fishes and little sprats.

Brief fragment: (F 63) "branch bearers."

KITCHEN OR PANNYCHIS

"Kitchen" suggests a domestically centred comedy, which the allusions to Poulytion's mansion (F 64), blowing on the fire (F 66), and the price of wheat (F 67) would confirm. The play is usually cited as "Kitchen," but twice (T 1 and Athenaeus, citing F 70) it has the double title of "Kitchen or Pannychis," and once (F 72) the Aristophanic scholiast cites only a "Pannychis." Pannychis can mean "all night festival," and some have inferred from this title and the allusion to Poulytion (F 64) that the play had something to do with the parody of the Mysteries held at his house in 415.

447

Testimonium

i Harpocration p. 160.14

ἶπνός . . . μέρος τι τῆς οἰκίας οὕτω καλεῖται, τὸ λεγόμενον παρ' ἡμῖν μαγειρεῖον· ἔστι γοῦν δρᾶμα Φερεκράτους Ἰπνὸς ἢ Παννυχίς, ἐν ᾧ δηλοῦται τοῦτο, ὅτι μέρος τῆς οἰκίας ἐστὶ.

Fragments

64 Photius p. 626.9

οὐχ ὁρᾷς τὴν οἰκίαν
τὴν Πουλυτίωνος κειμένην ὑπώβολον;

---

1 Poulytion (*PAA* 786265) was the owner of the house where Alcibiades and his friends performed the infamous parody of the Mysteries. His house would become the last word in luxury ([Plat.] *Eryxias* 394b, 400b; Pausanias 1.2.5).

But Pherecrates was known for his nonpolitical and non-personal comedy, and how safe a comic subject would that scandal have been? Given Pherecrates' fondness for domestic and women's themes, an all-night festival is certainly a possibility.

*But Pannychis has also been explained as a woman's name, very likely that of a hetaera—Eubulus would write a comedy with this title, and Pannychis is a documented name in Thessaly and Sicily in the fourth century, and the name of a prostitute in both Petronius (*Satyricon* 25) and Lucian (*Dialogues of the Courtesans* 9). Is Pannychis a high-class prostitute who can afford to put on a splendid evening's entertainment?*

The mention of Poulytion should help date the comedy, but is the house "under a mortgage" the same as being confiscated and sold by the state, the fate of the possessions of all those implicated in the scandal of the Mysteries? At any rate, a date in the 410s seems indicated.

Testimonium

i "Kitchen" . . . the name given to a part of the house, what we would call "cooking room." In fact there is a play by Pherecrates, *Kitchen* or *Pannychis*, in which this is made clear that ⟨the kitchen⟩ is part of the house.

Fragments

64 Don't you see that the house of Poulytion is under a mortgage?[1]

449

65 Photius (z) α 2309

τί οὐκ ἐπανεχώρησα δεῦρο κἀπέδραν;

66 Eustathius *On the Iliad* p. 898.7

ἀνέπλησα τὠφθαλμὼ πάλης φυσῶν τὸ πῦρ.

67 *Suda* α 2814

ὅδ᾽ ἔστ᾽ ἐφ᾽ οὗ ποτ᾽ ἦν ὁ πυρὸς ἄξιος.

68 Pollux 10.181

ἤδη μὲν ᾠὰν λουμένῳ προζώννυτε.

69 Pollux 10.183

σκηνὴ περίερκτος περιβόλοις κάνναισι.

70 Athenaeus 612a

κᾆτα μυροπωλεῖν τί μαθόντ᾽ ἄνδρ᾽ ἐχρῆν καθήμενον
ὑψηλῶς ὑπὸ σκιαδείῳ, κατεσκευασμένον
συνέδριον τοῖς μειρακίοις ἐλλαλεῖν δι᾽ ἡμέρας;

αὐτίκ᾽ οὐδεὶς οὐτὲ μαγείραιναν εἶδε πώποτε
5 οὔτε μὴν οὐδ᾽ ἰχθυοπώλαιναν.

71 Photius (b, z) α 1020

ὑποζυγίοις ἀλοάσαντ᾽ εὐθὺς ἐκποιῆσαι.

65 Why didn't I run away and come back here?

66 I filled my eyes with ash from blowing on the fire.

67 This is the man in whose day wheat was cheap.

68 Already you [pl.] are girding the fleece on him as he bathes.

69 A tent surrounded by a wicker fence.

70 Moreover, what's got into a man that he should sit high up beneath an umbrella selling perfume, establishing a meeting place for young men to chatter on all day?

Look, no one has ever seen a woman butcher or a female fish seller, for that matter.

71 To put out ‹the grain› for the beasts of burden after he has threshed it.

72 Σ Aristophanes *Peace* 1242b

μέμνηται δὲ καὶ Φερεκράτης ἐν Παννυχίδι τῶν κυμ-
βείων καὶ τοῦ κατακτοῦ κοττάβου.

ΚΟΡΙΑΝΝΩ

Testimonia

i *Suda* κ 2084

Κοριαννοῖ· Φερεκράτης κέχρηται.

72 Pherecrates in *Pannychis* mentions little cups and sinkable cottabus.

CORIANNO

This a comedy about which we would like to know more. Athenaeus cites it at length (F 73–36) and identifies the Corianno of the title as a prostitute. Presumably it is she who is keeping a house of some wealth and comfort and whose visitor and servant we see in F 75–76. The fragments give us an intriguing glimpse of domestic life, at least as comedy would present it. The whole tone is very much more in the style of later comedy or of Theocritus 15, although Aristophanes at Wealth *641–770 does give us a domestic scene with Chremylus' wife. The women are shown in the familiar comic stereotype as very fond of wine (F 75–76, perhaps also 81), and we hear about lentils that cause bad breath (F 73), figs as large as pots (F 74), and boiled saltbush (F 80).*

F 77 seems to present a young man telling an older one (his father?) that for a young man to be in love is natural, but inappropriate for an old man, while F 78–79 mention first a mad, then a toothless old man. Were they rival visitors at the home of Corianno? F 83 stresses that "every man" was filling a vessel or a basket or a bag—could this have been a looting scene such as that in Eupolis' Spongers*?*

Testimonia

i "For Corianno": Pherecrates has employed ⟨this form⟩.

ii Athenaeus 567c

καὶ ἄλλα δὲ πολλὰ ... δράματα ἀπὸ ἑταιρῶν ἔσχε τὰς
ἐπιγραφάς, Θάλαττα Διοκλέους, Φερεκράτους Κορι-
αννώ, Εὐνίκου ἢ Φιλυλλίου Ἄντεια, Μενάνδρου δὲ
Θαΐς καὶ Φάνιον, Ἀλέξιδος Ὀπώρα, Εὐβούλου Κλε-
ψύδρα.

Fragments

73 Athenaeus 159e

{Α.} φέρε δὴ κατακλινῶ· σὺ δὲ τράπεζαν ⟨ἐκ⟩φερε,
καὶ κύλικα κἀντραγεῖν, ἵν' ἥδιον πίω.
{Β.} ἰδοὺ κύλιξ σοι καὶ τράπεζα καὶ φακοί.
{Α.} μή μοι φακούς, μὰ τὸν Δί', οὐ γὰρ ἥδομαι·
5 ἢν γὰρ τράγῃ τις, τοῦ στόματος ὄζει κακόν.

74 Athenaeus 653a

ἀλλ' ἰσχάδας μοι πρόελε τῶν πεφωγμένων

οὐκ ἰσχάδας οἴσεις; τῶν μελαινῶν· μανθάνεις;
ἐν τοῖς Μαριανδυνοῖς ἐκείνοις βαρβάροις
χύτρας καλοῦσι τὰς μελαίνας ἰσχάδας.

75 Athenaeus 481a

{Α.} ἐκ τοῦ βαλανείου γὰρ δίεφθος ἔρχομαι,
ξηρὰν ἔχουσα τὴν φάρυγα. {Β.} δώσω πιεῖν.

ii Many other plays took their titles from hetaerae: *Thalatta* (Sea) by Diocles, Pherecrates' *Corianno*, *Anteia* by Eunicus or Philyllius, Menander's *Thais* and *Phanion*, *Opora* (Bounty) by Alexis, *Clepsydra* (Water-Clock) of Eubulus.

Fragments

73 (A) Well then, I shall recline. You, bring out a table and a cup and something sweet to eat, so that I may enjoy my drinking more.

(B) Here's a cup for you and a table and some lentils.

(A) Lentils, not for me, no by Zeus, I hate lentils. If you eat them, your breath reeks.

74 Bring out some of those baked figs for me.

Could you bring out some figs? Some of the black ones. Do you understand? Among those barbarians at Mariandynia they call black figs "pots."

75 (WOMAN) For I am coming from the baths well boiled, with a very parched throat.

(B) I'll give you something to drink.

{A.} γλίσχρον γέ μοὐστὶ τὸ σίαλον νὴ τὼ θεώ.
{B.} † εἰ λάβω κυρισοι † τὴν κοτυλίσκην; {A.}
μηδαμῶς
5 μικράν γε. κινεῖται γὰρ εὐθύς μοι χολή,
ἐξ οὗπερ ἔπιον ἐκ τοιαύτης φάρμακον.
εἰς τὴν ἐμήν νυν ἔγχεον τὴν μείζονα.

76 Athenaeus 430e

{A.} ἄποτος, ὦ Γλύκη.
{ΓΛΥΚΗ.} ὑδαρῆ ’νέχεέν σοι; {A.} παντάπασι μὲν
οὖν ὕδωρ.
{ΓΛΥΚΗ.} τί εἰργάσω; πῶς ὦ κατάρατε ⟨δ’⟩
ἐνέχεας;
{B.} δύ’ ὕδατος, ὦ μάμμη. {ΓΛΥΚΗ.} τί δ’ οἴνου;
{B.} τέτταρας.
5 {ΓΛΘΚΗ.} ἔρρ’ ἐς κόρακας. βατράχοισιν οἰνοχοεῖν
σ’ ἔδει.

77 Bachmann's *Lexicon* p. 114.12

ἀπαρτὶ μὲν οὖν ἐμοὶ μὲν εἰκός ἐστ’ ἐρᾶν,
σοὶ δ’ οὐκέθ’ ὥρα.

78 Photius p. 619.8

ὑοσκυαμᾷς ἀνὴρ γέρων.

79 Photius (b, z) α 2017

ἀνὴρ γέρων ἀνόδοντος ἀλήθει

(WOMAN) The spit just sticks in my mouth, by the Two Goddesses.

(B) If I get . . . the small flask?

(WOMAN) No, it's too little. It has made me sick ever since I drank some medicine out of it. Now pour ⟨some wine⟩ into this larger ⟨flask⟩ of mine.

76 (A) Glyce, it's undrinkable.

(GLYCE) Did she pour it out too watery for you?

(A) It's *all* water.

(GLYCE) What have you done? How did you mix it, you wretched girl?

(B) Two parts water, mum.   (GLYCE) And how much wine?   (B) Four parts.

(GLYCE) Go to hell. You should have been a wine pourer for frogs.[1]

1 The mixture of two parts water to four of wine would make for a powerful drink. The assignation of the three parts in this fragment is not clear. It is possible that B is Glyce, and Glyce as printed above is the hostess (Corianno?).

77 On the contrary it is fitting for me to be in love, but your time is long gone.

78 You're out of your mind, an old man at your age.

79 A toothless old man grinds away.

80 Photius (b, z) α 387

ἀδράφαξυν ἕψουσ᾽, εἶτ᾽ ὀκλὰξ καθημένη

81 Photius (b, z) α 2152

κατάχεον αὐτῆς κἀνύδρευσαι τὸν κάδον.

82 Photius p. 596.13

πάντως γάρ εἰσι τῶν φίλων ἑνός γε του.

83 Pollux 10.179

πᾶς δ᾽ ἀνὴρ ἔσαττε τεῦχος ἢ κόικ᾽ ἢ κωρύκους.

84 Hephaestion *Handbook* 15.23

ἄνδρες, πρόσχετε τὸν νοῦν
ἐξευρήματι καινῷ,
συμπτύκτοις ἀναπαίστοις.

ΚΡΑΠΑΤΑΛΟΙ

80 Boiling up [fem.] some saltbush and then sitting hunched down.

81 Draw some water and pour the jar over her.

82 They completely belong to some one of my friends.

83 Every man was stuffing a jar or a palm-leaf basket or leather bags.

84 Spectators, give your attention to my new invention, folded anapaests.

TIDDLERS

The title ("krapataloi") can mean "worthless or foolish things" or "small fish" (hence my title "tiddlers"), but Pollux (T 1) makes it clear that Pherecrates used it as the principal monetary unit in the Underworld, subdividing it into two "crumbs" and thence into eight "pips." This strongly suggests an Underworld setting for the comedy, or at least the appearance of characters from the Underworld, confirmed by F 100, which we are told was spoken by Aeschylus. Unless this is a very late comedy, Tiddlers is thus earlier than Frogs, *both of which had a descent to Hades and Aeschylus as a speaking character. F 96 has been put by some in the mouth of Joacsta, thus increasing the literary theme of the comedy, but this is not a compelling argument. F 85, like* Frogs 117–34, *may be directions on how to easily get to Hades.*

F 98 is in iambic tetrameter, often used in the comic agon in Aristophanes, and we may have a glimpse of some

Testimonia

i Pollux 9.83

ὄνομα δὲ νομίσματος καὶ κραπαταλοί, εἴτε παίζων
εἴτε σπουδάζων Φερεκράτης ὠνόμασεν ἐν τῷ ὁμωνύμῳ
δράματι· λέγει δὲ τὸν μὲν κραπαταλὸν εἶναι ἐν ᾅδου
δραχμήν, ἔχειν δ᾽ αὐτὸν δύο ψωθίας, τὴν δὲ ψωθίαν
εἶναι τριώβολον καὶ δύνασθαι ὀκτὼ κικκάβους.

ii Photius p. 164.17

κίκκαβος· ὀνοματοπεποίηταί τι νομισμάτιον ἐν Ἅι-
δου.

Fragments

85 Athenaeus 75b

ὦ δαιμόνιε, πύρεττε μηδὲν φροντίσας,
καὶ τῶν φιβάλεων τρῶγε σύκων τοῦ θέρους,
κἀμπιπλάμενος κάθευδε τῆς μεσημβρίας,
κᾆτα σφακέλιζε καὶ πέπρησο καὶ βόα.

86 Athenaeus 646c

λήψει δ᾽ ἐν Ἅιδου κραπάταλον {τριωβόλου} καὶ
    ψωθία.

sort of confrontation between two men, each thinking that he is owed something by the other. F 101–2 show Pherecrates consciously referring to the dramatic setting, in the first fragment perhaps inviting the spectators to have a drink. Athenaeus (464ef) cites Philochorus for wine and snacks being provided throughout the competition. In the second Pherecrates threatens the judges, not indirectly as do the Clouds and Birds, but in his own name.

Testimonia

i "Tiddlers" is the name of a currency, to which Pherecrates has given the name, either in jest or being serious, in his play of that name. He says that the "tiddler" is a drachma in Hades, and that it has two "crumbs," the "crumb" being a three-obol piece and worth eight "pips."

ii "Pip": a made-up name of a type of little coin in Hades.

Fragments

85 Not to worry, my dear fellow, catch a fever, eat some Phibalean figs in summer; when you are full, sleep until noon, and then writhe in pain, feel on fire, and scream.

86 In Hades you will get a tiddler and crumbs.

87 Pollux 10.89

{A.} μάχαιραν ἆρ' ἐνέθηκας; {B.} οὔ. {A.} τί μ'
  εἴργασαι;
ἀμάχαιρος ἐπὶ βόεια νοστήσω κρέα,
ἀνὴρ γέρων, ἀνόδοντος;

88 Photius (z, Sᶻ) α 3492

                              ἐβάδιζον δ' ἀπὸ
δείπνου· κνέφας δ' ἦν ἄρτι κοὐκ ἀωρία.

89 Athenaeus 366d

τακεροὺς ποιῆσαι τοὺς ἐρεβίνθους αὐτόθι.

90 Athenaeus 700c

{A.} τίς τῶν λυχνείων ἡργασία; {B.} Τυρρηνική.

91 Photius (b, Sᶻ) α 1905

οὐδεὶς γὰρ ἐδέχετ' οὐδ' ἀνέῳγέ μοι θύραν.

92 Photius (b, z) α 277

ὦ δέσποτ' Ἀγυιεῦ, ταῦτά συμμέμνησό μοι.

93 Pollux 10.45

πρὸς τῇ κεφαλῇ μου λάσανα καταθεὶς πέρδεται.

87 (A) Have you included a knife? (B) No.

(A) What have you done to me? That I, a toothless old man, should return home to beef without a knife?

88 I was [they were?] walking home from dinner—it was evening and not too late.

89 To make chickpeas tender on the spot.[1]

[1] "Chickpea" (*erebinthos*) at *Ach*. 801 and *Frogs* 545 can be slang for "penis."

90 (A) What is the craftsmanship of the light-stands? (B) Etruscan.

91 Nobody welcomed me or opened their door to me.

92 Lord Agyieus, keep this in mind for me.

93 Putting a chamber pot beside my head he farted.

94 Photius p. 306.26

καὶ νωτοπλῆγα μὴ ταχέως διακονεῖν.

95 *Suda* α 3037

ζητῶ περιέρρων αὐτὸν ἐξ ἑωθινοῦ.

96 Choeroboscus on the *Canons* of Theodosius (*GrGr* IV
1 p. 303.17)

ὡς ἄτοπόν ἐστι μητέρ' εἶναι καὶ γυνήν.

97 Priscian *Institutes of Grammar* 18.243

ὥς τοι κακὸν ὄζει † ΤΑΝΑΜΗΔΥΝ † ἀλλὰ γλυκύ

98 Bachmann's *Lexicon* p. 114.3

{A.} τί δαί; τί σαυτὸν ἀποτίνειν τῷδ' ἀξιοῖς; φράσον
    μοι.
{B.} ἀπαρτὶ δήπου προσλαβεῖν παρὰ τοῦδ' ἔγωγε
    μᾶλλον.

99 Athenaeus 645e

ταῦτ' ἔχων ἐν ταῖς ὁδοῖς ἁρπαζέτω τὰς ἐγκρίδας.

100 Σ Aristophanes *Peace* 749

ὅστις ⟨γ'⟩ αὐτοῖς παρέδωκα τέχνην μεγάλην
    ἐξοικοδομήσας.

94 For a whipped slave not to serve quickly.

95 I have been wandering about, looking for him since dawn.

96 How strange it is to be mother and wife.

97 It does have a bad smell . . . but sweet.

98 (A) Okay, how much do you think it right for you to recompense him? Tell me.

(B) Just the opposite, I rather . . . to receive something from him.

99 Holding these let him snatch the honey cakes in the streets.

100 (AESCHYLUS) I who constructed and handed on to them a great craft.[1]

[1] Cf. *Frogs* 1004 addressed to Aeschylus, "The first of the Greeks to raise a tower of lofty words."

101 Athenaeus 485d

τῶν θεατῶν δ᾽ ὅστις διψῇ λεπαστὴν λαψάμενος με-
στὴν ἐκκαρυβδίσαι.

102 Photius p. 647.22

τοῖς δὲ κριταῖς
τοῖς νυνὶ κρίνουσι λέγω,
μὴ ᾿πιορκεῖν μηδ᾽ ἀδίκως
κρίνειν, ἢ νὴ τὸν φίλιον
5   μῦθον εἰς ὑμᾶς ἕτερον
Φερεκράτης λέξει πολὺ τού-
του κακηγορίστερον.

6 Φιλοκράτης codd., Φερεκράτης Grotius.

103 Pollux 7.152

σῦκα δὲ τῶν διφόρων

ΛΗΡΟΙ

Fragments

105 Athenaeus 690d

ἔστην δὲ κἀκέλευον † ἐγχέασθαι νῶν μύρον †
βρένθειον, ἵνα τοῖς εἰσιοῦσιν ἐγχέῃ.

ἔστην δὲ καὶ / ἐκέλευον ⟨αὐτὸν⟩ Dobree, del. μύρον
Meineke.

101 Whoever of the spectators is thirsty ‹can› pick up a limpet cup and gulp it down.[1]

1 The text is uncertain. Various attempts have been made to render it metrically.

102 I say to the judges who are judging today: do not break your oaths or judge unfairly, or by the god of friendship Pherecrates will be presenting a very different story, a far more abusive one than this, aimed at you.

103 Figs of the double-bearing variety.

Brief fragment: (F 104) "to be unsuccessful."

ACCESSORIES

The Greek lēros *means something that is showy and worth little, hence "nonsense," and also according to Hesychius "golden ornaments on women's clothing" (λ 895). This raises the possibility of a chorus dressed in fancy "accessories." Certainly F 105–6, 112 have to do with expensive luxuries and decorations.*

Fragments

105 I stopped and ordered ‹him› to pour out some expensive perfume, so that he might pour it over those who entered.[1]

1 Translating the text with the conjectures of Dobree and Meineke.

467

106 Photius p. 366.3

μίτραν ἁλουργῆ, στρόφιον, ὄχθοιβον, κτένα.

107 Athenaeus 95d

ὡς οὐχὶ τουτὶ ῥύγχος ἀτεχνῶς ἐσθ᾿ ὑός.

108 Photius (z) ined.

τὸ δ᾿ ὄνομά μοι κάτειπε τί σε χρῆσται καλεῖν.

109 Athenaeus 228e

        ἀπὸ τηγάνου τ᾿ ἔφασκεν
ἀφύας φαγεῖν.

110 Pollux 10.79

λαβοῦσα μὲν τῆς χοίνικος τὸν πύνδακ᾿ εἰσέκρουσεν.

111 Photius p. 188.20

ἔπειθ᾿ ἕτερα τούτων ποιοῦντα πολλὰ κυντερώτερα.

112 Pollux 6.105, Athenaeus 424b

κυάθιον ἀργυροῦν

106 A purple headband, a sash, a purple blaze, and a comb.

107 Since this is definitely not the snout of a pig.

108 Tell me the name by which I should call you.

109 He kept saying that he ate sprats out of the frying pan.

110 She took hold of the bushel and knocked the bottom in.

111 Next doing many other things more disgraceful than this.

112 Silver ladle.

ΜΕΤΑΛΛΗΣ

*Both Athenaeus and Eratosthenes had their doubts about
the authorship of this play, among others. It has been sug-
gested that Pherecrates' plays were revised by later poets
(see Pollux 2.33), and this may account for the debate over
authorship.*

*The comedy clearly had a utopian theme, about a style
of life where things happened "on their own" (auto-
matēn—l. 6) and there was no need to work. In comedy
such places are either in the past, to be created in the fu-
ture, on somewhere "out there." In this case the ideal life
is to be found in the Underworld, into which one conjec-*

Testimonia

i Harpocration p. 203.8

μεταλλεῖς· Λυσίας ἐν τῷ πρὸς Διοχάρη, εἰ γνήσιος. οἱ
τὰ μέταλλα ἐργαζόμενοι μεταλλεῖς ὀνομάζονται. ἔστι
δὲ καὶ δρᾶμα Φερεκράτους Μεταλλεῖς, ὅπερ Νικό-
μαχόν φησι πεποιηκέναι Ἐρατοσθένης ἐν ζ΄ περὶ τῆς
ἀρχαίας κωμῳδίας.

ii Photius p. 32.11

Ἐρατοσθένης καὶ διὰ τοῦτο ὑποπτεύει τοὺς Μεταλλεῖς

iii Athenaeus 685a

ὁ δὲ πεποιηκὼς τοὺς εἰς αὐτὸν ἀναφερομένους Μεταλ-
λεῖς

470

MINERS

tures that the miners of the title, presumably the chorus, have broken and have brought back a description. The first speaker of F 113 is a woman, perhaps in keeping with the domestic and female themes elsewhere in Pherecrates.

Athenaeus tells us that Pherecrates' play was produced after Cratinus' Wealth-Gods, Crates' Beasts, and Teleclides' Amphictyons, all of which seem to belong to the 430s. Thus I would date the comedy to the early 420s. Pellegrino prefers a wider range of 427–416.

Recent Bibliography: G. Rehrenboeck, Wiener humanische Blätter 29 (1987) 14–25; *Pellegrino* (Utopie) 83–109.

Testimonia

i "Miners": Lysias in his *Against Diochares*, if genuine [F XLIII Carey]. Those who work in mines are called "miners," and there is even a play, *Miners* by Pherecrates, which Eratsothenes in Book 7 of his *On Old Comedy* [F 93] says was written by Nicomachus.

ii For this reason Eratosthenes [F 46] has his doubts about *Miners*.

iii The person who wrote the play *Miners* attributed to him [Pherecrates].

iv Athenaeus 268d

ἐχρησάμην τῇ τάξει τῶν δραμάτων ὡς ἐδιδάχθη· καὶ
εἰ μὴ ἐνοχλῶ τι ὑμῖν (τῶν γὰρ κυνικῶν φροντὶς οὐδὲ ἡ
σμικροτάτη), ἀπομνημονεύσω κατὰ τὴν τάξιν καὶ τὰ
τοῖς ἄλλοις εἰρημένα ποιηταῖς· ὧν εἷς ἐστιν ὁ Ἀττικώ-
τατος Φερεκράτης, ὃς ἐν μὲν τοῖς Μεταλλεῦσί φησιν.

Fragments

113 Athenaeus 268d–69c

{A.} Πλούτῳ δ᾽ ἐκεῖν᾽ ἦν πάντα συμπεφυρμένα,
ἐν πᾶσιν ἀγαθοῖς πάντα τρόπον εἰργασμένα·
ποταμοὶ μὲν ἀθάρης καὶ μέλανος ζωμοῦ πλέῳ
διὰ τῶν στενωπῶν τονφολυγοῦντες ἔρρεον
5 αὐταῖσι μυστίλαισι, καὶ ναστῶν τρύφη,
ὥστ᾽ εὐμαρῆ γε καὐτομάτην τὴν ἔνθεσιν
χωρεῖν λιπαρὰν κατὰ τοῦ λάρυγγος τοῖς νεκροῖς.
φύσκαι δὲ καὶ ζέοντες ἀλλάντων τόμοι
παρὰ τοῖς ποταμοῖς σίζοντ᾽ ἐκέχυτ᾽ ἀντ᾽ ὀστράκων.
10 καὶ μὴν παρῆν τεμάχη μὲν ἐξωπτημένα
καταχυσματίοισι παντοδαποῖσιν εὐτρεπῆ,
τεύτλοισί τ᾽ ἐγχέλεια συγκεκαλυμμένα.
σχελίδες δ᾽ ὁλόκνημοι πλησίον τακερώταται
ἐπὶ πινακίσκοις καὶ δίεφθ᾽ ἀκροκώλια
15 ἥδιστον ἀτμίζοντα καὶ χόλικες βοὸς
καὶ πλευρὰ δελφάκει᾽ ἐπεξανθισμένα
χναυρότατα παρέκειτ᾽ ἐπ᾽ ἀμύλοις καθήμενα.

472

iv [After citing Cratinus' *Wealth-Gods*, Crates' *Beasts*, and Teleclides' *Amphictyons*]

I have used the order in which the plays were produced, and if I am not boring you too much—for the Cynics I don't have the slightest concern—I shall also recite what has been said by other poets in that order, one of which is that most Attic ‹of poets›, Pherecrates, who says in his *Miners* [F 113].

Fragments

113 (WOMAN) There everything was mixed together by Wealth and made from all good things in every possible way. Rivers full of porridge and black broth with scoops of bread would gurgle and flow through the narrow ways, and delicious flat-cakes as well. So a morsel would slide easily and smoothly by itself down the gullets of the dead. Beside the rivers instead of shells were scattered haggises and steaming slices of sizzling black pudding. Moreover, there were baked fish fillets nicely prepared with every sort of seasoning, and eels smothered in beets. Close by on little platters lay melt-in-your-mouth sides of beef, legs and all, and boiled pig's trotters with the most heavenly smell, beef sausages, and delicious pork ribs browned and resting

παρῆν δὲ χόνδρος γάλατι κατανενιμμένος
ἐν καταχύτλοις λεκάναισι καὶ πύου τόμοι.
20 {Β.} οἴμ᾽ ὡς ἀπολεῖς μ᾽ ἐνταῦθα διατρίβουσ᾽ ἔτι,
παρὸν κολυμβᾶν ὡς ἔχετ᾽ ἐς τὸν Τάρταρον.
{Α.} τί δῆτα λέξεις, τἀπίλοιπ᾽ ἤνπερ πύθῃ;
ὀπταὶ κίχλαι γὰρ εἰς ἀνάβραστ᾽ ἠρτυμέναι
περὶ τὸ στόμ᾽ ἐπέτοντ᾽ ἀντιβολοῦσαι καταπιεῖν,
25 ὑπὸ μυρρίναισι κἀνεμώναις κεχυμέναι.
τὰ δὲ μῆλ᾽ ἐκρέματο τὰ καλὰ τῶν καλῶν ἰδεῖν,
ὑπὲρ κεφαλῆς, ἐξ οὐδενὸς πεφυκότα.
κόραι δ᾽ ἐν ἀμπεχόναις τριχάπτοις, ἀρτίως
ἠβυλλιῶσαι καὶ τὰ ῥόδα κεκαρμέναι.
30 πλήρεις κύλικας οἴνου μέλανος ἀνθοσμίου
ἤντλουν διὰ χώνης τοῖσι βουλομένοις πιεῖν.
καὶ τῶνδ᾽ ἑκάστοτ᾽ εἰ φάγοι τις ἢ πίοι,
διπλάσι᾽ ἐγίγνετ᾽ εὐθὺς ἐξ ἀρχῆς πάλιν.

114 Athenaeus 685a

ὑπ᾽ ἀναδενδράδων ἁπαλὰς ἀσπαλάθους πατοῦντες
ἐν λειμῶνι λωτοφόρῳ κύπειρόν τε δροσώδη,
κἀνθρύσκου μαλακῶν τ᾽ ἴων λείμακα καὶ τριφύλλου.

ΜΕΤΟΙΚΟΙ

This comedy is cited only by the second-century AD gram-
marian Apollonius Dyscolus (On Pronouns p. 113.17–20
Schneider), who records the unusual form emautos in the

on the finest wheat rolls. There was polenta too, snow-covered with milk in colanders as big as tubs and slices of beestings.

(B) Woman, you'll kill me if you stay here any longer, when you can dive into the Underworld.

(WOMAN) What will you say, when you learn the rest? Roast thrushes ready for boiling flew round our mouths, begging us to eat them, spread out beneath myrtle trees and anemones. Overhead hung apples, the fairest of the fair to see, growing from nowhere. And the girls in fine-spun shawls, just recently come to womanhood and their "roses" shorn, were ladling out cups full of fragrant dark wine through a funnel for those who wanted to drink. And when someone had eaten or drunk, immediately twice as much appeared all over again.

114 In a meadow full of the lotus flower, beneath the tree vines, walking on soft buckthorn and dewy galingale and a garden of chervil and tender violets and clover.[1]

[1] The lyric metre suggests a song by the chorus. At *Frogs* 326ff. the initiates in the Underworld also celebrate the meadow in which they play.

Brief fragments: (F 115) "only just," (F 116) "straight for the Lyceum."

METICS

nominative from Pherecrates' Metics, *but in another passage (p. 69.18), he attributes the same rarity to a* Metics *by Platon (F 83). Crates also is credited with a* Metics, *of*

ΜΥΡΜΗΚΑΝΘΡΩΠΟΙ

Fragments

117 *Etymologicum Genuinum* β 308

{A.} τί ληρεῖς; ἀλλὰ φωνὴν οὐκ ἔχειν
ἰχθύν γε φασι τὸ παράπαν. {Β.} νὴ τὼ θεώ,
κοὐκ ἔστιν ἰχθὺς ἄλλος οὐδεὶς ἢ βόαξ.

*which one fragment (F 26) remains. The most economical
approach is to recognise one comedy with this title, that by
Platon.*

ANT-MEN

*Two myths come together in this comedy. The first is that of
Deucalion and the Flood (Pindar Olympian 9), in which
Deucalion and his wife survive the great Flood and repop-
ulate the world. The second is a story (Hesiod F 205, Ovid
Metamorphoses 7.615–60) of the ant-men (Myrmidons)
created when Zeus turned ants into men to replenish the
population of Aegina after a plague. We may have here a
combination of the burlesque of myth and the theme of the
new world.*

*F 125 makes it clear that Deucalion, and presumably
then his wife, Pyrrha (speaker of F 125?), was a character
in the comedy. F 118–19 may come from an early scene
in the comedy, where Deucalion sees the storm approach-
ing and turns the loom pillar into a makeshift mast. See
Cratinus' Odysseus and Crew (F 143, 152) for a storm and
boat scene at the start of the comedy. In the traditional
myth Deucalion and Pyrrha recreate the human race by
casting stones behind them, which miraculously turn into
men. In this comedy they perhaps were responsible for, or
encountered, a new race of ant-men.*

Fragments

117 (A) What nonsense. They say that a fish has no voice
at all.

(WOMAN) You're right, by the Two Goddesses, no fish
at all, other than the grunt fish.

118 Photius (b, z) α 525

οἴμοι κακοδαίμων, αἰγὶς αἰγὶς ἔρχεται.

119 Pollux 7.73

ἀλλ' ὡς τάχιστα τὸν γέρονθ' ἱστὸν ποίει.

120 Photius p. 573.7

γελῶντα καὶ χαίροντα καὶ τεθολωμένον.

121 Photius (z) α 2766

ὕστερον ἀρᾶται κἀπιθεάζει τῷ πατρί.

122 Photius (z) α 2903

ξένη γυνὴ γραῦς ἀρτίως ἀφιγμένη.

123 Photius (b, z) α 1295

ἔχω δὲ πάντως ἱμάτιον· ἀμφέξομαι

124 Photius (z) ε 1015

καὶ τριβώνιον πονηρὸν οἶον ἐνριγισκάνειν

125 Athenaeus 335a

μηδέποτ' ἰχθύν, ὦ Δευκαλίων, μηδ' ἢν αἰτῶ
    παραθῇς μοι.

118 Oh no, woe is me, a squall is coming, a squall.

119 Quickly as you can, turn the "old man" into a mast.[1]

> [1] Pollux tells us that a vertical post, of a loom with the arms of a herm and the carved face of an old man, from which the fibres hung down, was called a *gerōn* (old man).

120 Laughing and happy and befuddled with joy.

121 Afterward he curses and prays against his father.

122 An old foreign woman just now arrived.

123 I do indeed have a garment. I shall put it on.

124 A cloak of poor quality, the sort to freeze in.

125 Do not ever serve me any fish, Deucalion, not even if I ask for some.

126 Σ Aristophanes *Wasps* 674c

ἆρα ποθ᾽ ὑμεῖς <
  > καὶ τῆς ὀροφῆς τὸν χοῦν
κατὰ τῆς κεφαλῆς καταμήσονται
λαγαριζόμενοι.

127 Pollux 10.91

ἀλλὰ καὶ τὰς κύτας οἱ ἐν ἐμοῖν ἀποβανθ᾽ ἃ μέλλομεν
ἀριστῆσιν.

κύτας F, κοίταις Meineke κίσταις Kock; οἱ ἐν ἐμοῖν F, ἐν
ἐμαῖς ἀπόκειθ᾽ Meineke; ἀριστῆσιν F, ἀριστήσειν Hemster-
huis.

128 Athenaeus 229a

σὺ δ᾽ ἀποτηγανίζεις.

129 Zenobius 4.23

ἢ τρὶς ἓξ ἢ τρεῖς κύβους

130 Pollux 7.17

Μανία θρεπτή

131 Photius (b, Sᶻ) α 1833

ἀνελεύθερον σῶμα

126 Won't you ‹ant-men?› someday . . . swarming together bring down a heap of dirt from the roof on ‹their?› heads?

127 But in my chests (?) . . . on which we are going to dine.[1]

  [1] The text is very uncertain, and is cited by Pollux for *kistē* (chest) or *koitē* (jar).

128 You are eating out of the fry pan.

129 It's either three sixes or three ones.

130 A maid-servant Mania.

131 A body that is not free.

ΠΕΡΣΑΙ

Persians *is cited ten times, seven times as the work of Pherecrates and three times, all by Athenaeus, as "Pherecrates or whoever wrote the* Persians *attributed to him" (T 2). The matter is further confused by the fact that on three other occasions Athenaeus cites the play as the work of Pherecrates, calling him at 268e "that most Attic of writers" (T 4).*

F 137 suggests that the play was another example of the utopian theme in Old Comedy, where there is no need for work and where the good things of life will happen "on their own" (F 137.3). The stereotype of Persia as a place of luxury and soft living (cf. Acharnians *61–125) may well be at work here. See F 138 and Metagenes'* Thurio-Persians.

Athenaeus (T 1) tells us that the comedy was later than

Testimonia

i Athenaeus 268d

ἐχρησάμην τῇ τάξει τῶν δραμάτων ὡς ἐδιδάχθη· καὶ εἰ μὴ ἐνοχλῶ τι ὑμῖν (τῶν γὰρ κυνικῶν φροντὶς οὐδὲ ἡ σμικροτάτη), ἀπομνημονεύσω κατὰ τὴν τάξιν καὶ τὰ τοῖς ἄλλοις εἰρημένα ποιηταῖς· ὧν εἷς ἐστιν ὁ Ἀττικώτατος Φερεκράτης . . . κἀν Πέρσαις δέ φησιν

ii Athenaeus 78d, 502a, 685a

Φερεκράτης δὲ ἢ ὁ πεποιηκὼς τοὺς Πέρσας

482

PERSIANS

Miners, *which I would date to the early 420s. F 141 re-*
cords that Pherecrates parodied Sophokles' Electra 86, *but*
the date for that comedy is notoriously uncertain, most
scholars tending to put it late in Sophocles' career, 413–
409. That would push Persians *down into the 400s, not at*
all an impossible date, but it is worth considering whether
Pherecrates actually was parodying Electra *or whether*
Sophocles' play might have been earlier than one usually
thinks.

Recent bibliography: G. Rehrenboeck, Wiener Studien
101 (1988) 47–57; *Pellegrino (*Utopie*) 111–26;* M. A.
Melero, SPhV 9 (2006) 131–45; M. Pellegrino, SPhV 9
(2006) 177–207.

Testimonia

i [Having cited Cratinus' *Wealth-Gods*, Crates' *Beasts*,
Teleclides' *Amphictyons*, and Pherecrates' *Miners*]
  I have used the order in which the plays were pro-
duced, and if I am not boring you too much—for the
Cynics I don't have the slightest concern—I shall also re-
cite what has been said by other poets in that order, one of
which is that most Attic ‹of poets›, Pherecrates, who . . . in
his *Persians* he says [F 137].

ii Pherecrates or the person who wrote *Persians*.

Fragments

132 Pollux 7.15

$$τὸ παιδίον$$
τὸ πολλαγόρασον κἀπὸ πολλῶν τηλιῶν.

133 Athenaeus 228e

ἐπὶ τηγάνοις καθίσανθ᾽ ὑφάπτειν τοῦ φλέω.

134 Athenaeus 502a

στεφάνους τε πᾶσι κὠμφαλωτὰς χρυσίδας.

135 Athenaeus 502ab

οὗτος σύ, ποῖ τὴν ἀργυρίδα τηνδὶ φέρεις;

136 Photius (z) α 2533

ἀποκυβιστᾷς τὴν δόσιν

137 Athenaeus 269c

τίς δ᾽ ἔσθ᾽ ἡμῖν τῶν σῶν ἀροτῶν ἢ ζυγοποιῶν ἔτι
    χρεία,
ἢ δρεπανουργῶν ἢ χαλκοτύπων ἢ σπέρματος ἢ
    χαρακισμοῦ;
αὐτόματοι γὰρ διὰ τῶν τριόδων ποταμοὶ λιπαροῖς
    ἐπιπάστοις

Fragments

132 The child who shops a lot, and from many stalls.

133 To sit down beside the frying pans and set the tinder alight.

134 Garlands for all and golden navel cups.

135 Hey you, where are you taking this silver cup?

136 You do not accept the gift.

137 What need have we now of your ploughmen or your yoke makers, of your sickle makers or coppersmiths, of seed or stakes? For on their own through the crossroads

ζωμοῦ μέλανος καὶ Ἀχιλλείοις μάζαις κοχυδοῦντες
   ἐπιβλὺξ
ἀπὸ τῶν πηγῶν τῶν τοῦ Πλούτου ῥεύσονται, σφῶν
5   ἀρύτεσθαι.
ὁ Ζεὺς δ᾽ ὕων οἴνῳ καπνίᾳ κατὰ τοῦ κεράμου
   βαλανεύσει,
ἀπὸ τῶν δὲ τεγῶν ὀχετοὶ βοτρύων μετὰ ναστίσκων
   πολυτύρων
ὀχετεύσονται θερμῷ σὺν ἔτνει καὶ
   λειριοπολφανεμώναις.
τὰ δὲ δὴ δένδρη τἀν τοῖς ὄρεσιν χορδαῖς ὀπταῖς
   ἐριφείοις
φυλλορροήσει, καὶ τευθιδίοις ἁπαλοῖσι κίχλαις τ᾽
10   ἀναβράστοις.

138 Athenaeus 685a

ὦ μαλάχας μὲν ἐξερῶν, ἀναπνέων δ᾽ ὑάκινθον,
καὶ μελιλώτινον λαλῶν καὶ ῥόδα προσσεσηρώς·
ὦ φιλῶν μὲν ἀμάρακον, προσκινῶν δὲ σέλινα,
γελῶν δ᾽ ἱπποσέλινα καὶ κοσμοσάνδαλα βαίνων,
5 ἔγχει κἀπιβόα τρίτον παιῶν᾽, ὡς νόμος ἐστίν.

139 Athenaeus 78d

ἢν δ᾽ ἡμῶν σῦκόν τις ἴδῃ διὰ χρόνου νέον ποτέ,
τὠφθαλμὼ τούτῳ περιμάττομεν ⟨τὼ⟩ τῶν παιδίων.

will rush forth rivers of black broth with shiny speckle cakes and Achilles buns, gurgling from the springs of Wealth, for us to draw from. Zeus will bathe the roof tiles by sending down a rain of mellow wine, and from the rooftops will flood down streams of grapes as well as cheese cakes along with pea soup and lily rice pudding. The trees on the mountains will be shedding roasted sausages, tender baby squid, and broiled thrushes.

138 Your belch is mallow, your breath is hyacinth, your voice honey clover, your smile roses, your kiss is marjoram, your touch parsley, your laugh is alexanders and your walk larkspur; pour the wine and shout out the third paean, as is the custom.[1]

1 The person addressed is a male, perhaps being accused of Persian luxury and effeminacy. See Eupolis F 176 and Cratinus F 105. The eupolidean metre suggests that this is part of the parabasis.

139 If after a while one of us spots a young fig, we smear it on the eyes of our children.

141 Σ Sophocles *Electra* 86

"ὦ φάος ἁγνὸν καὶ γῆς ἰσόμοιρ᾽ ἀήρ"· καὶ ταῦτα δὲ
Φερεκράτης παρῴδηκεν ἐν Πέρσαις.

ΠΕΤΑΛΗ

Fragments

142 Harpocration p. 181.16

{A.} οὗτος πόθεν ἦλθες; {B.} εἰς Κολωνὸν ἱέμην,
οὐ τὸν ἀγοραῖον, ἀλλὰ τὸν τῶν ἱππέων.

---

¹ There were two places called Colonus at Athens, the more
famous being the town just outside Athens, home of Sophocles,
and site of the cult of Poseidon Hippius ("god of horses"). Market
Colonus was located in the agora, where men looking to be hired
would gather.

141 "O holy light and air that has an equal share of light"
[Sophocles *Electra* 86]: Pherecrates has parodied this in
Persians.

Brief fragments: (F 140) "forbidden things."

PETALE

*If "Petale" was the name of a hetaera, then this comedy be-
longs with* Corianno *as another instance of a play with a
domestic and perhaps amatory theme. The name might de-
rive from* petalon, *a poetic word for "leaf," and the name
Petale is very likely the reading on an early fourth-century
gravestone (PAA 772915). F 143 is the most interesting of
the meagre remains, both for its reference to Cleisthenes,
the arch-effeminate of Old Comedy, one of the few per-
sonal jokes in Pherecrates, but also for the possibility that
the mechanē was made up like a giant pigeon, like the dung
beetle at the start of* Peace. *Pigeons were used in classical
times to carry messages (see F 38) and in later antiquity
were associated with the goddess of Love. If the speaker is
Petale herself, then there is a pun on Petale and* petou *(fly).
The three kōmōidoumenoi (Cleisthenes—F 143, Melan-
thius—F 148, and Megallus—F 149) do not help with
dating the comedy, since the first two had long careers in
comedy.*

Fragments

142 (A) Hey you, where have you come from?
　(B) I was heading for Colonus, not Market Colonus but
Colonus of the horsemen.[1]

143 Athenaeus 395bc

ἀλλ᾽ ὦ περιστέριον ὁμοῖον Κλεισθένει,
πέτου, κόμισον δέ μ᾽ εἰς Κύθηρα καὶ Κύπρον.

144 Photius p. 204.20

παίειν με τύπτειν λακπατεῖν ὠθεῖν δάκνειν.

145 Photius (b, z) α 648

πρόσαιρε τὸ κανοῦν, εἰ δὲ βούλει, πρόσφερε.

146 *Etymologicum Genuinum* (A) λ 180

τί δ᾽ αὐτὸ λίαν ὧδε λιπαρεῖς θεόν;

147 Pollux 7.163

                    κἀκ πιθῶνος ἤρυσαν
ἄκρατον.

148 Athenaeus 343c

κωμῳδοῦσι δ᾽ αὐτὸν ἐπὶ ὀψοφαγίᾳ Λεύκων ἐν Φράτερ-
σιν, Ἀριστοφάνης ἐν Εἰρήνῃ, Φερεκράτης ἐν Πετάλῃ.

149 Athenaeus 690f

Μεγάλλειον· ὠνομάσθη γὰρ καὶ τοῦτο ἀπὸ Μεγάλλου
τοῦ Σικελιώτου· οἱ δ᾽ Ἀθηναῖόν φασιν εἶναι τὸν
Μέγαλλον. μνημονεύει δ᾽ αὐτοῦ Ἀριστοφάνης ἐν
Τελμησσεῦσι καὶ Φερεκράτης ἐν Πετάλῃ.

143 O my little pigeon, so much like Cleisthenes, fly and carry me off to Cythera or Cyprus.[1]

1 Cleisthenes (*PAA* 575540) was the great effeminate of Old Comedy, mocked by Aristophanes for looking (and thus behaving sexually) like a woman. Cythera and Cyprus were sites of temples of Aphrodite.

144 To strike me, hit me, thrash me, push me, bite me.

145 Take up the sacred basket, and if you want, bring it here.

146 Why do you ask a god so much?

147 And from a jar they drew unmixed wine.

148 Melanthius is made fun of for gluttony by Leucon in his *Phratry-Members* [F 3], Aristophanes in *Peace* [804], and by Pherecrates in *Petale*.

149 Perfume of Megallus: this was named for Megallus of Sicily, but some say that he was an Athenian. Aristophanes mentions him in *Telmessians* [F 549] and Pherecrates in *Petale*.

ΤΥΡΑΝΝΙΣ

*F 152 shows that this play had a theme of male v. female.
The metre is trochaic tetrameters catalectic, often used in
the epirrhemata of a parabasis. Do we have in this comedy
a pair of semichoruses (men and women), each complain-
ing about the other? Compare Lysistrata 614–705, where
each side has two lyric sections, each followed by trochees.*

Fragments

150 Harpocration p. 76.9

κἄπειθ᾽ ἵνα μὴ πρὸς τοῖσι βωμοῖς πανταχοῦ
ἀεὶ λοχῶντες βωμολόχοι καλώμεθα,
ἐποίησεν ὁ Ζεὺς καπνοδόκην μεγάλην πάνυ.

151 *Suda* α 3750

ἆρ᾽ ἀράχνι᾽ ὥσπερ ταῖς σιπύαισι ταῖς κεναῖς;

152 Athenaeus 481b

εἶτ᾽ ἐκεραμεύσαντο τοῖς μὲν ἀνδράσιν ποτήρια
πλατέα, τοίχους οὐκ ἔχοντ᾽ ἀλλ᾽ αὐτὸ τοὔδαφος
    μόνον,
κοὐχὶ χωροῦντ᾽ οὐδὲ κόγχην, ἐμφερῆ γευστηρίοις·
σφίσι δέ ⟨γ᾽⟩ αὐταῖσιν βαθείας κύλικας ὥσπερ
    ὁλκάδας
5 οἰναγωγούς, περιφερεῖς, λεπτάς, μέσας γαστροίδας,
οὐκ ἀβούλως, ἀλλὰ πόρρωθεν κατεσκευασμέναι

TYRANNY

Some have thought that the title implies a theme of "women in power," but all tyrannis *means is "tyranny," and the title might be a woman's name, a rather appropriate one for a hetaera. "Tyrannis" is a documented woman's name at Athens, but principally in the Roman period. In F 150 "we" might refer to gods, and if so, there was a divine theme (and characters) in this comedy.*

Fragments

150 Then so that we might not be called *bōmolochoi* by always hanging about altars everywhere, Zeus made a very large chimney.[1]

[1] The etymology of *bōmolochos* is thus explained as *bōmos* (altar) and *lochan* (lurk).

151 Cobwebs, like those in empty bins?

152 Then for their husbands they had shallow drinking cups made, having no sides but the base alone, holding not even a shell's worth, like little shot glasses. But for themselves ⟨they had made⟩ deep cups, the size of wine freighters, round and thin, bulging out in the middle. This was no accident, but planned long in advance, so that they

αὖθ', ὅπως ἀνεκλογίστως πλεῖστος οἶνος ἐκποθῇ.
εἶθ' ὅταν τὸν οἶνον αὐτὰς αἰτιώμεθ' ἐκπιεῖν,
λοιδοροῦνται κωμνύουσι μὴ 'κπιεῖν ἀλλ' ἢ μίαν.
10 ἡ δὲ κρείττων ἡ μί' ἐστὶ χιλίων ποτηρίων.

153 Photius (b, z) α 1871

ὥστ' ἀνέρρωγεν τὸ φώνημ' εὐθὺς ὀξὺ καὶ μέγα

154 Hesychius γ 1004

γυμνῷ φυλακὴν ἐπιτάττειν

ΧΕΙΡΩΝ

This plays presents both one of the longest book fragments of Old Comedy (F 155) and a host of problems for the critic. The play's authorship was disputed in antiquity, principally by Athenaeus, who five times uses the phrase "the person who wrote Chiron *attributed to Pherecrates" (vel sim.) and at one point (363f) adds "be it Pherecrates or Nicomachus the rhythmist or whoever." But the Aristophanic scholiast (citing F 159) uses a similar description "in the* Chiron *attributed to Pherecrates." Because the date has seemed to some too late for Pherecrates (see below), its authenticity has been placed in real doubt.*

The title might suggest a burlesque of myth, but F 155 (in iambic trimeters) presents an episode with Music and Justice as characters and a very topical and contemporary context—the mistreatment of Music by modern dithyrambic poets, expressed in sexual double entendres. Female personifications are well documented for Old Comedy,

494

could consume the most wine without counting drinks.
Then when we accuse them of drinking up the wine, they
get rude and swear to have drunk "only the one." But that
"one" was larger than a thousand ordinary cups.

153 And so at once the utterance broke forth loud and
clear.

154 To command a naked man to stay awake.

CHIRON

*both as speaking roles (Comedy in Cratinus' Wine-Flask
or Poetry in Aristophanes' Poetry) and silent (Diallage in*
Lysistrata *or Basileia in* Birds), *while Justice appeared as a
character in the so-called "Dike play" by Aeschylus (F
281a). In this fragment Music is presented as a high-class
hetaera, who takes one lover at a time.*

*The other principal problem with this comedy lies with
incorporating all the details suggested by the fragments:
the topical scene about musical innovators, the memoirs of
an old man with a carefree past (F 156), a parody of* Iliad
*9.270–71 that suggests Achilles as a character (F 159, also
the promise of money in F 161), and finally the dactylic
hexameters (F 162) which, we are told, parody both Hesiod
and Theognis. Chiron was famous as the wise teacher of
heroes, and F 161 could be from a scene of instruction, al-
though the contemporary tone and the first-person plural
make the chorus (made of whom?) more likely. Is Chiron*

495

*the addressee of F 156, who "urged me in vain . . . when I
was young"? Then who would this sadder but wiser older
man be? If "people" refers to the spectators, then F 156
could come from a prologue where the old man is explain-
ing the plot.*

*We may date the play late in the fifth century, since
the last of the four musicians to have assaulted Music is
Timotheus (dated roughly 450–360), who was known at
Athens by the late 410s. But if the last three lines of F 155
do refer to Philoxenus of Cythera, the comedy would have
to be somewhat later, since Philoxenus (b. 435) is more a
poet of the fourth century. Is 400 BC too late for a comedy
by Pherecrates?*

Finally there is the so-called "Chiron vase," an Apulian

Testimonia

i Nicomachus of Gerasa *Handbook of Harmony* 4, p.
274.5 (Jan)

Τιμόθεος ὁ Μιλήσιος τὴν ἑνδεκάτην (χορδὴν προσ-
καθῆψε) καὶ ἐφεξῆς ἄλλοι. ἔπειτ᾽ εἰς ὀκτωκαιδεκάτην
ἀνήχθη χορδὴν τὸ πλῆθος παρ᾽αὐτῶν. ὥσπερ καὶ ὁ
Φερεκράτης ὁ κωμικὸς ἐν τῷ ἐπιγραφομένῳ Χείρωνι
καταμεμφόμενος αὐτῶν τῆς περὶ τὰ μέλη ῥᾳδιουργίας
φαίνεται.

ii [Plutarch] *On Music* (1141c)

ὡς καὶ Φερεκράτη τὸν κωμικὸν εἰσαγαγεῖν τὴν Μου-
σικὴν ἐν γυναικείῳ σχήματι, ὅλην κατηκισμένην τὸ

bell krater (V 9—c. 380), showing a comic scene with two
men (one named "Xanthias") pushing an aged "Chiron" up
some steps. The steps leading to a stage and a door, plus the
distinctive comic dress, clearly make this a scene from an
Old Comedy. A natural candidate would be Pherecrates'
Chiron, in which case we would need to work into the play
these two slaves, a pair of "nymphs" depicted in a separate
panel (the chorus?), and a young male off to the side, but
not wearing the phallus, padding, and grotesque mask of
comedy (Achilles?).

Recent bibliography: O. Imperio, in Tessere *75, E. Csapo,*
ICS 24/25 (1999/2000) 399–426; J. Henderson, in Rivals
135–58; M. de Simone, in Misc. A.R. Sodano *(2004) 119–*
37; Olson 156–57, 182–86, 318–20.

Testimonia

i Timotheus of Miletus ⟨added⟩ the eleventh ⟨string⟩
and others took this up in turn. Finally the number was in-
creased to the eighteenth string by them. So Pherecrates
the comic poet in his play entitled "Chiron" openly criti-
cises them for irresponsibility in their lyrics.

ii So Pherecrates the comic poet brings Music on stage as
a woman whose whole body has been badly abused. He

σῶμα· ποιεῖ τὴν Δικαιοσύνην διαπυνθανομένην τὴν
αἰτίαν τῆς λώβης καὶ τὴν Ποίησιν λέγουσαν . . . καὶ
Ἀριστοφάνης ὁ κωμικὸς μνημονεύει Φιλοξένου καί
φησιν ὅτι εἰς τοὺς κυκλίους χοροὺς μέλη εἰσηνέγκατο.
ἡ δὲ Μουσικὴ λέγει ταῦτα

Fragments

155 [Plutarch] *On Music* 1141c

{ΜΟΥΣΙΚΗ.} λέξω μὲν οὐκ ἄκουσα, σοί τε γὰρ
  κλύειν
ἐμοί τε λέξαι θυμὸς ἡδονὴν ἔχει.
ἐμοὶ γὰρ ἦρξε τῶν κακῶν Μελανιππίδης,
ἐν τοῖσι πρῶτος ὃς λαβὼν ἀνῆκέ με
5 χαλαρωτέραν τ᾽ ἐποίησε χορδαῖς δώδεκα.
ἀλλ᾽ οὖν ὅμως οὗτος μὲν ἦν ἀποχρῶν ἀνὴρ
ἔμοιγε < > πρὸς τὰ νῦν κακά.
Κινησίας δέ <μ᾽> ὁ κατάρατος Ἀττικός,
ἐξαρμονίους καμπὰς ποιῶν ἐν ταῖς στροφαῖς
10 ἀπολώλεχ᾽ οὕτως, ὥστε τῆς ποιήσεως
τῶν διθυράμβων, καθάπερ ἐν ταῖς ἀσπίσιν,
ἀριστέρ᾽ αὐτοῦ φαίνεται τὰ δεξιά.
ἀλλ᾽ οὖν ἀνεκτὸς οὗτος ἦν ὅμως ἐμοί.

---

1 Melanippides of Melos, probably active in the middle third
of the 5th c., is credited with compositions that did not use the
usual strophe + antistrophe construction (Aristotle *Rhetoric*
1409b26–29). See Campbell *GL* V 14–29.

makes Justice ask her the cause of her ill-treatment and
has Poetry [*sic*] say: [F 155.1–25] . . . Aristophanes the
comic poet also mentions Philoxenus [F 953] and says that
he introduced < > songs into his dithyrambs. Music says
the following: [F 155.26–28].

Fragments

155 (MUSIC) I will tell you and gladly. For your heart
takes pleasure in hearing and mine in telling. Melanip-
pides was the start of all my troubles, being the first of
them to grab me and loosen me up and make me slacker
with twelve strings. But still this man was acceptable to
me, compared with my current woes.[1] Then Cinesias[2],
that damned Athenian, by inserting off-key modulations in
his stanzas, so completely destroyed me that in the cre-
ation of his dithyrambs his right seems to be his left, like
objects in a mirror.[3] But even he was an acceptable man

---

[2] Cinesias of Athens (*PAA* 569985), a frequent target of com-
edy (*Clouds* 333 + Σ, *Birds* 1372–1409, *Frogs* 152–53, 366 + Σ,
1437, *Assemblywomen* 329–30, F 156; Strattis *Cinesias* F 14–22;
Platon F 200) for both his personal habits and his musical
(dis)abilities. Campbell *GL* V 40–61.   [3] The passage is usu-
ally taken as Cinesias' innovations have so perverted the normal
dithyramb that everything is in reverse, like the reflection in a mir-
ror (polished shield). Borthwick, *Hermes* 96 (1968) 62–73, argues
that it refers to movements in performance —cf. *Frogs* 152–53 for
Cinesias' pyrrhic dance—that is, the performers don't know
which way to move.

Φρῦνις δ' ἴδιον στρόβιλον ἐμβαλών τινα,

15 κάμπτων με καὶ στρέφων ὅλην διέφθορεν,
ἐν ἑπτὰ χορδαῖς δώδεχ' ἁρμονίας ἔχων.
ἀλλ' οὖν ἔμοιγε χοὖτος ἦν ἀποχρῶν ἀνήρ·
εἰ γάρ τι κἀξήμαρτεν, αὖθις ἀνέλαβεν.
ὁ δὲ Τιμόθεός μ', ὦ φιλτάτη, κατορώρυχε
καὶ διακέκναικ' αἴσχιστα. {ΔΙΚΑΙΟΣΤΝΗ.} ποῖος

20   οὑτοσὶ
<ὁ> Τιμόθεος; {ΜΟΤΣΙΚΗ.} Μιλήσιός τις πυρρίας
κακά μοι παρέχεν οὗτος, ἅπαντας οὓς λέγω
παρελήλυθεν, ἄγων ἐκτραπέλους μυρμηκιάς.
κἂν ἐντύχῃ πού μοι βαδιζούσῃ μόνῃ,

25 ἀπέδυσε κἀνέλυσε χορδαῖς δώδεκα.

ἐξαρμονίους ὑπερβολαίους τ' ἀνοσίους
καὶ νιγλάρους, ὥσπερ τε τὰς ῥαφάνους ὅλην
καμπῶν με κατεμέστωσε

156 Stobaeus 4.50b.46

εἰκῆ μ' ἐπῆρας ὄντα τηλικουτονὶ
πολλοῖς ἐμαυτὸν ἐγκυλῖσαι πράγμασιν.
ἐγὼ γάρ, ὦνδρες, ἡνίκ' ἦν νεώτερος,
ἐδόκουν μὲν ἐφρόνουν δ' οὐδέν, ἀλλὰ πάντα μοι

5 κατὰ χειρὸς ἦν τὰ πράγματ' ἐνθυμουμένῳ·
νῦν δ' ἄρτι μοι τὸ γῆρας ἐντίθησι νοῦν,
<καὶ> κατὰ μίτον τὰ πράγματ' ἐκλογίζομαι.

for me. Then Phrynis thrust in his own whirlwind and just about killed me, turning and twisting me with his twelve harmonies on five strings.[4] But still he treated me all right and if he did me wrong, he soon made it up to me. But now, my dear, Timotheus has buried and scraped me most indecently.

(JUSTICE) What's this Timotheus like?[5]

(MUSIC) A certain redhead from Miletus. He has caused me real problems and far outdone those other men I mentioned, leading me along his bizarre ant paths. If he meets me when I am out walking by myself, he has me stripped and undone on twelve strings.

Off-key and unholy superfluous trills, and just like a cabbage he [Philoxenus] has stuffed me full of wrigglers.

[4] Phrynis of Mytilene won a victory at the Panathenaia "in the archonship of Callias" (406?) and was made fun of by Aristophanes (*Clouds* 969–71 + Σ) for his new musical "twists and turns." He was also a character in Eupolis' *Demes*. Campbell *GL* V 62–69.

[5] Timotheus of Miletus (c. 450–360) was famous for his musical innovations, considered "too effeminate" by some, and was said to have influenced Euripides in the last years of his career. He was thus active at Athens by 410. A considerable fragment of his *Persians* survives. See J. Horden, *The Fragments of Timotheus of Miletus* (Oxford 2002).

156 In vain you [sing.] urged me at my age to get myself involved in many matters. For when I was young, people, I didn't understand anything at all, although I though I did, but everything just came ready-made into my mind. But now old age is finally giving me sense, and I work out matters carefully point by point.

157 Athenaeus 368b

νὴ τὸν Δί᾽ ὥσπερ αἱ παροψίδες
τὴν αἰτίαν ἔχουσ᾽ ἀπὸ τῶν ἡδυσμάτων,
† οὓς ὁ καλεῖας † ἀξιοῖ τοῦ μηδενός.

158 Athenaeus 653e

ἀμυγδάλας καὶ μῆλα καὶ μιμαίκυλα
καὶ μύρτα καὶ σέλινα κἀξ οἴνου βότρυς
καὶ μυελόν.

159 Σ Aristophanes *Frogs* 1308

{A.} δώσει δέ σοι γυναῖκας ἑπτὰ Λεσβίδας.
{B.} καλόν γε δῶρον ἔπτ᾽ ἔχειν λαικαστρίας.

160 Athenaeus 388f

ἔξεισιν ἄκων δεῦρο πέρδικος τρόπον.

161 Σ Plato *Sophist* 220a

τοῖς δέκα ταλάντοις προσθήσειν ἔφη,
⟨   ⟩ ἄττα πεντήκοντα.

162 Athenaeus 364a-c

μηδὲ σύ γ᾽ ἄνδρα φίλον καλέσας ἐπὶ δαῖτα θάλειαν
ἄχθου ὁρῶν παρεόντα· κακὸς γὰρ ἀνὴρ τόδε ῥέζει·
ἀλλὰ μάλ᾽ εὔκηλος τέρπου φρένα τέρπε τ᾽ ἐκεῖνον.

157 By Zeus, just as side dishes get their reputation from their seasonings, which . . . considers worthless.

158 Almonds and apples and fruits from the strawberry tree, myrtle berries and celery and grapes from the vine, and marrow.

159 (A) He will give you seven women from Lesbos.
(B) What a nice present to get, seven sluts.[1]

  [1] A parody of *Iliad* 9.270, this fragment plays on the reputation of Lesbian women as experts in fellatio.

160 He will come out unwillingly, like a partridge.

161 He says that in addition to the ten talents he will add another fifty.

162 When you have invited a friend to a really fine feast, do not get upset when you see him arrive, for that's how an inferior man behaves. But relax, put a smile in your heart, and welcome him.

ἡμῶν δ' ἤν τινά τις καλέσῃ θύων ἐπὶ δεῖπνον,
5 ἀχθόμεθ' ἢν ἔλθῃ καὶ ὑποβλέπομεν παρεόντα,
χὤττι τάχιστα θύραζ' ἐξελθεῖν βουλόμεθ' αὐτόν.
εἶτα γνούς πως τοῦθ' ὑποδεῖται, κᾆτά τις εἶπεν
τῶν ξυμπινόντων, "ἤδη σύ; τί οὐχ ὑποπίνεις;
οὐχ ὑπολύσεις αὐτόν;" ὁ δ' ἄχθεται αὐτὸς ὁ θύων
10 τῷ κατακωλύοντι καὶ εὐθὺς ἔλεξ' ἐλεγεῖα·
"μηδένα μήτ' ἀέκοντα μένειν κατέρυκε παρ' ἡμῖν
μήθ' εὕδοντ' ἐπέγειρε, Σιμωνίδη." οὐ γὰρ ἐπ' οἴνοις
τοιαυτὶ λέγομεν δειπνίζοντες φίλον ἄνδρα;

ΨΕΥΔΗΡΑΚΛΗΣ

Fragments

163 Athenaeus 122e

εἴποι τις ἂν τῶν πάνυ δοκησιδεξίων
ἐγὼ δ' ἂν ἀντείποιμι· "μὴ πολυπραγμόνει,
ἀλλ' εἰ δοκεῖ σοι, πρόσεχε τὸν νοῦν κἀκροῶ."

But if one of us is holding a sacrifice and invites someone to dinner, we get upset when he arrives and scowl at his being there, and we hope he goes back outside as soon as possible. Somehow he gets the message and is starting to put his sandals back on, when one of the other guests says, "Hey you, leaving already? Why aren't you drinking? You, take off his sandals?" The man hosting the sacrifice gets upset at the person who is interfering and immediately rhymes off those elegiacs: "Do not make anyone stay with us against his will, Simonides, and do not wake a sleeper up."[1] Is this not the sort of thing we say over wine, when we entertain a friend?

[1] See Theognis 467–69.

FALSE HERACLES

This comedy is known only from one citation by Athenaeus. This may be the same play as Heracles the Mortal, *also attested with only one fragment. Do we have a comedy where a man disguises himself as or pretends to be Heracles?*

Fragments

163 ⟨That's what⟩ one of those who think themselves so clever might say, but I would reply, "Don't be such a busybody, but if you agree, pay attention and listen."[1]

[1] From the prologue where a character is explaining the plot to the audience? For the too-clever spectator see *Peace* 43–49 and Cratinus F 342.

ΑΔΗΛΩΝ ΔΡΑΜΑΤΩΝ

164 Athenaeus 535b

οὐκ ὢν ἀνὴρ γὰρ Ἀλκιβιάδης, ὡς δοκεῖ,
ἀνὴρ ἁπασῶν τῶν γυναικῶν ἐστι νῦν.

165 [Didymus] *Disputed Readings in Plato* p. 400 Miller

† ὁ δ᾽ Ἀχιλεὺς εὖ πως ἐπὶ κόρρης αὐτὸν
ἐπάταξεν, ὥστε πῦρ ἀπέλαμψ᾽ ἐκ τῶν γνάθων

166 Photius (b, z) α 816

ὦ Ζεῦ πολυτίμητ᾽, ἆρ᾽ ἀκούεις ἅ σε λέγει
ὁ πανοῦργος υἱός;

167 Athenaeus 644f

ὑπὸ τῆς ἀπληστίας
διακόνιον ἐπῆσθεν ἀμφιφῶντ᾽ ἔχων.

168 Photius (b, z) α 273

{Α.} τί δ᾽ ἔπαθες;
{Β.} ἄγρυκτα κἄλεκτ᾽, ἀλλὰ βούλομαι μόνῃ
αὐτῇ φράσαι σοι.

169 Zonaras p. 1030

σκέψαι δέ μου
τὸ μέτωπον, εἰ θέρμην ἔχουσα τυγχάνω.

UNASSIGNED FRAGMENTS

164 For Alcibiades, it seems, though not ⟨yet⟩ a man, is now a man for all women.[1]

[1] The joke depends on the double meaning of the word *anēr* (adult male, husband). See Eupolis F 171.

165 Achilles struck him firmly in the face and fire shone forth from his mouth.   [*Chiron*?]

166 O much-respected Zeus, do you hear what your wicked son is saying about you?
    [*Corianno* or *Heracles the Mortal* or *False Heracles*?]

167 Because of his insatiable appetite he would start eating the under-crust, even though he had a cake with candles.   [*Heracles the Mortal* or *False Heracles*?]

168 (WOMAN) What's wrong with you?
    (B) Unutterable and unspeakable things, but I am willing to tell only you.[1]

[1] Meineke placed these lines immediately before F 155, A being Justice and B Music.

169 (WOMAN) Check my forehead and see if I have a fever.

170 Athenaeus 55b

τρώγων ἐρεβίνθους ἀπεπνίγη πεφρυγμένους.

171 Heraclides *On the Greek City* 1.25

ἥνπερ φρονῇς εὖ, φεῦγε τὴν Βοιωτίαν.

172 Σ Homer *Odyssey* 2.289

τὴν γαστέρ᾽ ἦων κἀχύρων σεσαγμένους.

173 Photius (b, z) α 782

ὕβριστον ἔργον καὶ κόβαλον ἠργάσω.

174 Photius (z) α 3453

ἢ τῆς ἀχέρδου τῆς ἀκραχολωτάτης

175 *Epimerismi Homerici* π 131

{Α.} ποῖ κῆχος; {Β.} ἐγγύς, ἡμερῶν γε τεττάρων.

176 Photius ε 46

ἀεί ποθ᾽ ἡμῖν ἐγκιλικίζουσ᾽ οἱ θεοί.

177 Photius p. 524.1

ἀρκεῖ μία σκόνυζα καὶ θύμω δύο.

170 He choked himself while eating roasted chickpeas.

171 If you [sing.] have any sense, avoid Boeotia.

172 Their stomachs crammed with pulse stalks and bran husks.

173 You [sing.] have done an outrageous and knavish deed.

174 Or from the most prickly pear tree.

175 (A) So then, where to? (B) Not far, just four days' travel.

176 The gods are always playing tricks on us.

177 One sprig of fleabane and two of thyme are enough.

178 Photius (b, z) α 238

ἕωθεν ἧκε πρὶν ἀγορὰν πεπληθέναι

179 Pollux 7.194–95

μηδὲν κοτυλίζειν, ἀλλὰ καταπάττειν χύδην.

180 Σ Aristophanes *Acharnians* 86a

τουτὶ τί ἐστιν; ὡς ἀνεκὰς τὸ κρίβανον.

181 Photius (b, z) α 400

Ἀδώνι᾽ ἄγομεν καὶ τὸν Ἄδωνιν κλάομεν.

182 *Suda* δ 121

ὑπέλυσε δήμαρχός τις ἐλθὼν ἐς χορόν.

183 Orus F A 57

δεῖπνον παρασκεύαζε, σὺ δὲ καθίζανε.

184 Photius (Sᶻ) α 3404

οὐδ᾽ εἰς Ἑταίρας οὐδ᾽ Ἀφροδίτου πώποτε.

185 Photius (b, z) α 1485

πάλιν αὖθις ἀναθυῶσιν αἱ γεραίτεραι

178 He was here at dawn before the agora was full.

179 Not to sell by the cupful, but to dole out indiscriminately.

180 What is this? The bread pan is bulging.

181 We are celebrating the Adonia and weeping for Adonis.

182 Some demarch has got into the chorus and has undone.[1]

[1] A demarch was the local official in charge of each of the demes and was especially responsible for financial matters involving members of his deme.

183 You, prepare dinner, but you, sit down.

184 Nor ever to the shrine of Hetaera or that of Aphroditus.

185 The older women have got the hots again.

[*Old Woman*?]

186 Photius α 1771

ἀνδροκάπραινα καὶ μεθύση καὶ φαρμακίς.

187 Basil on Gregory Nazianus 15.2

μείξοφρυς
μέλαιν᾽ ἐπιεικῶς κατ᾽ ἐμέ.

188 Athenaeus 67c

ἀνεμολύνθη τὴν ὑπήνην τῷ γάρῳ.

189 Orus F A 17

ὁ λαγώς με βασκαίνει τεθνηκώς.

190 Athenaeus 56ef

ῥαφανίς τ᾽ ἄπλυτος ὑπάρχει,
καὶ θερμὰ λουτρὰ καὶ ταρίχη πνικτὰ καὶ † κάρνα.

191 Bachmann's *Lexicon* p. 150.28

οἷον αὖ τὸ πνῖγος, ὡς ἀσελγές.

192 Pollux 7.90

καττύομαι τοὺς καρκίνους.

193 Aristophanes *Lysistrata* 158

τὸ τοῦ Φερεκράτους, "κύνα δέρειν δεδαρμένην."

186 She's as lewd as a goat, a drunkard, and a witch.
[*Corianno*?]

187 She's reasonably dark, like me, with eyebrows that meet.

188 He has fish paste smeared all over his moustache.

189 The hare has annoyed me by dying.

190 There is an unwashed radish and hot baths and baked salt fish and nuts.

191 How stifling the heat is, it's brutal.

192 I am stitching up my crabs.[1]

1 "Crabs" being a type of shoe.

193 In the words of Pherecrates: "To skin a skinned dog."[1]

1 This is Lysistrata's reply to the question, "What do we do if the men ignore us?". Her answer plainly refers to women using leather dildos (made from dog skin?) for sexual pleasure (cf. *Lysistrata* 108–10 and F 592). "Dog" was also a slang term for penis.

194 Photius (b, z) α 1665

κάδους ἀνασπῶν

195 Zenobius 5.3

ἀβυρτάκην τρίψαντα καὶ Λυδίαν καρύκην.

196 Orus F A 79

{A.} πότε σὺ < > ἤκουσας αὐτοῦ; {B.}
πρωπέρυσιν, ἔτος τρίτον

197 Eustathius *On the Iliad* p. 801.57

νῦν δ' ἐπιχεῖσθαι τὰς κριθὰς δεῖ, πτίττειν, φρύγειν,
ἀναβράττειν,
ἄνειν, ἀλέσαι, μᾶξαι, <πέψαι>, τὸ τελευταῖον
παραθεῖναι.

198 Photius p. 583.10

ὁ δὲ παῖδα καλεῖ καὶ τευτάζει τούτῳ δεῖπνον
παραθεῖναι.

199 Eustathius *On the Iliad* p. 1369.43

ὁ χορὸς δ' αὐτοῖς εἶχεν δάπιδας ῥυπαρὰς καὶ
στρωματόδεσμα.

200 Eustathius *On the Odyssey* p. 1484.50

ἡγούμεθα τῆς πόλεως εἶναι ταύτας σωτῆρας.

514

194 Drawing up buckets of water.

195 Having mixed up a salad paste and a Lydian blood sauce.

196 (A) When did you hear from him?   (B) The year before last, two years ago.

197 Now we must have the barley corns poured out, hull them, parch and boil them, work them, grind them, knead and ‹bake› them, and finally put it on the table.

[*Servant-Trainer*?]

198 And he summons a slave and instructs him to serve this man a meal.

199 Their choruses would have dirty sheets and bed sacks.[1]

[1] Aristophanes F 264 uses very similar language of choruses in the past, "the chorus would dance wearing sheets and bed sacks." The metre (anapaestic tetrameter catalectic) is that normally used in the parabasis proper. Is Pherecrates' chorus addressing the spectators about comedy?

200 We think that these ‹women?› are the saviours of the city.

[*Tyranny*?]

THE POETS OF OLD COMEDY

201 Eustathius *On the Odyssey* p. 1528.45

κυάμους, ἀφάκην, ζειάς, αἴρας, ἀκεάνους.

202 Pollux 2.27

ὦ ξανθοτάτοις βοτρύχοισι κομῶν.

203 Hesychius ε 4973

βριθομένης ἀγαθῶν ἐπίμεστα τραπέζης.

204 Photius (z) α 3413

ἵν’ ἀφυπνισθῆτ’ οὖν ἀκροᾶσθ’· ἤδη γὰρ καὶ
λέξομεν.

205 Photius (Sᶻ) α 3397

ὦ Χάριτες, ἀφροδίσιόν τις ὑμέναιον ὑμνεῖ γαμικόν.

206 Choeroboscus (*GrGr* IV 1 p. 307.18)

ἀλλ’ ὁρῶ τὰς γυνάς

207 Eustathius *On the Odyssey* p.1428.60

Ἀθηναῖος δὲ καὶ Ἑρμίππου τοῦ κωμικοῦ παράγει τὸ
Χία δὲ κύλιξ ὑψοῦ κρέμασται περὶ πασσαλόφιν. περὶ
ἧς ὅτε κατενεχθῇ ἐκ τοῦ πασσάλου πάιζει ὁ Φερε-
κράτης ἐπὶ διαβολῇ γυναικῶν.

201 Beans, tares, rice-wheat, darnel, hard seeds.

202 Hey you [masc.], showing off your blond curls.

203 Of a table brimming over in full measure with good things.

204 Now listen here so that you [pl.] may wake up, for we shall speak right now.[1]

1 The metre is eupolidean, a metre used in the parabasis (cf. F 34, 102). "You" must be the spectators, but if this is from a parabasis, why would they need to "wake up," unless Pherecrates is being deliberately ironic about his play's merits? See also Eupolis F 205.

205 O Graces, someone is singing a romantic marriage song.

206 I see the women.

207 Athenaeus [480e] quotes from Hermippus the comic poet, "A Chian cup hangs high on its peg" [F 55], about which Pherecrates makes a joke against women, when the cup is brought down from the peg.

247 Phrynichus *Sophistic Preparation* p. 74.9

θυμέλη· νῦν μὲν θυμέλην καλοῦμεν τὴν τοῦ θεάτρου
σκηνήν . . . Φερεκράτης δὲ τὰ θυλήματα, ἅπερ ἐστιν
ἄλφιτα οἴνῳ καὶ ἐλαίῳ μεμαγμένα, οὕτω καλεῖ "θυ-
μέλην."

253 Photius p. 219.16

ληκούμεσθ᾽ ὅλην τὴν νύκτα.

266 Photius p. 522.15

Σκιτών· ἀσθενής· οὐδενὸς ἄξιος· οὕτω Φερεκράτης.

Σ Aristophanes *Knights* 634a

Σκίταλοι μὲν οὖν οἱ εὐτελεῖς καὶ πονηροί· ἦν γὰρ
Σκίτων κναφεύς τις εὐτελής, ἐπὶ πονηρίᾳ κωμῳδού-
μενος.

247 *Thymele*: we now call the stage-building in the theatre a *thymele* . . . but Pherecrates also calls the sacrificial cakes, barley kneaded with wine and oil, *thymele*.

253 When we get screwed all night.

266 Sciton: weak, worthless, so Pherecrates.

"Scitaloi": those who are vulgar and wicked, for Sciton was a vulgar fuller, made fun of in comedy for wicked behaviour.[1]

[1] Sciton is a documented name at Athens (*PAA* 824360).

Brief fragments: (F 208) "his blood boiled," (F 209) "beasts without feet," (F 210) "unwashed, with unruly hair."

(F 211) "open wide," (F 212) "gluttonous" [of horses], (F 213) "of Adonis," (F 214) "hearing," (F 215) "fisherman," (F 216) "strangely," (F 217) "in one gulp," (F 218) "I will set up," (F 219) "I will endure," (F 220) "female slave."

(F 221) "first cousin's son," (F 222) "silliest," (F 223) "give back," (F 224) "he looks straight at," (F 225) "I decline," (F 226) "to peel," (F 227) "to jack off," (F 228) "old-fashioned," (F 229) "most unusual" [fem.], (F 230) "growing."

(F 231) "more elderly" [fem.], (F 232) "to feel," (F 233) "lowing," (F 234) "ring maker," (F 235) "in-between time," (F 236) "teachers [of musicians]," (F 237) "that which keeps one awake, stopper of drowsiness," (F 238) "perianal abrasions," (F 239) "bring out," (F 240) "tutor."

(F 241) "hunting nets," (F 242) "other," (F 243) "sifted," (F 244) "treating slaves well," (F 245) "good condition," (F 246) "be alive," (F 248) "must sit down," (F 249) "to explain in detail," (F 250) "barley grains."

(F 251) "to have a thick head," (F 252) "son of a thief," (F 254) "motherland," (F 255) "donkey's giblets," (F 256) "you don't mean what you say," (F 257) "curly headed," (F 258) "to slap," (F 259) "ringlets" [of women's hair], (F 260) "front bencher."

(F 261) "loafers" [type of shoe], (F 262) "I abuse," (F 263) "decayed," (F 264) "stolen treats," (F 265) "feast of the Scira," (F 267) "discovery," (F 268) "talkative," (F 269) "woman in command," (F 270) "pivots" [of the vertebrae].

(F 271) "swinishness," (F 272) "wasp tails" [small, pointed pieces of wood], (F 273) "quickishly," (F 274) "turned the other way" [to the left], (F 275) "dry chippings," (F 276) "under-mouthpiece" [of an aulos*], (F 277) "web," (F 278) "plant," (F 279) "fearful," (F 280) "hare's flesh," (F 281) "to place in a pot" [of killing infants], (F 282) "because."*